C

vs.

Catholic University

6/6/15
Rockville, MD

Other books by Larry Witham

Rodzianko: An Orthodox Journey from Revolution to Millennium, 1917–1988

Curran
vs.
Catholic University

A Study of Authority and Freedom in Conflict

by
Larry Witham

Edington-Rand, Inc.
Riverdale, Maryland

Library of Congress Catalog Card Number: 91-70531

ISBN: 0-9628685-0-7

Manufactured in the United States of America
Cover design by Gil Roschuni
Typesetting by Edington-Rand, Inc., Riverdale, MD
Printed by McNaughton & Gunn, Saline, MI

Printed on acid-free paper

For more information, write or call:

Edington-Rand, Inc.
P.O. Box 511
Riverdale, MD 20738
301-927-1949

Contents

For Anna, Rodger, Wendy and Ted

Foreword

William James's characterization of the "sin-sick" soul in his classic work *Varieties of Religious Experience* is well known to many. Doubtless one of the reasons is that it so well describes the personalities of many religious geniuses. The person who struggles with the status-quo and attempts to make real her vision of what should be is an ever-present part of the story of the religious quest. Whether one thinks of Moses leading his people out of bondage into a land of envisioned blessing or of the great missionary of intuitive Buddhism, Bodhidharma, bringing the teachings of the Buddha to China, the paradigm is similar: The seeker is transformed from a state of discontent to one of enlightenment by a conversion experience that forever changes the way he looks at the faith he has inherited. On the basis of that experience, he goes forth to share the insights he had gained. His struggles with doubt and indecision are reborn as a struggle against the shadows of ignorance and fear that cloud people's minds.

At first glance it seems absurd to see Charles Curran in the same light as Bodhidharma or Moses. Father Curran is not by anyone's account a firebrand. He is not a prophet claiming new revelations from on high. His claims are far more modest, his work more pedestrian. He is a very decent fellow who has spent his life teaching young people about right and wrong and ministering as a priest of the Catholic Church. Yet the characterization of Father Curran as sin sick is plausible in one important way. He is a man who was converted, and that conversion has been the basis for much of what has followed since then. While not pretending to know the intimate workings of his soul, it is obvious that as a young man studying for the priesthood in Rome on the eve of the Second Vatican Council he was profoundly moved by the promise of rapprochement between Catholicism and the modern world. That his area of study is moral theology, the one that, for whatever reasons, has preoccupied the Vatican in the years since the council, accounts for both his notoriety and his troubles. But clearly Charles Curran, like so many others of his generation, is a believer in the idea that a new age dawned in the church in 1960, and what remains for the faithful is the task of applying the insights of the council fathers and their vision for a renewed church and a more just society. The struggles that he encounters, the rebuffs he suffers, are simply part of the process. They will not change his mind or dull is resolve. He has been formed and has formulated a hermeneutic for the age.

His opponents, be they in the Vatican or in the pews, have their own hermeneutic for our age. They vary from the moderates who think that the church needs time to regroup after so many years of experimentation to those who are convinced that the whole project of the council was a mistake. They range from the old guard who remembers well a time when the church seemed a more secure place to the young who never felt the sting of tyrannical authority against their callow cheeks. For them Charles Curran is a symbol of all that is wrong with the contemporary church. His unwillingness to submit to authority appears as mere rebellion; his persistence as egotistical stubbornness.

All of this needs to be said as a foreword to this work by Larry Witham, because what he has produced here is not simply a detailed account of Curran's dispute with his former employer, The Catholic University of America. It is also a chronicle of our age. It tells the story of the struggle between two ways of looking at the world, at our times, and at our church. As a reporter for *The Washington Times* Witham covered the Curran story as it unfolded. He had the advantage of being present at the trial and interviewing lawyers on both sides. Drawing on these sources and on the extensive written record of court proceedings he has compiled the most comprehensive account of the Curran case yet done. To his skills as a reporter Witham adds the ability to thoroughly contextualize current events through an energetic effort at providing the historical background for the issues raised by the case. The result is a very responsible, very complete telling of the story that will satisfy the heartiest appetite for detail.

Witham rightly sees the whole affair as a missed opportunity to deal with the conflict between authority and freedom in a positive, fruitful way. I should simply like to add that, although one might have imagined a more happy ending, it was unlikely that things would have turned out differently. Despite what many of our best minds in this century and in the past would have hoped for the future, there remains a tension—perhaps a fundamental tension—between democracy and church authority as those ideas have been understood by Rome and by citizens of our land. On the eve of Vatican I, Pius IX, drawing on the inspiration of Gregory XV's *Mirari Vos,* issued the Syllabus of Errors that explicitly condemned the idea of separation of church and state along with the notions of popular sovereignty implied in liberal democracy. Obviously the church has come a long way since then, and the Second Vatican Council with its American-inspired "Declaration on Religious Liberty" was a milestone on that journey. But a century—despite the mad hype of futurists of today—is simply not a long time in the history of an institution nearly two millennia old.

The tension between personal liberty and authority, then, remains. Normally the tension can be ignored. Usually the cautious, the timid, and the wise who represent the majority of the church's middle management prevail and preserve the delicate peace. Rather than be shocked that the Curran affair happened, we would be better advised to be thankful that the battle was fought in the courtroom and not on the battlefield or at the executioner's stake, as it has been at times.

We have only recently begun the arduous task of working out the proper balance between liberty and authority, and much needs to be done. In this patient and objective account of the Curran case the fundamental issues with which the church of the twenty-first century must deal are presented in the real context of human conflict, frailty, and virtue. We can ignore this important work only at our peril.

John Farina

Preface

Newspaper reporters in the midst of long developing stories have often asked the question: Is there a book to be made of these events?

That news room chemistry sparked this account of the "Curran affair." It met all the requirements for a bell-ringing newspaper story—conflict, change, personalities, a historic institution, intrigue, and drama, not to mention religion and sex. Yet behind that daily commotion stood lasting concerns worth deeper exploration. The Curran story reveals a struggle over first principles, a headlong quest for faith, harmony, freedom, and religious authority in our world.

As religion writer at *The Washington Times,* I covered the "Curran affair" off and on since 1986 and finally gave it concentrated attention in December 1988 by attending the eight-day trial. Curran had sued The Catholic University of America for breach of contract. In February 1989 the court ruled in the university's favor. Three months later I decided to write this story and the basic text was completed by November of 1989. I came back to the manuscript at the end of 1990 for final revisions.

The book attempts to achieve four goals. The easiest has been to present a readable narrative. In telling the story, the second goal came almost automatically—to make this a book of record. This has been done by focusing the account on the eight-day trial, a crucible into which the whole twenty-year dispute between Curran and the Vatican flows.

Narration of the trial itself is the third goal. There are several ways this could be done, from describing select highlights to laying out the chronology of testimony. In choosing the latter approach, I have risked that the trial portion of the book might read like a dry legal transcript rather than the terse, dramatic dialogue of a Hemingway story. I have tried to do both: portray the trial record and muster a colorful narrative.

To keep the trial narrative uncluttered, the background subjects have been set off in their own preliminary chapters. Here too, the leaning is toward a simple treatment of topics such as the magisterium, moral theology, and Catholic higher education. Their condensation perhaps excludes the nuance experts like to see, but the intent is to state succinct themes.

My fourth goal, like Hercules's twelfth labor, has been the hardest, for it goes against the grain of most daily journalism. If not a sharp or partisan point of view, I have at least given this book a theme to stand on. The theme of authority and freedom in conflict produces my point of view: Roman Catholicism is a tradition of hierarchical authority. Some wings of the church are calling for a Catholic democracy. I have begun with the church as it is. Judges do no less. The courts have ruled that the highest governing body of a religious organization, in this case a pope and his bishops, defines what it is.

Reviewing the books and articles on modern dissenters or free thinkers in religious bodies, I found that a particular theme is pervasive. The plot is David against Goliath, the heroic individual versus the authoritarian institution. If only to be different than these types of accounts, I have not assumed that a dissenter is an automatic hero. As Catholic theologian Avery Dulles once wrote in the journal *America,* "Dissent should be neither glorified nor vilified." Its value depends on the circumstances. I have tried to recount the circumstances fairly and have left it to the reader to make the value judgments.

Almost the entire book has been written from the public record, whether newspaper accounts, church documents, or the trial transcript. Because of the amount of material available and the disputes over interpreting it, I did not interview any of the principals in this story. The only exceptions were the chief lawyers for Curran and for Catholic University. I am therefore indebted to Paul Saunders, lawyer for Charles Curran, for his interviews and detailed corrections on the trial chapters. Likewise, Kevin Baine, lawyer for Catholic University, was extremely helpful in interviews and in reviewing the text.

Two of this story's main actors—William J. Byron, president of Catholic University, and Curran—have written books published in the aftermath of the trial. These works have further informed me on their views. Byron's *Quadrangle Considerations* (Loyola University Press, 1989), is a collection of his talks on higher education. Charles

Curran's *Catholic Higher Education, Theology, and Academic Freedom* (Notre Dame University Press, 1990) includes reflections on his legal case. I am also indebted to the Curran work for pointing out to me in my eleventh hour of editing a few more facts, sources, and quotable quotes. About the same time that galley proofs of the Curran book were available in late 1990, a history of Catholic University was also released. *The Catholic University of America: A Centennial History* (Catholic University Press, 1990), by professor and provost emeritus C. Joseph Nuesse, helped confirm and hone my brief version of the university's history.

I should also thank Pope John Paul II for making 1990 a year of significant Vatican documents on the issues of theological dissent and Catholic higher education. In June 1990 he approved release of the *Instruction on the Ecclesial Vocation of the Theologian* by the Congregation for the Doctrine of the Faith. In September the pope released his own *Apostolic Constitution on Catholic Universities.* These sources indeed cap a decade of debate in the church and nicely provide an ending point for many of the issues raised in this book.

The density of quotations in trial, which produced 1,933 pages of transcript, has led me to eschew footnotes through that part of the book. In Parts 1 and 2, I have used citations for endnotes. In Part 3, the witnesses in trial speak for themselves. The main legal filings and trial records for *Charles Curran vs. The Catholic University of America* are listed in the bibliography.

The book could not have been completed without the help and encouragement of others. I wish to thank William Bole, correspondent for *Religious New Service,* for his comments on early drafts of some chapters. Tyler Tucker, who edited my *Times* stories on the Curran trial, first suggested that a book be written. *Times* education writer Carol Innerst and Jay Mallin, then superior court reporter, commented helpfully on some chapters. Woody West, *Times* associate editor, improved the manuscript with his patient reading, questions, and markings. Mary Margaret Green did some very fine editing. Philip Gold of *Insight* magazine gave counsel on an important chapter, and the magazine's chief research librarian, Richard O'Keeffe, assisted me on Catholic terms, usage, and citations.

Bruce Miller, librarian for theology, philosophy, and canon law at Catholic University, and his assistant librarian, David Gilson, have been generous guides. Anne Smith of the university's public information office made helpful comments as well. In the final stages of this work, Alice Gallin, Avery Dulles, George Weigel, Robert Spaeth, and Charles Rice gave valuable critiques of the manuscript and in some cases offered corrections. Finally, John Farina's editorial advice encouraged me to sharpen the manuscript's thesis, a literary element he understands well after a decade of writing and editing books on Catholic subjects.

In all, I have both accepted and rejected much that was counseled, making me the final source of shortcomings in this work. And to those who understand my shortcomings best, my wife Kazui and son G. Emmett, I am grateful for their love, patience, and support.

Washington D.C.
January 1991

PROLOGUE

Authority and Freedom

A battle is underway for ownership of the name Catholic. The combat, waged in thought and deed, involves two claimants to the legacy of Saint Peter, one advocating assent to authority and the other insisting on the right to freedom.

Though this deep-seated contest is not new in the long history of the Roman Catholic Church, it is today called a "crisis." It evokes a portrait of the American church as a weary sentry stationed too long on the front lines. To understand the modern outbreak of the age-old clash between authority and freedom, few episodes are more instructive than the battle of Charles Curran, a moral theologian, with the Vatican and The Catholic University of America.

Curran's dispute with church officials and institutions for more than twenty years can by no means be told in black and white, for it waxed and waned and is layered with personalities, church politics, social changes, and public perceptions. Yet the primary source of tension in the diverse and dynamic tradition of Catholicism arises from this uneasy interaction between authority and freedom, and for its modern reading the Curran case is archetypical.

"The problem of authority and obedience, responsibility and freedom is a very deep reality today," Curran wrote in 1966, when the church and its related universities were in progressive ferment.[1] In 1988, he took the witness stand in civil court as a result of that "problem." He defended his ability, as a professor and priest at Catholic University, to combine academic freedom with his commitment to the church. "This is the principle I fought for for twenty years," he said.[2]

Across the Atlantic, in Rome, a counterforce had been deployed to preserve a papal seat of authority seen as having lost its sway in the West. Vatican vigilance finally pried Curran from his university position. Pope John Paul II, speaking of that outcome, made the reasons plain: "We could not permit a Catholic theologian teaching in a Catholic university to teach that which is contrary to church teaching."[3]

Church history shows that dissent sometimes was coopted creatively, invigorating the church as it was incorporated into the established system. Thomas Aquinas, condemned in his own thirteenth century, later became *the* doctor of the church. The German Jesuit Karl Rahner, spurned before the Second Vatican Council of 1962–65, is now called one of its leading theological lights. At other times the church was less generous, rejecting outright those acts of dissent it viewed as being in stark opposition to established norms or as unmanageable culturally and politically. This raises a key question in the Curran affair and how it transpired. Was his dissent truly against acceptable Catholic belief and practice, or was it made volatile by the social circumstances of the Roman church?

The story that follows will show that both explanations apply, though greater weight may be given to the second. The hierarchical Catholic leadership unleashed centrifugal forces at the Second Vatican Council by declaring that the church was "the people of God" and by opening its arms to the modern world and "the signs of the time."[4] Pontificates after the council attempted to offset those forces, and that corrective posture became the most rigorous under John Paul II. In that light, Curran's dissent cast a far darker shadow than it might in calmer times. Arguably, his intellectual methods or conclusions were not matters as alarming to the Holy See as his attitude—his unwillingness to assent to Vatican concerns and his tendency to parlay his dissent into public protest.

This story attempts to describe both the historical setting for the contemporary clash between authority and freedom and the intellectual issues at its heart.

An apt analogy for the Catholic Church is the solar system, with its sufficiently strong center of gravity generated by a sun. Like the solar system, the church maintains its unity as so many Catholic planets move freely about. The majesty of the church has been its ability to sustain such an equilibrium through the ages and across the continents. It has succeeded because at the heart of Catholicism is an ideal, that authority and freedom can balance sufficiently for the church to live. Authority is necessary because the church draws its existence from a presumably unchanging divine revelation that must be preserved and protected. Freedom is necessary for the human person to respond, unfettered, to the revelation of God.

In application, however, the choices people make upset the great balance. Those choices, and the ensuing conflicts, are as old as the church itself. On the one hand, a New Testament gospel promises, "The truth will make you free." Truth connotes authority and order; it says that freedom is found by living within its certainties and structures. On the other hand, an epistle of Saint Paul declares, "Where the Spirit of the Lord is, there is freedom."[5] In church history, the latter has meant a quest for liberty, augmented by a denial of authoritative structures, whether as institutions or teachings. Curran and the Vatican both want freedom in God, but one stresses "spirit" and the other "truth."

The early church was vibrant with those who sought freedom in the spirit. Montanism, the most forceful "heresy" of the third century, resisted control by the institutional and secularizing church. Orthodoxy reacted by ushering in the principle of teaching authority. The two camps sparred through generations until the skirmishes erupted into a full-scale war, the sixteenth century Reformation.

At different epochs in the church's life, the sheer force of culture, political society, and collective human habit solidified Catholicism. Today, those buttresses are thin and fragile. With dwindling external supports, the church must find its cohesion internally if it is to avoid breaking apart. The *sensus fidelium,* or consensus of the faithful, has been the internal buttress, and it too is disintegrating. Modern times have accentuated the choices between authority and freedom and the conflicts they bring. The Curran affair is just such an accent.

"THERE IS PROPERLY no history; only biography," Ralph Waldo Emerson said.[6] From that vantage, Curran's story is more than an account of particulars—a theologian, a university, a pope, and a string of Vatican officials. For in this saga, many of the modern currents in the church converge and gain force. The strength of that confluence is also determined by the terrain, which is largely American.

In the United States, the ideas of theological freedom and secular democratic freedom have intertwined—indeed, they have become almost interchangeable in definition or popular conception. The American philosopher George Santayana posed a question early in this century that perhaps could be asked only in America: "What will liberty bring to the free man?"[7] Such an abundance of freedom in America has prompted two reactions: the search for a bastion of religious truth and a multiplying pluralism, one that finds its extreme in a panoply of private religion, opinion, and choice. The contemporary "democratic faith," as it has been called, has provoked debate on whether assent to authority is, indeed, healthy at all.

This is not only a secular discussion but also one heard within the Catholic community. In the model of psychologist Eugene Kennedy, Catholics with a healthy outlook on their faith operate from a position of personal autonomy. They seek what is authoritative but not authoritarian.[8] To the Vatican, this sounds more like ideology than psychology. Cardinal Joseph Ratzinger, the Vatican's watchdog of orthodoxy, says the model of autonomy is the symptom of philosophical liberalism: the tenet that the powers of independent thought are superior to received tradition. In effect, Ratzinger's office says, philosophical liberalism abhors revelatory tradition as "a cause of servitude" and makes it "*a priori* suspect and its truth . . . contested."[9]

One more American element that cannot be excluded from the Curran affair is the contribution of the mass media. It gave power to a 1967 strike supporting Curran at Catholic University and to the 1968 public dissent over *Humanae Vitae,* the encyclical upholding the church ban on birth control. Since then, Curran's allies and church authorities both have been keenly aware of the effects of their internal disputes writ large on the evening news. The final action taken against Curran was meant to stem the "confusion" of his teachings, which arguably had their largest impact because of mass-media simplification. An obscure dissenter could have been left alone. One who put the entire church in a fishbowl was a thorn in the flesh that the church could not ignore.

Beyond the American context, the Curran affair affected three important realms of the Roman Catholic Church: its teaching authority, called the *magisterium*; Curran's field of expertise, moral theology; and Catholic higher education. In all three arenas, authority and freedom wrestle to find coexistence, and the contest is vital to the future of Catholicism.

The Magisterium

Curran's work has always recognized the magisterium, but at the same time has held that dissent is possible because of the magisterium's varied dimensions. In Curran's view, some assertions of faith are to be accepted, as that is what makes someone a cognizant Catholic and not a Hindu, yet other beliefs are not so absolute and should be open to probing and possible change. When that probing takes place, the natural question is, "Who is in charge of the magisterium?"

For John Paul II and many Catholics, this question of religious authority is settled. There is no use treating it like a secular political issue to be subjected to majority vote. During John Paul's tenure, the Holy See has laid out clear rules on doctrines of faith, standards for morality, and lines of authority. The good theologian, in this pope's view, tries to make these rules more profound and credible. Dissent is possible in exploring the dynamics and contradictions within those standards, but it has virtue only when it is long-suffering. If a dissenting position is true, by this view, it will win out in the end. Until then, as a recent Vatican decree on theologians says, they are "to suffer for the truth, in silence and prayer."[10] As difficult as that may be, some of the church's most speculative thinkers have accepted this self-imposed humility. "I can be in error, but I cannot be a heretic," said Meister Eckhart, a fourteenth century Dominican who was tried and condemned for heresy.[11] The German mystic conceded that his intellect could stray. But in the freedom of his will there was no rejection of church authority.

Thinkers such as Curran beg to differ, for they say both theologians and the faithful of the church have a role in directing the magisterium. To them, calling for the silence of theologians is preposterous. For even in a church of revealed religion, power must be shared. Imposed order is to be feared more than too much freedom.

In this democratic age, argues American Catholic theologian Richard McBrien, the church can no longer be considered a flock. "The more educated they become, the less willing they have been to see themselves a 'simple faithful' and 'sheep.'"[12] Curran and his associates thus see themselves as the loyal opposition. They believe in a magisterium. But they believe it can change, as an age-old battle cry suggests: *Ecclesia semper reformanda*—the church is always in need of reform.

Moral Theology

Curran's area of expertise, moral theology—the quest for knowing right and wrong behavior—is the Maginot line of engagement between the advocates of authority and the advocates of freedom. This focus on private and family morality comes at a time when doctrines about God, the universe, and salvation are of lessening interest to the majority. The great contentions over dogma and skepticism were waged during the Enlightenment and in the heyday of nineteenth century scientism and modernism.

Now the debate is far more personal; it is not just about belief but about the most intimate aspects of living, which produce both social and financial consequences. Medical science, technology, and the growing pluralism of social mores have directly challenged simple precepts of good and bad action, right and wrong choices. The question Catholics must ask is, which authority should dictate their behavior—the mores of Madison Avenue and Hollywood or the stern mandates of a pope in Rome? There is, of course, a range in between. But the two most powerful poles—individualistic and authoritarian—best define the church's basic choices in secular culture.

The church's struggle to uphold a durable system of morality and ethics is the same challenge that faces contemporary society. Does humankind assume there are objective truths—certain moral absolutes—that abide for all time for all people? Or is morality a question of personal preference and circumstance, a subjective reality that makes each person responsible for interpreting what is good and right?

For Catholicism, the issue has been who defines these moral

absolutes. The papacy has done so in its decrees against birth control, homosexuality, divorce, and abortion—all of which have positive corollaries in the sanctity of life, family, fidelity, and harmony with natural law.

These are the same questions that occupied Charles Curran. He stood for a school that presented alternatives to the Vatican's moral absolutes, criticizing them as inflexible laws. He envisioned an age of ideals that still accomplished the same ends of good Christian living. Curran was not the first to declare his dissent in the realm of moral theology, but he is today's most prominent advocate of the "new" moral theology and perhaps one of the last to arise during the post-Vatican II era.

Catholic Higher Education and Academic Freedom

Authority and freedom can play tremendous havoc with each other in the university, the place of Curran's work. As a professor who taught for twenty-one years at a historic Catholic university, Curran was but one voice in the debate over Catholic identity in institutions of higher learning. The judge in the Curran trial candidly observed the connection. "It is apparent that this dispute is merely a piece of a larger struggle that has been raging in Catholic higher education for many years," he said.[13]

When Catholicism was *the* culture, as in the Middle Ages of Europe, the university was born as an integral part of the church. As church and state, religion and culture, began dividing in Europe and finally separating in America, the Catholic university was on its own. It emerged as a contained community in an alien, though not necessarily inimical, environment.

Only in the past thirty years have Catholic colleges and universities tried to move beyond their religious and ethnic enclaves. That has increased their encounters with the church's classic stumbling-block question: How to respond to church authority and yet be free and autonomous in the secular world? Internal to the Catholic college or university, the conflict is between the revealed truths of the church and the claims of academic freedom — a key defense Curran used for his dissent. Externally, Catholic institutions are compelled to enter the secular arena of education. While still flying the banner of Catholic identity, these universities compete for recognition, influence, and funding. In that environment, freedom weighs in more heavily than religious authority, and this can upset a delicate balance within Catholicism.

As the Curran saga reveals, educators, theologians, and church authorities differ on just when this danger of losing balance may arise at a Catholic university. They all seek a symmetry of authority and freedom, but from different vocational viewpoints.

THE CURRAN CASE has one other unique claim on history: It came under the scrutiny of a civil court of law. Curran's 1987 lawsuit against Catholic University hinged on a contract dispute. In its most technical aspects, the complaint challenged the university's handling of his administrative suspension, the due process he deserved as a professor, and his rights under tenure. Yet in essence that legal dispute came down to authority facing freedom.

The court could not touch matters of doctrine or internal church decision-making. But the trial could explore questions about academic freedom and religion, church authority, and what constitutes Catholic colleges and universities. By entering the Superior Court of the District of Columbia, the Curran dispute entered into an entirely new forum in which the church's assertions on authority and freedom were going to be tested. In a land dedicated to separation of church and state, and therefore loath to put religion on trial, the court's venue had limits. It nevertheless allowed a wide-ranging contest of the agility of each side to argue its case.

For the first time in American church history, cardinals, theologians, professors, and administrators took the witness stand. Curran argued that the university was a civil realm, an institution bound by civil laws and the guarantee of rights provided by a contract. Catholic University responded that although it was indeed an autonomous civil institution, its very identity stemmed from religious loyalty to declarations of the Holy See; its legal right to respond to Rome was an exercise of religious freedom, guaranteed by the Constitution. For Curran's legal attack, this was a religious cloak used to deflect pure and simple civil contract obligations.

The Curran case revived a rigorous sparring over theology and the nature of the church that some thought had ended, watered down by polite consensus and indulgence. In the Middle Ages, for example, the fittest of the competing beliefs in the Catholic Church survived long university disputations. During the Reformation, Martin Luther openly declared "Here I stand" in public disputation with the best theologians the Vatican could muster against him.

The discussion between Curran and the Vatican was confined to correspondence and one brief visit to Rome. Curran lamented that he was "quite disappointed by the quality of the dialogue."[14] His supporters later called for a new process in investigations of theologians, to include face-to-face inquiries and full opportunities to present a defense after hearing the charges made in person by the investigators.

As the quest to find true authority and true freedom in the church intensifies, will the court increasingly become the venue of this debate? Doubtless the church hopes not. And the state will do all it can to disallow it. But in America such litigation is the way people make their claims. Charles Curran may not be the last theologian or church member to agitate for reform of the church under the mantle of rights asserted in the legal context.

BY 1990 THE POPE was completing his twelfth year in office. The battle lines over the proper places of authority and freedom had become clear.

Critics called the course taken by John Paul II an effort to restore the old Catholic Church, to roll back the reforms of the Second Vatican Council. The term "integralism" was revived to compare John Paul's approach to that of the assertive Pope Pius X, who condemned "modernism" in 1907. The infighting that followed Pius' condemnation of critical studies of scripture and doctrine in France was eased by decree of Benedict XV in 1914 and quelled entirely in 1921, when Benedict disbanded the chief antimodernist secret society. The same tug of war continues today between those who lionize papal authority and those who seek worldly guidance in "the signs of the times."

Making the charge of a revived "integralism" stick to the Polish pope has been a difficult task. He was a university man, a solid thinker who had addressed many of the subjects that were at issue during his pontificate. Knowing that the church is a voluntary association with no coercive powers to retain its membership, he nevertheless took the initiative, setting the terms of the debate in quick succession after the conclave of September 1978 elevated him to the papacy. By 1987 he had given 746 speeches, amounting to 3,626 pages of documents—three times the volume produced by Paul VI.[15] Much of that he spoke to frame authority and freedom in his terms.

When Vatican II closed, many good Catholic minds conceived of models of the church different from the one John Paul promotes. They continue to disagree, especially regarding the nuances of myriad council documents. Yet to define the church's essential purpose and identity, the most helpful measurement is the church's argument for uniqueness. In short, what does it provide that no other tradition can? What does it claim to do better? Conceived on divine revelation and organized on an apostolic succession traced to Saint Peter and Rome, the church presents itself as a mediator for a transcendent God and a path to salvation. This claim comes not by research, vote, or consensus, but by a belief in revealed truth.

America's pluralist setting does not make irrelevant this Catholic claim to uniqueness. But trends in American religion are shaping American Catholicism, much as water sculpts limestone. According to one well-founded diagnosis, the Catholic Church suffers the same strains as all organized religion. While the level of spiritual interest is high among Americans, the desire to affiliate with organized religion has declined.[16] Another trend, however, plays positively for Catholicism. People turn to religious groups not as social clubs but to find the ultimate meaning of life. The ability of the Catholic Church to continue asserting its claim to a revealed and authoritative truth meets this need. In part, the nature of Catholic belief and the pope's demand that the church be "countercultural" has given it a rate of membership growth just shy of the rate for evangelical Protestant bodies. As the liberal churches' membership declines in inverse proportion to their efforts to blend into society and replicate many of its secular services, Catholics and evangelicals—not to mention Muslims and Mormons—maintain an identity by insisting on unique doctrinal claims. For many people these religious elements are what give life ultimate meaning.[17]

In an ecumenical age, Christians can overlook minor differences between various church traditions. The major distinctions, however, are not easily ignored. The Eastern Orthodox fix authority in the historic church councils, and Protestants find it in the Scripture. Roman Catholicism has placed it in the papacy, keeper of the keys. For Catholicism to be true to itself this form of authority must be assured. Where, then, does freedom come in?

IN MY RESEARCH AND reflection on the Curran story, I have been led to draw a basic conclusion about freedom, one from which this narrative must flow. As the Roman Catholic Church is constituted today, freedom is defined by its relationship to authority. In the classic theological claim that still radiates from the Holy See, freedom is found by living within the truth and order of the hierarchical church.

Many in the church today would hold that this is no longer the case, for the church is in the process of a historic liberation, sanctioned by the Second Vatican Council but resisted by a formidable old guard. For better or worse, there is sparse evidence that this proposed "liberation" has come or that it can even be achieved unless the line is crossed toward Protestantism. Some hope for the day when freedom is the keystone of Catholicism. It may already be a reality for others, those who keep the name Catholic but in all respects go their own way. For the historic church, however, authority still reigns.

Given this immanent reality, the Curran affair was a missed opportunity—but not just for the cause of freedom. If handled differently it might have been a catalyst to unite warring factions in the church around a mutually acceptable fountainhead of authority. What happened, however, followed another axiom: "What begins in mysticism ends in politics." In the Curran case, a dispute over principle gave way to political expedients as each side tried to win. The predominance of the political in the Curran affair obscured a deeper concern, namely the search for effective religious authority in a world that sorely needs it.

By its nature, the Catholic Church is obliged to meet this challenge. Today, there are few, if any, spiritual institutions to which Americans can look to see authority as a success story—a tale of respect, honor, humility, cooperation, righteousness, love, sacrifice, and their salutary effects on the world.

For its part, the Holy See must make authority convincingly selfless, trustworthy, and fair, but without caving in to mere clamor. The Vatican cannot be expected to supply its foes with the rope to hang Saint Peter. On the part of theologians and the faithful, some measure of deference is due. That is a hard request, for Catholicism is permeated by a Western ethos that has lost its ability to welcome authority. Indeed, this is one way to describe the spiritual crisis of the West: It is in a situation where "self" is defiant, incapable of transcending its limits and fears to submit to something higher.

The life and times of Charles Curran open many vistas on the nature of freedom in the Catholic Church. His story offers no solution to freedom's divorce from authority, but it clarifies the claims of each. When Curran took a church-related institution to court, he was the plaintiff, and therefore the burden of proof was upon him. We could say these legal rules also apply to the battle between authority and freedom in the church. Catholicism has been put on trial to determine its future, but in this trial, too, the burden of proof is on freedom.

PART ONE

The Story

ONE

Freedom in the Air

The American public, including most Roman Catholics, first heard of Charles Curran on a balmy April day in 1967. According to the evening news, 6,600 students and 600 faculty members closed down The Catholic University of America during a strike in support of the young priest. The all-clerical board of trustees, alarmed by Curran's liberal approach to moral theology, had decided behind closed doors not to rehire him.

Charles Curran, at age thirty-three, was the right man in the right place and the right time in the church and in America. After that spring day in Washington D.C., a combination of media exposure, prolific writing, and cultural mood destined his rise.

During the 1960s, the Catholic Church and American society were changing dramatically. Curran was a personification. He was young and open to new ideas. His first book, *Christian Morality Today,* was a 138-page paperback with a stylistic cover, and it cost students only $2.45 when it was published in 1966. One of its nine chapters was titled, "Formation in Freedom and Responsibility." In the university environment Curran was a part of a fresh debate about governance and academic freedom at Catholic institutions of higher learning. Moreover, American culture was deep in a rebellion against authority, manifest on college campuses and focused, though not in theological terms, on Curran's area of expertise, sexual ethics. The changes were tumbling forth under the aura of the Second Vatican Council, which had closed in 1965 with the most optimistic outlook the church had yet taken on its interaction with the modern world.

Freedom was in the air as authority watched from behind its many citadels in the church and in society. Curran's life was like a path that led into the midst of it all.[1]

AS A THIRD-GENERATION Irish Catholic, Curran traced his past to that immigrant group which by dint of its English tongue excelled in America. While German, Italian, Polish, and other Catholic ethnic groups from Europe focused on preserving their language-based identity, the Irish assimilated quickly or channeled their energy into a range of fields, especially the priesthood.

Born the son of a Rochester, New York, insurance manager in 1934, Charles Edward Curran was one of four children. His studious nature soon inclined him toward the church, despite contrary wishes by his father, and at age thirteen Charles entered a minor seminary. It was 1947 when he entered St. Andrew's, a time when the Catholic Church was still a product of the First Vatican Council of 1870, though its American community was fast entering the social and economic mainstream of America. On a definite track to the priesthood, Curran finished his college education at St. Bernard's Seminary, to which he would have ties for the next fourteen years.

Curran followed the wishes of the bishop of Rochester to pursue graduate study in moral theology at the North American College in Rome. He would be needed as an instructor at St. Bernard's. Curran went to Rome at the end of an era. In 1958, Curran's third year there and the year John Paul XXIII was elected pope, he was ordained to the priesthood. After the nineteen-year conservative reign of Pope Pius XII the advocates of new approaches to Catholic theology eagerly battled for a foothold. On the field of moral theology the generals for change were two German theologians, Josef Fuchs and Bernard Häring. After receiving his doctorate in sacred theology from the Gregorian University in 1959, Curran continued his study and came under their influence. Both theologians criticized what they called the "classicist" view of moral theology, that moral action can be deduced from fixed, static natural laws that exist apart from history and persons and make certain actions always wrong. Through the centuries this approach had made moral science a matter of using manuals to identify those wrong actions, determine the weight of a transgression, and then provide the proper penance.

Fuchs and Häring denied this view of absolute negative norms. They introduced the subjective, or personal and existential, element of the conscience and relationship to God as a measure of morality.

And like many modern philosophers, they abandoned the static view of human nature and viewed it as changing in history.

Curran enrolled at the Redemptorists' Academia Alfonsiana to seek a second doctorate, now in moral theology, and there came under the influence of Häring, author of the imposing work *The Law of Christ*. The forty-seven-year-old Häring took Curran, age twenty-five, under his theological wing.

Although Curran would tend to hold traditional church positions on moral theology until 1964, the chipping away began in 1961. In his doctoral dissertation he defended the morality of "the prevention of conception after rape." Science had joined moral logic in moral explorations, and Curran became versed in human reproductive biology. With this as a starting point, he realized that many of the past moral teachings of the church were ignorant of scientific facts. That realization, combined with the new "personalist" approach, gave him the tools of the historical critic. In the future he would dedicate himself to arguing that several key moral teachings of the church—against contraception, divorce, premarital sex, masturbation, homosexual acts, and deviation from Sunday observances—were products of human knowledge at one time in history, subject to change in another historical age.

When Curran returned to New York and began teaching at St. Bernard's in 1961, the primary question in moral theology was contraception and responsible parenthood. Only by 1963 had a cautious attack on the condemnation of artificial birth control emerged among theologians, though it was quickly picked up by the popular media in the next five years. From his studies in Rome, Curran had the theoretical background to argue for changes in this teaching, among others. But it was pastoral experience with lay Catholics that finally convinced him. As a frequent leader of prayer and study groups with married couples and seminars for Catholic chaplains, he came to believe that the experience of people was a primary factor in determining morality. Ironically, Pope John Paul II also took this "personalist" attitude as his beginning point when he was a student and priest. But the two churchmen came to different conclusions about experience's effect on "the truth." What was wrong, Curran asked himself, with good Catholics wanting to limit the size of their families when they had good reasons to? Curran had started on his collision course with traditional moral theology.

Before long, the auxiliary bishop of Rochester alerted Curran that his theology was too progressive and avant garde, too heavily influenced by "the German theology." Partly for his new approach and its popular expression through his occasional essays, and partly because of the dearth of interesting moral theologians in the United States, Curran became known outside St. Bernard's. In March 1963 he was invited to present a paper on Catholic moral theology at a Harvard University colloquium. At first he shied from the invitation because of his youth, but he was persuaded finally to attend. Then at a theology convention that year, Walter Schmitz, dean of the school of sacred theology at The Catholic University of America, approached Curran with a job proposal. In addition to Schmitz's formal follow-up letter, inquiries about teaching also came from the University of Notre Dame and Fordham University. Curran passed them on to his ordinary, Bishop James E. Carney. Carney, an alumnus and board member of Catholic University, was reluctant to send the progressive young Curran to stir up his alma matter. What he told Schmitz was that Curran could not be replaced at St. Bernard's.

By fall of 1964, when he first wrote that he disagreed with the church condemnation of birth control by married couples, Curran was clearly in the progressive camp. He taught summer sessions at Catholic University in 1964 and 1965, the year in which he made his opposition to the ban on contraception quite public in a talk given to priests in Niagara, New York. He backed changes in priestly practice, endorsing general absolution at group penance and eschewing many private masses for a lesser number held with others. Back from his summer stint in Washington, Curran was informed by Bishop Carney that his teaching at St. Bernard's would end. He was too progressive for the Rochester seminary. When the topic of the Catholic University job arose, Curran said he might want to be a parish priest, but he was urged on to Washington.

His public activities put him on the radar screen of traditional Catholics, many of whom were preparing to fight the coming changes of Vatican II. Curran's nemesis was a New York lay Catholic, Hugo Maria Kellner. On February 19, 1965, Kellner began writing letters to the bishop of Rochester complaining about Curran's teachings. Before long, the treatises on Curran were being sent nationwide, including to the faculty and administrators at Catholic University. Of seven known Kellner tracts, three targeted Curran. They had some effect. A talk Curran was to give at Fordham to New York priests in the spring of 1965 was cancelled.

Curran arrived at Catholic University in September that year with a cause that had already evoked sympathy. Disputes had flared on campus over academic freedom and controversial speakers, pitting some professors against the administration. Faculty members in the religion departments assured Curran they supported his right to hold provocative opinions. It was a boost the thirty-one-year-old theologian needed.

Since 1957 the rector had been William McDonald, an Irish-born and Irish-educated priest who had begun at Catholic University as a professor of philosophy in 1940.[2] A decade later he succeeded Bishop Fulton J. Sheen in the university's chair of Philosophy of Religion. During his second five-year term as rector, McDonald was made auxiliary bishop of Washington. On his watch the university bloomed. Enrollment increased eighty-eight percent, faculty went up seventy percent, alumni giving rose twenty-three fold, investment in the campus tripled—twenty-one units or additions were built—and faculty salaries jumped one hundred-twelve percent. But many faculty members thought McDonald ruled the university with too firm and orthodox a hand. McDonald also represented a historic irritation: the American complaint of being governed by a foreign-born prelate. The Irishman had risen quickly, also serving as editor-in-chief of *The New Catholic Encyclopedia* and becoming president in 1960 of the International Federation of Catholic Universities, and for some professors that cultivated resentment.

In his first month at Catholic University, Curran was summoned by the vice rector, Monsignor Joseph McAllister, apparently prompted by a Kellner circular. He was told to be careful about espousing his views on birth control. But what Curran had determined to be his framework and method for moral reasoning invariably led him down the path of controversy on other moral issues. At Catholic University, he held a graduate seminar on the church's moral teaching that masturbation was a grave sin, and from it developed a paper delivered before a meeting of the Catholic Theological Society of America in June 1966. On this topic, he employed existential and historical views to argue that the act was less serious than the manuals asserted. New data, he said, should alter the church's teaching.

Curran's opinions on freedom, morality, birth control, mixed marriages, and Sunday observances were all put on the record in his first book, *Christian Morality Today,* a collection of his essays since 1963. On observances and penance, for example, he was unabashedly positive. Better than a gloomy and negative penance, he advised, a wife should bake her husband his favorite cake as an act of reparation. "It is much more beneficial than mumbling a few prayers because it serves to remind a wife that her entire day is the living of the vow she made on her wedding day," he wrote.[3]

In that decade, those pushing back old church horizons made an assumption. It was a cautionary note: Write for fellow theologians and some fellow priests but as little as possible for bishops and never for the general public. Before his first term at Catholic University had passed, Curran had spilled over that limit. Twice more he was called in by the vice rector, first in December 1965 over a statement he had signed for the White House Conference on Population. It said that church teaching on family planning should not dictate policy in a religiously pluralistic society. The more awkward of the two encounters came in September 1966. That month the *National Catholic Reporter* ran an article based on a series of Curran's talks and a phone interview. Curran had also become active in the Institute for Freedom in the Church and was quoted in the article as forecasting the doom of authoritarian moral teachings. They would be replaced by a form of ethics based on "the experience of Christian people," he said. "We today are beginning to break away from absolutism and this is precisely where the risk, the danger, the insecurity, the name-calling starts coming."[4]

Under new pressures from church authority, Curran discovered a way to defend himself, one he would employ in years to come. His explanation for the article was that it was "somewhat inaccurate." This was not the first time a newspaper had been cited for oversimplifying statements or using them out of context, but it raised enough of a credibility issue that the *Reporter* defended itself. It ran a column stating that Curran in fact had been given the article to read and had made slight changes.[5] In the cat-and-mouse debate,

Curran would say church teaching should be changed but then add that the media overlooked his nuanced reasoning. Nearly twenty years later, in protesting a Vatican investigation of his writings, he similarly said his controverted positions "are always carefully nuanced."[6] So in 1966 when the vice rector wanted an explanation for the *Reporter* article, Curran said it was impossible to convey in one document. He advised the rector to read all his articles, a time-consuming proposition.

The faculty members in Curran's department rallied to his support. They passed a resolution in October 1966 asking the rector to end the inquisition. These were times when faculty members at several Catholic universities were being forced to take a stand. Turmoil had erupted at two major Catholic institutions in 1966, and Curran's colleagues at Catholic University were in the mood to show some solidarity. For now, they hoped that open conflict and infighting would not be necessary at their campus as it was elsewhere.

At the University of Dayton in the fall of 1966, a philosophy professor charged four colleagues in philosophy and theology with publicly opposing church teachings.[7] The university investigated and ruled that the four were innocent, a decision that spurred eight other faculty members to call the investigation a whitewash. Those eight were censured by the school administration for their criticism. All this prompted the local archbishop to begin his own investigation, an intervention that alarmed the American Association of University Professors (AAUP) and brought down its opposition to the archbishop's involvement. By 1967 the archbishop had backed off, and the administration was standing firmly beside the four professors who had been accused originally. The original accusers resigned.

The year 1966 also had been the time when a conflict at St. John's University in Queens, New York, snowballed into a series of firings as union-organizing faculty members clashed with what they called a "paternalistic, anti-intellectual administration."[8] The dispute began in 1963 when the largely clerical administration refused to recognize a newly formed chapter of the AAUP. That policy changed, but a teachers' union was barred. The firings and an unsuccessful attempt at a mass strike in January 1966 sent ripples across other campuses and reminded of the latent tension between faculty members and university governance.

Through all of this the Vatican had remained quiet. But it had noticed the potential for more turmoil. It was especially concerned about those professors who, in the midst of this, were teaching faith and morals to young American Catholics. In 1966 the Congregation for the Doctrine of the Faith opened a file on Charles Curran.

DESPITE THE WARNINGS he had received at the university, Curran seemed to be on the track to tenure, the professor's Nirvana. By the end of his two-year contract, he had published a book and so could apply for promotion to associate professor. The request was approved by a school of theology committee and the academic senate. To some on the university's board of trustees, however, Curran was a risk. Archbishops Philip Hannan of New Orleans and John Krol of Philadelphia, joined by McDonald, reported on his unorthodox views. Although McDonald warned that rejecting Curran would trigger "serious campus repercussions," the April 10 meeting in Chicago voted not to renew his contract.[9] McDonald summoned the young theologian along with his dean, Walter Schmitz, on April 17 to hear the news. McDonald gave neither specific charges nor an explanation for the board's action. Later, the pro-Curran forces accused the rector of not telling the board that the committee and senate had recommended Curran's appointment; it was likely the board knew this but felt more compelled by the Krol report. It also was widely believed that the papal nuncio, Archbishop Egidio Vagnozzi, wanted Curran fired.

By some accounts, this conflict was what a discontented faculty and some in the activist student organizations were waiting for. In the mid-1960s, every campus worth its salt was seething to express some kind of challenge to authority. Society was in tumult. Race riots broke out in the Watts ghetto of Los Angeles in the spring of 1965, and by the end of that year the first "Peace in Vietnam" march drew thousands to Washington. Sandwiched between these events and the explosion of student violence across America in 1968-70, the year of the Curran affair was yeasty. As the old *Washington Star* said in an editorial, the campus protest was the release valve for years of pressure that had accumulated in the relationship between the trustees and the campus, especially the faculty. "The case of Father

Curran served more as an occasion for rather than the cause of their revolt," it said.[10]

On the day he learned the news, Curran said he would make his dismissal public but agreed to a twenty-four-hour cooling period. An ad hoc Committee for the Reinstatement of Father Curran was formed. The next day, Tuesday, McMahon Hall was the scene of a pro-Curran rally of about four hundred faculty members and students, more than half of them wearing the robes of priests and nuns. Wednesday at noon, as campus demonstrations continued—two thousand students demonstrated in front of McDonald's residence that morning—the theology faculty met and concluded, "We cannot and will not function unless and until Father Curran is reinstated."[11] They invited the other faculty members to revolt as well. That day Curran made a public appearance at a 2 P.M. press conference—his first.

On Thursday, Catholic University was effectively closed down. Still, a carnival atmosphere filled the campus as students rallied, musicians entertained, and the entire faculty met. They formed the Assembly of Faculty Professors and voted 400–18 to strike. Some sixty-six hundred students and six hundred faculty members finally became involved.

In a campus speech before some three thousand students, transmitted on national news that Friday, Curran declared, "The issues involved in this dismissal are greater than any one man. Catholic professional theologians need the opportunity to pursue their science with responsible freedom."[12] At a press conference afterward, he demanded reinstatement and called for a meeting between faculty and trustees to "discuss and clarify the basic underlying issues."[13]

Proposals were made for mediation so classes could resume, but nothing came of it. The trustees and administration then offered Curran a hearing before five bishops, but he rejected that. The battle lines were drawn quickly, with the students, faculty, and some of the nation's hierarchy on Curran's side and alumni and others in the hierarchy backing the trustees.

The real issue was the "administration's right to hire and fire its employees," the alumni association president said. "The next thing you know, the university will decide to paint a building red, but the students will say, 'No, paint it brown,' and they will go out and picket."[14]

Archbishop Lawrence Shehan of Baltimore said Curran should be "restored to his former status" and Cardinal Richard Cushing of Boston spoke of the ineptitude of the trustees, his fellow bishops, in the action. "It makes no sense to appoint people to a university board who know absolutely nothing about running a university," he said.[15]

On Sunday, at a demonstration of more than two thousand students on the campus mall, it was announced that Cardinal Patrick O'Boyle, archbishop of Washington and chancellor of the university, would meet with Curran and the faculty of the school of sacred theology the next day. Afterward a thousand protesters walked to nearby Trinity College, where Curran, in white and purple vestments. celebrated a Mass. Students continued to demonstrate before and after the meeting the next day to keep up the pressure. That evening at 6 P.M. O'Boyle mounted the steps of the John K. Mullen Memorial Library and said the board's action was rescinded. He made it clear, however, that the decision "must not be interpreted as in any way reflecting theological issues injected by the news media. In particular, it in no way derogates from the teachings of the church . . . on birth control."[16]

The remark was salient because of what also had happened the week of the strike. For several years a papal commission had been researching the church's teaching on birth control, and that week the *Reporter* published a majority report of the commission that took a liberal stance: Change the teaching, the report said. This revelation fueled the hopes of those fighting to change the disputed moral teaching, and it doubtless stirred the ferment at Catholic University.

Curran was given a new three-year contract and rank of associate professor beginning September 1967. He received two years of credit for teaching at St. Bernard's so his appointment carried him through the seven-year probationary period required for the next step—a tenured contract. Classes resumed on Tuesday, and Curran celebrated a victory Mass that evening by Curran at the monumental National Shrine of the Immaculate Conception, adjacent to the Catholic University campus.

When the dust settled, O'Boyle met April 29 with faculty representatives, who pressed for changes they had presented to the chancellor earlier in 1967. These included McDonald's departure. The sixty-three-year-old McDonald finished his second five-year term that year, a natural time to phase out. By September he was gone, serving as auxiliary to the archbishop of San Francisco. For the next year, John P. Whalen, a more progressive priest who was a professor of theology, was the interim rector. By the time a full rector, to be called president, came into office in the spring of 1969, the university had been refashioned; under new bylaws its governing board was half composed of lay trustees, ending the clerical dominion that once had served as a direct line of Vatican oversight.

THROUGH THE STRIKE Curran became known as a leading dissenter, but now he was to be launched onto the national scene. Rumors about what the papal commission would finally say about birth control had floated around since the group was appointed in 1962. Since the spring of 1968, the prevailing hearsay had been that Pope Paul VI would restate the ban on artificial contraception. A network of theologians around the country was quickly prepared to launch a public dissent from the imminent encyclical.[17] But the first manifestation of the coming conflict occurred in a document for Washington and Baltimore priests. The "Guidelines for the Teaching of Religion" in those dioceses asserted that priests and teachers should uphold the ban. The Association of Washington Priests took the document to theologians at Catholic University to guide them in their theological dissent.

Curran was spending the summer of 1969 at St. Bonaventure University in Olean, New York, when he was called by the old *Washington Star* about the guidelines. Curran's critical comment appeared on the front page on July 28. Ironically, that night the correspondent for *Time* magazine in Rome called Curran to alert him that the encyclical was to be released the next day. On Monday morning, July 29, *Humanae Vitae* shook the Catholic world. After so much anticipation that church teaching would be relaxed, it echoed the same official position as the 1930 encyclical on marriage, *Casti Connubii*: If the procreative act "is deliberatively frustrated in its natural power to generate life [it] is an offense against the law of God and of nature, and those who indulge in such are branded with the guilt of grave sin."[18] Curran flew back to Catholic University and was the chief author, with ten other theologians, of a statement of dissent. "Spouses may responsibly decide according to their consciences that artificial contraception in some circumstances is permissible and indeed necessary to preserve and foster the values and sacredness of marriage," the statement said.[19] Through the network of dissent, eighty-seven theologians signed on to the statement by that night. It was sent to 1,200 Catholic theologians. Six hundred would affix their names.

At the Mayflower Hotel a few blocks down from O'Boyle's chancery, the Association of Washington Priests had already reserved a room for their July 30 press conference to protest the guidelines. Now, that moment was given over to the theologians. Curran led the Tuesday morning news event, a declaration of dissent that he later said was happening for "the first time in recorded modern history."[20] Almost half of the twenty-one dissenting theologians at Catholic University were members of the ecclesiastical faculties. What was more, dozens of archdiocesan priests signed the dissenting document.

Two days later some lay members of the papal commission on contraception also stated their dissent in a press conference. At that event, Curran sought to widen the impression of consensus by saying that the theologians' statement was not incompatible with what the American bishops had said in their support of the encyclical. That was too sanguine for the bishops, however, especially in the media spotlight. To disassociate from the theologians Auxiliary Bishop Joseph Bernardin of Atlanta, then general secretary of the National Conference of Catholic Bishops, issued a statement clarifying its alliance with the papal position.

The Washington priests were O'Boyle's initial concern, and he summoned them to recant or face suspension. There was dissent in other dioceses around the country, but O'Boyle, finding himself at storm center, took the strongest hand. He called for obedience to the encyclical "without equivocation, ambiguity, or simulation."[21] Some twenty-five to thirty priests were penalized, with suspensions ranging from no preaching to not hearing confession.

As the dissent spread, a group of bishops and theologians met on August 18 in New York at Whalen's invitation to discuss implications of the encyclical and dissent. No problems were solved. O'Boyle sent a special delivery letter to dissenting professors on the religion faculty and eleven days later, on August 20, held a consultation. O'Boyle had both civil and canon lawyers at the meeting, as well as a court reporter transcribing the testimonies. After an open hearing, he gave the professors ten days to state in writing to him their positions on dissent and birth control. The professors reacted strongly. They objected to the short deadline, knowing that without the students on campus to stage protests their arsenal was diminished. O'Boyle relented and gave them until October 1. "Frankly, I believe I will have to refer the matter to the board of trustees and ask for a special meeting of the board," O'Boyle said.[22] For the professors, the meeting with O'Boyle indicated that he opposed dissent itself, no matter what the mode or manner.

To address this distinction between dissent and its outward form, among other issues, the trustees met September 5 at the Madison Hotel in downtown Washington. Some faculty representatives who sided with Curran attended as well as some bishops not on the board. O'Boyle read a letter from the Vatican's secretary of state, Cardinal Amleto Cicognani. It commended O'Boyle's firmness with the priests and, though counseling restraint, also suggested that the dissenting theologians be dealt with, too, unless they recanted. Cardinal James McIntyre of Los Angeles motioned that the dissenters on the faculty be fired. O'Boyle too was impatient, and he responded by throwing down the letter. For two weeks the professors had gotten away with their dissent, O'Boyle said. "I move we fire them all."[23] By the time the twelve-hour meeting ended, however, the motion was thought imprudent. Accordingly, McIntyre withdrew it.

As an alternative, the board called for an inquiry to find out if the theologians had violated their responsibilities as professors, especially "the style and method of organizing and publicizing their dissent."[24] The dean of the school of engineering and architecture, Donald E. Marlowe, was asked to head one of two committees that reviewed the issue. The so-called Marlowe committee, which became the lasting symbol of the campus inquiry, probed into the propriety, rights, and implications of the public dissent. The committee did not meet until October 31, but the process began September 9 when Whalen proposed four questions for the theologians' response. The next day five of the professors met for three hours with executives and counsel of the American Association of University Professors, which, like a union, could sometimes organize collective bargaining for professors in contract disputes. They said Curran should get a lawyer. The American Civil Liberties Union offered to help, but one of the dissenting theologians at Catholic University got assistance from his brother in a major New York law firm.

That professor was Robert Hunt, who had joined the theological faculty about the same year as Curran. His brother, John H. Hunt, was a partner at Cravath Swaine & Moore and gave gratis representation to Curran and the others before the Marlowe hearings. Although Curran and the others felt they were being put on trial and asked that specific charges be lodged against them, the committee did not proceed that way. Instead, it simply took testimony from thirty-eight witnesses and studied more that three thousand pages of exhibits for the next five months.

In April 1969, the Marlowe committee issued its report on the dissent of July 30, 1968. "The content and style of the [dissenting] statements are well within the bounds of academic propriety," the report said. It concluded: "The rights of a faculty member to determine the content of his public statement without fear of reprisal, even though such statement may embarrass his institution in its relationship with its various constituencies, cannot be challenged." To illustrate when a scholar can dissent from noninfallible church teaching, the Marlowe report cited a pastoral letter released by the National Conference of Catholic Bishops in November 1968, *Human Life in Our Day*. The pastoral's "Norms of Licit Theological Dissent" listed three conditions: The reasons are serious; the manner of the dissent does not impugn teachings of church; it does not give scandal. The Marlowe report stated that even under these standards, Catholic University's statutes "are patently incompatible with modern American university practice" regarding academic freedom.[25]

Although the Marlowe report became the symbol of reform toward freedom at Catholic University, there was a hitch. It had to be adopted by the trustees to be binding. At its April 12, 1969, meeting in Houston, the board asked Cardinal Krol to set up a commission to study the Marlowe report and respond. At the next board meeting, in June, the trustees passed a resolution that said "acceptance" of the report "does not imply complete agreement that all findings are supported in the record." The trustees said they trusted the theology faculty's Catholic commitment but then quoted from a recent church document to clarify their view on a theologian's role: "As an individual he is bound to accept the authentic teaching of the church and to submit to its legitimately exercised authority. As a theological scholar he is bound by the nature of the discipline to take into proper account the pronouncements of the church."[26] There was no public confrontation, but the Marlowe committee and the trustees were far from agreement.

Nevertheless, many on the faculty and in the administration viewed the report as a guarantor of academic freedom. After Whalen, Nivard Scheel, a Xavierian brother, became acting rector. In his May 1969 baccalaureate address he alluded to the results of the Marlowe committee. "What we were doing was what a university ought to do, that we were being truly a university, and at the same time, we were being truly Catholic."[27] Catholic University also used the Marlowe report in its 1970 statement to its accrediting agency, Middle States Association of Colleges and Schools, after the bylaw changes.

But the triumph was not complete. That fall of 1969, the Catholic University faculty chose Old Testament professor Roland Murphy to succeed Schmitz as dean of the school of theology. But the choice of a new president, Clarence Walton, aborted that. Walton rejected the recommendation because Murphy had signed the dissent on *Humanae Vitae*. Murphy resigned.

CURRAN'S NOTORIETY continued to grow. In mid-1969 he was elected to the one-year post of president of the Catholic Theological Society of America. Newspapers quoted him more frequently for his provocative talks and ideas. The proposal for the new revised Code of Canon Law "ought to be bombed out of existence,"Curran said, speaking in 1970 as outgoing president of the society.[28]

In October of 1971, Curran was granted tenure at Catholic University as "ordinary professor." Other honors came his way. In 1971 he became the first Catholic elected president of the Society of Christian Ethics. The next year, the Catholic Theological Society nominated Curran for its Spellman Award, founded and funded by Cardinal Francis Spellman of New York. Cardinal Terrance Cooke, now overseer of the prize money as Spellman's successor in New

York, resisted the selection of Curran. So the board of the theological society created its own award, named for the late John Courtney Murray, a Jesuit and American dissenter, and gave that to Curran.

During the 1970s, Curran taught about forty students, all graduate level, in his moral theology courses each year. Several of his doctoral students entered the field of moral theology. In the next two decades his scholarship established its place, though neutral observers have said it was not the stuff of intellectual history. Indeed, Curran has said moral theology does not produce classics, as does speculative theology. Its aim is the practical.

That bent, in fact, encouraged voluminous writing—the final weight behind Curran's reputation. By 1975 he had written twelve books, edited two others, and written seventy-two articles. There were more by 1987: He had written nine more books and fifty-one articles and edited for books.[29] A look in the English section of most European Catholic bookstores usually will turned up something by Charles Curran. His writings generally were accessible to lay readers. Eventually six monographs would be written on Curran's work, some of them doctoral dissertations by students in Austria, Belgium, Canada, and Italy. His intellectual critics happily noted, however, that even by 1990 no major disciple of the Curran school was on the horizon.

With much of the soil in moral theology exhausted by 1974, Curran took no new positions regarding sexual ethics and moved on to social ethics. (On abortion, he did develop a theory of law's relationship to morality that concluded a constitutional amendment should not be sought to overturn Roe vs. Wade). Curran wrote in 1975 that just distribution of the world's resources was the most pressing social ethics issue. Catholic social ethics, he discovered, had advanced beyond moral theology in its methods. It embraced, he said, historical consciousness, an inductive methodology, and deeper recognition of a person's freedom and dignity.

Paralleling Curran's academic career was his public life. During the 1970s his notoriety was buoyed on a tide of speaking invitations. In all of this, by most accounts, Curran remained a sincere and responsible priest. "He lives simply and has a remarkable ability to combine a life of serious scholarship with generous availability to a variety of persons," his ordinary, Bishop Matthew Clark of Rochester, said publicly some years later. Even his opponents within the American church called him "Charlie," as he would wish friend and foe to address him.

Though given to talking extensively about himself, Curran had his reasons. A great amount of attention was thrust on him. And out of conviction, he said, he labeled positions as his in order to distinguish them from official church teaching. Meanwhile, Curran remained part of a shrinking quantity at major universities—professors who enjoyed instructing. By the 1980s, that was a salient critique of higher education: Professors had assistants teach their courses while they focused on research. Whatever students or administrators thought of Curran's positions, his devotion to the classroom was evident.

And yet all his public and private virtues finally cut both ways. They combined to make Curran the closest thing around to a popularizer of the more progressive school of moral theology and sexual ethics. The corollary to his public rise was, of course, increased opposition from conservative Catholic groups, especially in their national press. This came with a vengeance by the late 1970s.

The Vatican, too, was aware that while Curran was an academic, his ideas had gained public currency. Despite the nuance and footnotes, Curran's work reached an ordinary faithful largely unprepared to discern alternatives or optional argument to his positions. What would strike them was the conclusion: A traditional "do not" in the church can now be a "maybe" or a "yes."

After nearly a decade of uneasy silence between Curran and the official church, Catholic University got a new president in 1978. Curran visited Edmund Pellegrino to apprise him of the past disputes on dissent and academic freedom. In Pellegrino's account, Curran was friendly and open but clearly was trying to swing the president into his camp in preparation for future battles with the Vatican.

The next year, in 1979, Curran took a sabbatical, a time of relative freedom and pursuit of personal interests. The year was deceptively quiet, for in the Vatican an old manual typewriter was clacking away on his file at the Congregation for the Doctrine of the Faith. It typed out excerpts from Curran's works. Then came a letter dated July 13, 1979, that told Curran the congregation "has judged it necessary to examine some of these writings."[30] It had been sent by Cardinal Franjo Seper, then prefect of the congregation.

Curran was stirred by the correspondence. He called other moral theologians he knew in Belgium, France, England, and Germany to see if they, too, had been contacted. They had not. On the moral theology front, he was the only one.

TWO

Vatican File 4866

As the Second Vatican Council ended in 1965, the Vatican began anew its surveillance of theological dissent. Files were opened on progressive theologians, and when Pope John Paul II arrived in 1978 the accumulation of information begged action. The new pontiff faced this question: Had theological freedom overrun respect for the authority of the magisterium?

Three years before Curran received the 1979 Vatican letter with "observations" about his ideas, formal dialogues had already begun with two European theologians. Edward A. Schillebeeckx, a Dutch priest, and Swiss-born Hans Küng were the first casualties in a new era of conflict over dissent. The contact made with Curran in 1979 brought the trend to the United States.

Schillebeeckx and Küng had been negotiating with the Vatican over their theological stands since 1976, but the boom was lowered at the end of 1979. First came the Dutchman, whose exploration of the human side of Jesus alarmed some Vatican theologians who though that he had ventured far from the traditional language of the Council of Nicea, that Christ was divine as well as human. Schillebeeckx's work was also perceived as softening the doctrine of the uniqueness of the ordained priesthood. After a few years of correspondence with the Congregation for the Doctrine of the Faith, he went with his Dominican superior to meet with Vatican officials in December 1979.

Though the media expected a great and dramatic heresy trial, the two-day hearing led to a friendly parting. A compromise statement was forged. Then the Vatican announced that Schillebeeckx's theological views on the priesthood were "at variance with the teaching of the Church," but he remained a theologian in good standing.[1]

The Küng case created far more turmoil. He refused to go to

Rome for talks. As Schillebeeckx was winding up his consultation at Vatican City on December 15, 1979, a decree was issued on Küng: "He can no longer be considered a Catholic theologian nor function as such in a teaching role," the Vatican said.

The Swiss-born theologian and priest had challenged the primacy of the papal office and the teaching claims of the hierarchy and had blurred the line between the ordained priesthood and "the priesthood of all baptized peoples." To his critics, he was downright Protestant in his sentiments. Küng had left behind the medieval German atmosphere of the University of Tübingen to become a prolific publicist and writer, often generating ill will in the process. Critiques of orthodoxy had been too subtle to arouse the Vatican, he said, "so I had to sound the alarm . . . There are cases, and this is one of them, where it is expedient to engage in polemics."

After his appointment to a chair at Tübingen in 1962, he gained considerable power in the battle of ideas during the Second Vatican Council and believed he set the tone thereafter. "My inquiry into infallibility gave rise to the greatest debate among Catholic theologians since Vatican II," he said. Küng's works had come under scrutiny, off and on, since 1963, but only when the council closed did they become a formal issue for the Congregation for the Doctrine of the Faith. Negotiations over a threat of discipline did not begin until 1976.

When Küng was stripped of his status as an official Catholic theologian in 1980, likening himself to Galileo and the exiled Andrei Sakharov in frigid Siberia, John Paul wondered at the complaint. "Does a theologian who no longer accepts completely the doctrine of the church still have the right to teach in the name of the church, and on the basis of a special mission received from her?" the pope asked rhetorically in a letter commending the German bishops' action. "Can he himself still wish to do so, if some dogmas of the church are contrary to his personal convictions?"[2]

WHEN CURRAN RECEIVED his first warning from the Vatican, the July 1979 letter with "observations" about his teachings, word had leaked out to the Catholic press. One report said that Curran and Schillebeeckx were both summoned to Rome. When news reporters called, Curran denied the rumor and said he was bound only to write letters. In fact, the timing of the "observations" may have been related to American incidents more than developments on the European scene.

On February 19, 1979, Curran was scheduled to give a talk on "Christian Social Ethics in the Twentieth Century" for the Catholic campus ministry at Louisiana State University. Bishop Joseph V. Sullivan of Baton Rouge denied the event access to the campus's Catholic center. Staff members at the conservative Catholic newspaper, *The Wanderer,* had culled revealing quotes from Curran's writings, and the list was released with Sullivan's approval.

On April 29, the secretary of the congregation sent a supportive letter to Bishop Sullivan. But apparently the Vatican was still unsettled, if divided, on the issue in those first months of John Paul's reign. Sullivan was summoned to Rome by intervention of the papal delegate in Washington, Archbishop Jean Jadot, who has been described as either "pastoral" or as "liberal" in his agenda. It was not the normal *ad limina* visit made by each bishop every five years but a special consultation with the prefect of the Congregation for Bishops.

At issue was Sullivan's performance as a bishop and his failure to consult and work in solidarity with the other bishops, Sullivan later confided to close associates.[3] He believed his maverick stand against Curran, a theologian of growing popularity, prompted the summons. A memo was sent to the American hierarchy, he said later, advising against such independent actions by bishops. The Louisiana flap only increased Curran's notoriety. In mid-June of that year, he was invited to give a talk on human sexuality at Marquette University. His appearance, sponsored by the office of religious education of the Archdiocese of Milwaukee, led to protests before the talk and tight security during it.

It was after these events in early 1979 that the Vatican issued its "observations" on Curran's writings.[4] The sixteen-page document was sent to Cardinal William Baum of Washington, who had succeeded O'Boyle in 1973. Nearly three weeks later, on August 2, Cardinal Baum told Curran at the archdiocesan chancery that the Vatican was investigating his theological positions. He was shown the congregation's missive.

Curran took a copy of the letter to some canon lawyers to ask if the protocol number on it—4866—meant anything. It meant that file

48 was begun in 1966. The congregation said the primary flaw in his theology was the lack of due respect for noninfallible teachings. After the charges were stated in that letter, no additional ones were added. Nor had Rome said he should curtail his public dissents. Curran continued to state some forms of dissent between 1979 and 1986 but decided to refrain from any public statements about the investigation, a decision he stuck to until 1986.

By his fifteenth year in Washington, Curran was to deal with his third archbishop, who was also chancellor of the university. Archbishop James A. Hickey arrived from Cleveland in 1980. He had some experience in the administration of higher education, but his strength was as a pastoral leader and loyalist to the pope. Hickey was a past head of the North American College in Rome. He was promptly briefed on the Curran investigation.

Communications to Curran from the Vatican came through Hickey and once or twice through the apostolic delegate at the Vatican embassy in Washington. Most of the time, Curran passed responses to the Vatican through Hickey, who wanted to help the dialogue along. He once worked with Curran on a particular response letter. Curran also sent responses through the delegate. In an August 1984 letter to William J. Byron, The Catholic University of America's Jesuit president since 1982, Curran offered to move from the department of theology to the department of religion and religious education, which is not an ecclesiastical faculty, if the investigation would in turn be closed. With no authority to close a Vatican investigation, university officials rejected the offer. They also believed such changes were technicalities, not offers to obey the Vatican.

Curran began meeting with Hickey and Joseph Bernardin of Chicago, now a cardinal and chairman of the board of trustees at the university, as early as 1984 to try to reach a compromise. Then in October 1985 the Vatican asked Curran to recant. "The positions you have maintained on various important elements of moral doctrine are in open contrast with the teachings of the magisterium," the letter said. "The Congregation now invites you to reconsider and retract those positions which violate the conditions necessary for a professor to be called a Catholic theologian."[5]

Hickey and Bernardin met with Curran at the downtown Univer-

The bishops were taking pains to avoid the enmity that often attended a theological quarrel, common enough in church history to be called a special kind of hatred, *odium theologicum*. At that juncture of gap narrowing, Curran presented a compromise. He offered to not teach sexual ethics, which he had not taught since about 1970 anyway, and the Vatican could declare what it considered errors in his writings. In return, however, his status on the faculty would not be touched, ensuring that he would remain a "Catholic theologian in good standing."

Curran was crafting his compromise based on some of the precedents set when other theologians were disciplined—and there were more after his case. The Vatican needed some concession, and better he suggest it than leave it to them entirely.

The Schillebeeckx resolution was along lines amenable to Curran—that is, Schillebeeckx's positions were critiqued officially and the critique was declared, but he remained a theologian in good standing. In early 1980, the German bishops had withdrawn Hans Küng's license to teach as a Catholic theologian. Tübingen, though a state university, had a theology faculty that was ecclesiastical, appointed by the German bishops, and that is where Küng had taught. He continued to teach at Tübingen, but not under church auspices. Another case from that period was the French Dominican Jacques Pohier, whose 1979 book, *Quand je dis Dieu,* was scrutinized for straying from orthodoxy. He was barred from teaching matters of faith or celebrating the Eucharist publicly.[8] In 1984, Brazilian Franciscan Leonardo Boff was summoned to Rome for his advocacy of liberation theology. He was charged with teaching erroneously that church power is with the people, not the hierarchy, and in May 1985 he was silenced for a year—a proscription he obeyed.[9]

Curran's compromise, which would have left him intact at Catholic University, got support from some but was far from acceptable to the Vatican. The tension with Rome only seemed to increase. At this point Hickey suggested Curran use his privilege to meet Cardinal Joseph Ratzinger, head of the office investigating his teachings. To him the compromise could be put directly.

Ratzinger was archbishop of Munich in 1979 when Curran was advised of the investigation of his writings, but by 1981 the German theologian was to become chief doctrinal watchdog. Being head of the office once called the Holy Office of the Inquisition gave mythic proportions to his post, especially as his detractors fanned that inquisitional image. But Ratzinger was more complicated than an old-line conservative, for his background was mixed.

As a German priest among the so-called "Rhine Fathers" in the 1960s, he was considered progressive in his contributions to the Second Vatican Council: To antireform conservatives then he was doubtless a dangerous liberal. He was a founder, along with other German theologians such as Hans Küng, of the liberal journal *Concilium.* Indeed, one historian said, "Ratzinger's writings of this period radiated with enthusiasm for the new climate of freedom, lively pluralism, and active lay participation."[10]

By the end of the council, however, he was firmly in the moderate camp, breaking with the Rhine Fathers, whose proposals he saw as too sweeping. He also jettisoned the council's optimistic prognosis—that the church and the world were progressing together on a natural path to freedom and goodness. In those circumstances, he chose authority over freedom for what he believed was the good of the church. Hans Küng calls the choice tragic. "Joseph Ratzinger is afraid," he said. "And just like Dostoevsky's Grand Inquisitor, he fears nothing more than freedom . . . something one would not have thought possible in light of the remarkable theological work which this man produced in the 1960s."[11]

Ratzinger saw not freedom but wild centrifugal forces from the council knocking down too much certainty and too much tradition. All that was once valued as supernatural was replaced by the groping to fulfill human needs and exigencies. And, the cardinal believed, Vatican II was being used to justify it all. Summarizing the final session of the council, he said, "Many today seek for modernity, not for truth," an observer noted.[12] Ratzinger felt called to shore up the tradition. Drawing the line on errant theologians and clarifying a few rules was clearly his Vatican mandate when Charles Curran moved into sight.

For the March 1986 meeting in Rome between Curran and Ratzinger, theologian Bernard Häring prepared the way for Curran, and did it bluntly. Upstairs at the congregation's office in Vatican City, Häring opened the meeting by showing Ratzinger a list of mistakes the Vatican office had made that had upheld orthodox church doctrine in past centuries. But minds were made up, apparently, and the meeting resolved nothing; Curran's compromise proposal was rejected. Afterward, the seventy-four-year-old Häring counseled that Christians live on hope. But, he added, "You're not going to win this, Charlie. They're going to get you."[13] In a few years, Häring would be calling for the abolition of Ratzinger's office.

The first press release in the case was a joint one by Ratzinger and Curran after the Rome meeting. Flying back to Washington, Curran held a press conference at Catholic University on March 11, 1986. He revealed the October letter about recanting. "I cannot and do not retract," he said. Dissent from noninfallible teaching is possible, he added, and continued: "I have never been told who my accusers are. I have been given no opportunity of counsel. The congregation itself has performed the roles of both accuser and judge." Ratzinger labeled the charges specious: "Your own works have been your 'accusers' and they alone," the cardinal had said earlier in correspondence, noting also the abundance of Curran's advisers during the investigation.[14] Like dominos, the reaction came. Curran's bishop in Rochester issued a statement supporting him. While Bernardin was in Rome, according to news reports, he met with Vatican officials to appeal for the compromise presented earlier.[15] Past presidents of the Catholic Theological Society of America endorsed Curran.

Students and faculty members supporting the theologian geared up for a national campaign, but this was not 1967 or 1968. Former students of Curran's held a rally, and more than two hundred people gathered March 15 for a pro-Curran campus teach-in. Friends of Catholic Theology, which had formed a year earlier to promote American experience in Catholic theology, took up Curran's cause, later incorporating as a nonprofit entity. Battle lines were drawn, just as in the past, but apparently among a much narrower audience at Catholic University. Times had changed, symbolized in the most obvious, visible difference: Curran had protested in black clerical garb and collar in 1967, as nuns in habits by the droves had carried picket signs in his support; during his March 11 press conference at Catholic University, the thirty or so professors crowded into the room were mostly priests wearing casual coats and ties, as did Curran. Much had already been "liberated" at that campus. The urgency was gone.

As the days led toward a showdown, morale at the school of religious studies was hit hard, but campus life went on obliviously. This generation of students was living in a decade of reaction to the sexual revolution, while at the same time casual disagreement with church teaching was so commonplace that one professor's dissent did not stand out. A new pope was in charge, and a third of the American bishops were his appointees. The president of the National Conference of Catholic Bishops, Bishop James Malone of Youngstown, Ohio, subscribed to the Vatican action against Curran.

And unlike the past, the lead editorial in the student paper, *The Tower,* said Curran should recant. "The right of the church to protect faithfully her teachings and guide those who would teach as Catholic theologians is paramount," it said.[16] The students who knew of the issue were divided, however, and with a shift of students on the editorial board, Curran got a positive editorial nine months later.

For the theological community and some other academics, it was a time to stand ground. Curran and his intellectual allies argued that he was in the mainstream of current moral theology and that he was simply singled out by the Vatican as a deterrent, much as the Internal Revenue Service audits or prosecutes a movie star to educate the public. Curran estimated that fifty percent of all moral theologians held the same positions as he.

"This is more serious than 1968," Curran said. "This is intervention by the Holy See."[17] University of Notre Dame theologian Richard McBrien called it the Vatican's biggest blunder. Catholic University's school of religious studies faculty voted to give a good word for Curran and support the compromise proposal, as did the psychology faculty. *Commonweal* magazine called the demand to recant "a genuine scandal, an action by Rome so dismaying that it requires something beyond outrage."[18]

Curran sent his reply to the Vatican on April 1—he would not recant. The Catholic Theological Society adopted a statement June 14 advising the Vatican against disciplining Curran, focusing on the right to dissent rather than the issues of moral theology. As in the past, Curran turned to the American Association of University Professors to understand his legal rights and to see what leverage the professors' collective might have to fight his removal.

FINALLY, HICKEY RECEIVED the July 25, 1986, letter from Ratzinger to Curran telling the theologian he was neither "suitable nor eligible to exercise the function of a professor of Catholic theology." Based on the "definitive judgment in this case," Hickey was to take "appropriate action." The pope, on June 10, had approved both the letter's "content and procedures followed."[19]

On August 18, when Hickey could schedule it, Curran came to the archbishop's residence at 4 P.M. and was handed the letter. For the welfare of the university, Hickey said, he would begin the proceedings to withdraw Curran's canonical mission, a sort of license allowing him to teach theology in the name of the church. They talked about due process. Curran's main concern was how the decision affected his tenure. Hickey said the board would determine that. Curran had until September 1 to decide if he wanted the due process hearing allowed him. As they parted, the battle for the media began. To Curran's chagrin, Hickey showed him a notice already released for a press conference the next day.

Byron and Hickey together announced the Vatican's decision on August 19. Officials in Rome were telling reporters there that the decision on Curran significantly expanded the area in Catholic theology that is not up for debate.[20] The action set a precedent for disciplining theologians over moral teachings rather than the customary doctrinal ones. Hans Küng had questioned doctrines of papal primacy and Edward Schillebeeckx the nature of Christ, theological issues settled in dogma or church councils. Now, the Curran case brought practical questions of sexual morality under the jurisdiction of right belief and doctrine. The action presaged an effort by church authorities to define better which moral teachings are binding. Vatican officials also said Curran's effort to prove that the Catholic population agreed with him, an appeal to public opinion, made the Holy See even more determined to maintain its control.

Curran held his own news conference at Catholic University and said he would fight the decision. He said he believed the Vatican had singled him out because he was an American. "I'm from the United States, and there has been friction between the Vatican and the church in the U.S.," he said. Was he an American target? he was asked. "I think very much so."

"You're dealing with the issue of sexuality—a most volatile issue. Put sexuality and authority together and you're bound to have neuralgia."[21]

Three days after the declaration on Curran, John Paul was having lunch and talking with *Time* correspondent Wilton Wynn. The subject of Curran naturally arose. "There is already too much confusion, and that kind of teaching only added to the confusion," the pope said to Wynn. The journalist reminded the pope that Curran said he dissented only from noninfallible moral teachings. At this, the pope leaned forward at the table and put his hands over his eyes to focus on choosing the right words. "Of course, the church has made no solemn declaration of infallibility regarding moral issues, but infallible declarations on any subject have been extremely rare in the history of the church," John Paul said. "If you believe only those declarations, you have very little left to believe."

There is an "ordinary magisterium" also to be obeyed, he said, adding that neither the Ten Commandments nor Jesus' call to love thy neighbor have been made infallible teachings. "Does that mean you have a right to dissent on those teachings?" he asked.[22]

Although it seemed so, all the theologians in the United States were not in Curran's camp. Two weeks after the declaration on Curran was disclosed, the Fellowship of Catholic Scholars, a conservative group formed in 1977, held a press conference backing the Vatican. This was a case of "truth in advertising," said theologians William May of Catholic University and Richard Roach, both reformed dissenters from the days of *Humanae Vitae*. Curran is "a friend, a good man . . . a good Catholic, in many ways a holy man," May said. "And I think he is sincere in what he holds . . . just as I think [South African President] P.W. Botha is sincere in what he thinks. But I think he is wrong."[23] Curran met more opposition speaking at a forum in Los Angeles with the city's Archbishop Roger Mahony, who backed the Vatican's position in debate before an audience of 1,500. "I believe that in these cases the theologian or theologians have seriously moved beyond their role of 'theologian' and have usurped the role of 'pastor' held by the bishops and pope," Mahony said.[24]

Curran remained concerned about his tenure and wrote to Byron in November asking about his rights. "Simple fairness and justice demand that I receive an answer to this question," Curran wrote. Byron responded, saying there appeared to be "no direct relationship" between tenure and the canonical mission.[25] Curran had been on sabbatical that year. But since he was staying on campus in anticipation of his faculty hearings, on September 2 the dean of the school of religious studies asked that he teach a few courses in the fall term. The first signs of administrative intervention now appeared; that request to teach was denied.

To follow were the course assignments for the winter term, beginning in January. The 1986 Christmas break was coming to a close and the directory of classes and professors had already been issued to students. Included in a preliminary list for the school of religious studies was Charles Curran for three graduate-level courses; Social and Political Ethics, Moral Theology and Practice, and Bible and Moral Theology. Curran said that because there were no findings against him by the faculty committee, which would not meet until April, he would teach his classes. But in November, Catholic University's vice president for academic affairs overruled the religion school and replaced Curran's name with T.B.A.—to be announced.

On January 9, Hickey told Curran he was suspended, an action based on a punitive section in the canonical statutes for the ecclesiastical faculties. Backed by the bishops on the board, Hickey wanted an agreement from Curran in two weeks that he would not teach. Curran called the action "unwarranted" and contended that it "prejudges the issue before the committee and ultimately the board of trustees."[26] Curran offered to be a professor at large, but that was rejected. As chancellor, Hickey also spurned the advice of two clergymen on campus, Curran's department chairman, David Power, and William Cenker, dean of the school of religious studies; they opposed the suspension.

An argument now took place over the nature of the department, Curran's right to teach, and Hickey's authority to intervene. Hickey restated his intention to the dean and chairman, but Curran persisted, saying the canonical suspension did not touch classes in which he only taught nonecclesiastical degree students. He estimated seventy-five percent of his students were in that category. Hickey's policy in the face of this was to reject Curran's delineation of two student groups, holding instead that the school of religious studies "is one department, one ecclesiastical faculty."[27]

Doubting Hickey's authority over the nonecclesiastical faculties, which were governed by their own committees, Curran did not relent. A January 13 meeting between Hickey, the dean, and the chairman produced no compromise. The term was to open in two days and it appeared that Curran was intent on striding into the classroom. To block that, Hickey informed Curran that he had until noon January 14 to promise he would refrain from teaching. If he did not, the cardinal would invoke Canon 812 in the 1983 Code of Canon Law. The canon, feared for its sweeping power, said: "It is necessary that those who teach theological disciplines in any institute of higher studies have a mandate from a competent ecclesiastical authority." Never yet used, it allowed the local bishop to remove a faculty member unconditionally. Fighting against what he considered an unjust suspension was important, "but I did not want to have that be the occasion for the invocation of Canon 812 in the United States," Curran said later.[28]

Curran met Hickey's deadline, and the next day, January 15, he held a press conference as classes at Catholic University began. "If there is a story today, the story is Curran blinked," the media-savvy Curran said about his backing off.[29] The three courses had been cancelled the day before; no substitute teacher had been found. Later that month, Hickey made clear that Curran was not to direct any doctoral dissertations either.

Byron called the suspension a necessary administrative decision until the board of trustees acted. Failure to take the action, Hickey said later, "would be perceived to be an act in defiance of the declaratory judgment rendered by the Holy See."[30] Curran believed the suspension from teaching the spring courses, despite no faculty findings against him, was a breach of his teaching contract. With the help of the prestigious law firm that had aided him in 1968, he filed a civil lawsuit for breach in the Superior Court of the District of Columbia in February 1987. The suit sought his reinstatement. The university filed to dismiss. In doing so, it submitted the confidential hearings of the trustees, starting a process that eventually put the entire behind-the-scenes story on the public record.

With Curran in the limbo of suspension, the university governors grappled with his fate. In 1967 it had been an issue of firing him; now it was a question of what it meant to discipline a professor who already had the ironclad protection of tenure.

In recent times there were only two prominent test cases regarding the tenure of Catholic University theology professors who came into disfavor with church authorities. Daniel C. Maguire, a priest and professor in what was then the department of religion and religious education, believed his tenure protected his employment as he applied to leave the priesthood, to be laicized. That was granted, but his bishop in Philadelphia ordered him to resign from the faculty; Vatican codes required theology professors to be clergy. Maguire fought the directive on the grounds of his apparent tenure. Finally, however, his records were flawed by faulty employment information, leaving him technically short of the requirements for receiving tenure. Maguire resigned in 1971 and went on to become the most liberal Catholic moralist in America.[31]

The second tenure case crossed a bridge similar to Curran's in 1967, minus the campus protests. Canon law professor James H. Provost was approved for tenure by the academic senate and other appropriate committees. His liberal interpretation of the new Code of Canon Law, however, prompted bishops on the board of trustees to consult with Rome and deny him the *nihil obstat*—meaning, nothing stands in the way. On appeal, Provost clarified his positions and the trustees granted him tenure in August 1986—just as Curran was being handed the Vatican declaration.[32]

Now the question was Curran's status. His tenure extended over fifteen years. Could he be disqualified from teaching in nonecclesiastical faculties? To what was his tenure attached, the university, the school, or the department? And in making any final decision, was it by authority of the Ratzinger letter itself or by the decision of the board itself? These were new and subtle questions, and none on the board, including the chancellor and university president, wanted to resolve them too quickly.

Curran asked for the ad hoc faculty committee hearing at the end of September. Between then and April, when the committee was formed, both Curran and the university administration prepared for what might come—a resolution or a legal battle.

PART TWO

The Issues

THREE

Magisterium and Dissent

At the height of the public dispute between Charles Curran and the Vatican's Cardinal Joseph Ratzinger, a time of student organizing, petition-circulating, and scores of media interviews, the moral theologian said he wanted this to be "a teaching moment."[1]

The allusion arose more from an assumption about the nature of the church than from Curran's lifelong vocation as university professor. He was of the view that everyone in the Catholic Church is a teacher, not just of dogma, but of his or her own Catholic experience. And hence, all parts of the Catholic family are included in the *magisterium*—the teaching authority of the church. "The hierarchical teaching office cannot be identified with the total teaching function of the Church," Curran has said. "The primary teacher remains the Spirit who dwells in the hearts of all Christians."[2]

Central to the Curran affair was this tension between conflicting claims of teaching authority. It was yet another manifestation of the collision between authority and freedom, personified now in the bishops as "pastors" and the academics—those with what Curran calls "faithful expertise."[3]

In the long tradition of dissent, Curran located himself among the respectful practitioners. His positions on moral theology, he said, dissented from noninfallible teachings of the church but paid respect to the infallible ones—the doctrines of faith. "We are dealing here with the noninfallible hierarchical teaching," Curran said, defending himself in a 1985 correspondence during the investigation of his writings. "My disagreements are on the level of complex, specific actions which involved many conflicting circumstances and situations. By their very nature these specific, concrete questions are removed from the core of faith."[4]

Curran's dissent did far more than touch on the widespread debate between what was infallible and what was noninfallible church teaching. Theological leadership had shifted from the seminaries to the universities in recent decades, and that was where Curran worked. It was full circle from the Middle Ages, a "providential" change made necessary because "theology had become too far removed from the modern world with its ebullient secularity," theologian Avery Dulles said.[5] University theologians took up the advocacy of academic freedom, adding another layer to the possibility of dissent. For the ordinary Catholics of the day, church doctrine was being given with an emphasis on conscience—the free but informed personal choices regarding faith and morals. Especially in the area of moral theology, which was Curran's bailiwick, the freedom of conscience was another tug of war between authority and dissent.

IN AN ERA THAT extols freedom and independence, the very idea of the magisterium was bound to face obduracy. Magisterium derives from the Latin term for "master," a title given to authority figures ranging from a teacher to a ship captain.[6] In the context of the Catholic Church, the term was narrowed to mean the bishops' teaching authority. There had been some flexibility in sharing that teaching power with theologians, but that was during the Middle Ages.

At the First Vatican Council of 1870, the teaching authority of the pope and his bishops was made supreme. Indeed, the chapter defining papal infallibility was titled, "On the infallible magisterium of the Roman Pontiff." The Second Vatican Council largely continued this use, speaking of the "authentic"—in Latin meaning authoritative—magisterium of the papacy, in which the bishops shared through the convocation of a council. Vatican II's "Dogmatic Constitution on the Church" (*Lumen Gentium*), asserted "that the bishops have by divine institution taken the place of the apostles as pastors of the Church, in such wise that whoever listens to them listens to Christ and whoever despises them despises Christ and him who sent Christ."[7] As transmitters of the magisterium, the bishops must teach "only what has been handed on," said the council's "Dogmatic Constitution on Revelation" (*Dei verbum*). They are servants of the Word of God: "At the divine command and with the help of the Holy Spirit, it [the magisterium] listens to this devoutly, guards it with dedication and expounds it faithfully."[8]

The journey to this position was a long and varied one, beginning at the foundation of the church.[9]

In biblical times there was a great variety of teaching positions. In the first centuries, tension arose among pastors, prophets, and teachers. Early in the third century prophets disappeared as an identifiable group. Bishops and theologians were left to vie for the dominant role. Irenaeus, bishop of Lyons in the early second century, argued for bishops' teaching authority. Two Alexandrian Greeks, Clement and Origen, said theologians like themselves shared that authority as well. The Latin churchman Tertullian, who ended as a heretic following Montanism, held that bishops were church disciplinarians, not teachers.

Heretical attacks on the church in the third and fourth centuries, however, anchored the bishops as the final teachers of the church. "Irenaeus formulated the doctrine of apostolic succession of ministers as the form and guarantee of the authentic tradition, against gnosticism," Yves Congar noted.[10] Gnosticism's elite claim that religious knowledge was held by a select group demanded a response that made church doctrine available to all. In effect, episcopal authority protected "the democracy of doctrine."

In the Middle Ages, from the tenth to thirteen century, the bishops lost much of their temporal authority to rising princes and rulers. Consequently, the papacy along with the religious orders assumed more teaching authority. By the thirteenth century a "magisterium of Doctors of the Church" had emerged and "the popes themselves relied on the universities to publish collections of decretals or councils," Congar said.[11] At the end of that period, Thomas Aquinas expounded on teaching authority, creating a framework that would last, at least in theory, until today. Aquinas said that teaching authority emanates from two "chairs," that of the bishop and that of theologian. The bishop in his cathedral was the *magisterium cathedrae pastoralis*. At the university was the theologian, who had *magisterium cathedrae magistralis*. Theologians of the late Middle Ages played a significant role in ecumenical councils. This was so at

Constance in 1414, a well-attended council that deposed two popes, transformed the papacy from an absolute into a constitutional monarchy, and tried and burned the reformer John Huss. The extreme was reached in 1439 at the Council of Basel, where three hundred "doctors" dwarfed thirteen priests and seven bishops.

That chorus of theologians, however, was drowned out by the Counter-Reformation. The Protestant rebellion demanded a Catholic Church militant. Theologians, who were nearly all clergy, worked with the bishops at the Council of Trent but then receded. Bishops reemerged, exerting teaching authority like legislators. Teachings of the church were presented in approved formulas. Here was the beginning point of what some historians call the "teaching church" and the "learning church," a split identified in the mid-1700s and commonly accepted a century later. The breach, as it continues today, is largely between bishops and theologians, with the laity taking sides. Throughout the church's history, however, the mass of ordinary Christians never presumed to play a role in forming or issuing the official doctrines of the church. That would come with the appellation "people of God," a concept from Vatican II taken to extremes in the formulation of liberation theology.

Tension remains between the bishop and the theologian. It arises from their entwined roles over centuries. As historian Jaroslav Pelikan noted: "During the years 100 to 600, most theologians were bishops; from 600 to 1500 in the West, they were monks; since 1500, they have been university professors . . . Each of these life styles has left its mark on the job description of the theologian, but also on the way doctrine has continued to develop back and forth between believing, teaching, and confessing."[12]

Today, some theologians yearn, perhaps romantically, for the time when bishops were indeed great theologians. Saint Augustine of Hippo, Pope Gregory the Great, Ambrose of Milan, Basil the Great, archbishop of Cappadocia, Gregory Nazianzen of Constantinople, Gregory of Nyssa, and others combined pastoral and theological authority. Such stature is lamentably less frequent today, theologian Richard McBrien said. "Unfortunately, there are some bishops who assume because they are bishops they are also master theologians, in fact that they are the principal theologian in their diocese."[13]

The Jesuit scholar Francis Sullivan, in his survey of the teaching office, *Magisterium,* concludes that for the good of the church, and given these historic times, the bishop must have precedence over the professor. "Competent scholars can speak with authority in their own field, but they do not have the kind of authority that has come to be associated with the word magisterium," Sullivan said. "When conflicts arise as to the terms of its creeds, or to its interpretation, those with pastoral responsibility must have the authority to judge which of the conflicting opinions is in accord with the faith of the church."[14]

Critics of a hierarchical magisterium say it declares truth by legislation, not necessarily by the best philosophical argument. And in times like these, when ease of movement, information, and education have diversified sources of teaching and the church's ability to respond, a top-down legislative approach is ineffective. McBrien has said, "That hard and fast distinction between the teaching church and the learning church has only recently begun to disappear."[15] Modern Catholic writers have called for a revival of a double magisterium, drawing their justification from Aquinas, so that the hierarchy and the theologian share the rostrum. One objection to that view says that Aquinas's proposal came in a different era, a time when a common mind bound all thinkers in the church. However, the Vatican's 1990 *Instruction on the Ecclesial Vocation of the Theologian* said Aquinas never viewed the two roles as equal. "St. Thomas was absolutely certain that the right to judge in matters of doctrine was the sole responsibility of the 'officium praclationis,'" it said.[16]

With the declaration at Vatican II that the church is the "people of God," the newest pressure has been toward expanding teaching authority still more. A three-tier magisterium would then include the people at the broadest base. Above would stand the scholars, theologians, and religious educators. The pope and his bishops would share the apex.

INTIMATELY RELATED TO teaching authority is the Catholic belief in infallibility. Over the centuries that condition has been ascribed to the entire church as an institution, kept true by the Holy Spirit. It was ascribed to councils of bishops and finally in recent times to the pope. Because of the late development of conciliar and papal infallibility, there is little in the Bible or early Christian experience to convey it. But, according to this logic, if the Holy Spirit leads the church infallibly, there must be a channel. As channels, the papal and conciliar mediators won the church's confidence by making decisions on faith and morals that were salutary to humanity and the church. Yet this root belief in leading by the Holy Spirit fuels the conflict of authority and freedom. Both bishop and theologian may assume they have such guidance and yet totally disagree.

The belief that ecumenical councils were infallible first appeared in the ninth century. The papacy's status evolved over centuries from "the servant of the servants of God" and the "Vicar of Peter" finally to "the Vicar of Christ." While papal primacy was established by the twelfth century, papal infallibility was not asserted until the late 1200s. Such a papal power was debated and challenged until 1870, when the First Vatican Council defined it as infallible.

Vatican I's decision on papal infallibility included the term "consensus," a way to describe the participation of the bishops in the pope's authoritative declarations. But the process retained the juridical authority of the pope. The Second Vatican Council revised that mildly with the idea of "collegiality." It decreed that authority is vested in the whole college of bishops. But for all the established tradition of those councils, they have "no authority unless united with the Roman Pontiff, Peter's successor, as its head, whose primatial authority, let it be added, over all, whether pastors or faithful, remains in integrity."[17] Hence, Vatican II's dogmatic constitution ensured that the pope's supremacy was not decreased. In effect, the bishops' was increased. In today's church, the magisterium is commonly explained by the distinction between the defining power of the pope's "extraordinary" magisterium and the "ordinary" magisterium, a power that even bishops and catechists can evoke.

Since Vatican II, the idea of papal infallibility has been heavily qualified by the work of theologians. This group criticizes a trend, begun with the generation of Vatican I, called "practical infallibility" or "creeping infallibility." During that period of conflict between national bishops' groups and the papacy, populist support of the pontiff was aroused and grew. Fueled by that devotion, by the early twentieth century believers commonly viewed the man elected to the papacy as infallible in his own right. For a segment of Catholics today, every papal word still has that aura. By a strict definition, however, a pope and his teaching are infallible only when he defines, from the chair of Peter, a dogma of the church. Neither John XXIII, Paul VI, nor John Paul II (at least up until 1990), have become infallible channels by virtue of such statements.

As such, papal infallibility is explained by some theologians as being a negative power. "It simply assures the church that when the pope . . . presumes to define a matter of faith and morals [it] will at the very least be immune from any fundamental error," according to McBrien.[18] But as a positive power, in this view, such a papal declaration does not have the guarantee of being made in the best possible formulation for all time. In effect, it can be improved upon—which means it can be changed.

THE PREMISE OF DISSENT is that church teachings, whether issued by papal declaration or by the bishops in council, can be incomplete. Indeed, the dissenter says, these authors of Catholic faith and morals are not always right. This possibility is generally accepted as extending to noninfallible teachings. But there are some who would take it further—even infallible declarations may need timely revisions. The underlying reason is that there are always human limitations in transmitting God's truth. And as history progresses, the language and presumption of a past doctrinal formulation can become outdated. A theologian's task, indeed purpose, is to probe and scrutinize church doctrines in search of these inadequacies.

This approach, as a basis for dissent, is exemplified in the critique of papal infallibility. Historians agree that several nontheological factors influenced what became a theological doctrine.[19] The First Vatican Council was called at a time when rival nationalist movements, especially Gallicanism in France, had joined bishops and nobles in alliances against the papacy. A declaration of infallibility, which Italian prelates pushed through the church bureaucracy, gave the pope final authority over all statements and actions by bishops or councils. So when the doctrine of papal infallibility is argued, it must base itself on more than the motives of that time.

The long trail of mistakes by the magisterium opens to probing theologians another door for doubt and dissent. There have been official reversals in church teachings on just war, interest taking, the right of the accused to remain silent, the purpose of sexual relations in marriage, and religious liberty. Many of the corrections were made with the help of theologians. By some accounts the early popes Liberius (352–56), Vigilius (537–55), and Honorius (625–38) decreed church teachings that later, with theological assistance, were overturned.[20] But how much popes took the advice of theologians in issuing a church position is up for debate. Benedict XII, an Avignon pope of the mid-fourteenth century, apparently heeded their voice. Though a monk of common French stock, he had a doctorate from the University of Paris and listened to theological minds around him during his reform of the Vatican's bureaucracy, known as the Curia, and his attack on nepotism.

Yet to make too sharp a distinction between the role of a church authority and that of a theologian is hazardous. That would imply that a bishop, let alone a pope, is automatically dulled by his administrative office, while the theologian runs free with insight and knowledge. History does not back that stereotype, though both the theologian and church official have been known to guard jealously their respective turfs. Could John Paul II and Cardinal Ratzinger, both with academic backgrounds and original writings on theological problems, be considered theologians? If so, their disagreement with Curran would be one theologian's view against another's. The difference is that John Paul and Ratzinger have the levers of power.

Those theologians who do not have such administrative power obtain it by forming schools of thought, which, if influential enough, can control a faculty or a wing of the church. They might also win the heart of the news media. They typically would stake their authority on being at the front end of theological "development." One such view holding prominence today is that historic change fundamentally affects church dogmas. It is a perspective that was bolstered, perhaps unintentionally, by the Second Vatican Council. This understanding was reinforced later by the Congregation for the Doctrine of the Faith, which issued a 1973 document to warn against "certain errors of the present day." While *Mysterium Ecclesiae* aimed to defend the church's infallibility, it nevertheless pointed out that doctrinal formulations, once suitable for their setting, can be seen differently with a change in cultural and historical period. Hence, "the transmission of divine revelation by the church encounters difficulties of various kinds." Such revealed knowledge is limited by the concerns and "changeable conceptions of a given epoch" and can also be conditioned by "the expressive power of the language used at a certain point of time."[21]

The broadest assault on hierarchical authority came from the Swiss-born theologian Hans Küng, a man who practiced what he preached and got censured. In his 1970 book *Infallible? An Inquiry,* Küng said that Vatican II's assertions on the magisterium were invalid. Indeed, the Küngian trend of argument in the church is what prompted *Mysterium Ecclesiae.* Küng said, "The statements about an infallibility of the college of bishops, based on the traditional, unhistorical theory of a direct and exclusive apostolic succession of the bishops, exegetically, historically, theologically, have feet of clay." There can be no such thing as an "infallible proposition." In the place of juridical authority to maintain the church, Küng asserted that the Holy Spirit, working through all its members, will weed out error and guide the people of God.[22]

While other theologians would not go as far as Küng, whose style was acerbic as well, his broad notion did have its influence. Hence, McBrien has said: "If the church is the whole people of God and the Holy Spirit is in the whole, then we have to be prepared for the possibility now and again . . . that the Holy Spirit who is in the church may be prompting the church at large [in] one way when another segment of the church, in this case the hierarchy, may have in fact badly expressed or badly understood an issue, and may thereby be putting themselves at cross purposes with the community."[23]

After Vatican II, the late German Jesuit theologian Karl Rahner counseled theologians to steer a course between assent and freedom. While church doctrine must "speak to" modern man in his new context, it must remain a confession of faith. Though new language may be good, it would be a "false path" for theologians to "think and say anything and everything they wish," he said.[24]

So in the final analysis, did Vatican II teach the legitimacy of dissent from noninfallible teaching? "It did so implicitly by its actions, we may say, but not explicitly by its words," theologian Avery Dulles said. He pointed out that the theological commission responsible for Article 25 of the dogmatic constitution of the church "refused to make any statement, one way or another, about dissent." In deed, however, the council employed prominent theologians whose views were suspect under Pius XII and, Dulles said, "Without explicitly contradicting pervious papal doctrine, the council took many positions that in fact corrected what had been taught."[25]

Before modern communication was available, dissent from official teachings by theologians went unnoticed. Now, mass media quickly spreads both the official view and the dissenting one. Doctrinal decrees are up for public evaluation by assorted experts, and opinions multiply. Invariably, public controversy follows. With this impetus, theologians and bishops began in the 1960s to formulate guidelines for proper kinds of dissent. The different distinctions they make are revealing. Although Vatican II did not make an explicit statement, the German bishops issued a pastoral letter on the matter in 1967. They said a dissenter is justified only if he tried to develop a teaching positively, if his theological expertise is adequate, and if his motives are free of conceit or selfishness.[26] The next year, the American bishops, in the pastoral letter *Human Life in Our Day,* gave their three criteria for proper dissent: There must be serious reasons; it must not impugn the teaching of the church; and it must not cause scandal, or bewilderment, to the church.[27]

For some American theologians, the key measure of a teaching's legitimacy is consultation and public acceptance. In dissenting one must ask if the formulation of the official church teaching makes sense, not only in light of the church fathers and the Bible, but in the language of the issue it is addressing. Second, is there evidence that all legitimate schools of thought contributed to the teaching, including a minority view? Finally, was the teaching accepted by the "people of God?" John Henry Newman, in his essay "On Consulting the Faithful," pointed out that indeed popes did seek out the opinions of Christian people before defining doctrine.[28] Such an airing today has the same risks and benefits as before, for it might be the Spirit that is heard through the masses but it might also be public opinion. For most Catholics, however, this concern arises more at the personal level, where the conscience speaks.

THE ACTIVE INGREDIENT in modern dissent is the reliance on conscience. What is one to do when a doctrinal teaching seems wrong? Thomas Aquinas, no opponent of church authority, seemed to make conscience king. "Anyone upon whom the ecclesiastical authority, in ignorance of the true facts, imposes a demand that offends against his clear conscience, should perish in excommunication rather than violate his conscience," he said.[29] Aquinas did not mean to suggest, his commentators say, that all consciences are objectively true to the mark.

In fact, sometimes he takes opposite, though not contradictory, positions on authority and freedom of conscience. This highlights the importance of knowing Aquinas but also how easily he can be used as a proof-text to make a point. If he is emphatic about following the conscience, he is equally so about obeying authority.

When put the question about following the opinion of "diverse teachers," Aquinas said there was no excuse for picking the wrong one. "Therefore, no one who assents to the opinion of any teacher in opposition to manifest testimony of Scripture or in opposition to what is officially held in accordance with the authority of the Church can be excused from the vice of being in error."[30]

A majority of sincere Catholics must naturally waver between the two poles of authority and freedom of conscience. Some Catholic writers, however, have described the Catholic community as having a strictly dual personality, a community of people who chose either authority or freedom. Eugene Kennedy's *Tomorrow's Catholics, Yesterday's Church: The Two Cultures of American Catholicism,* makes that distinction.[31] There are those wedded to an institutional church, with its given certainties, and those who are heedless of the institution and accepting of ambiguity as they follow their consciences. This group, Kennedy holds, are tomorrow's Catholics. McBrien has outlined a similar contrast. "For those who believe the unity of the church is rooted in a kind of uniformity, then any sort of difference of opinion on moral issues represents an undermining of the unity which we are supposed to display to the world outside," he said. "For those who insist that unity is impossible unless it is truly voluntary, unless it is unity of persons, the unity of free human beings, then the possibility, even the likelihood of diversity, pluralism, even of conflict in moral matters, is something that one simply expects and lives with."[32]

The intersection of personal conscience and church teaching was addressed in Vatican II's "Declaration on Religious Liberty" (*Dignitatis humanae*). Article 3 makes that case: "It is through the conscience that man sees and recognizes the demands of the divine law. He is bound to follow this conscience faithfully in all his activity so that he may come to God, who is his last end. Therefore he must not be forced to act contrary to his conscience."[33]

But just as the teachers of the magisterium can have human limitations, the conscience of each individual is limited. Decisions of conscience are incomplete or partial because persons, in the Catholic understanding, cannot entirely know themselves as God alone can. A conscience can, indeed, be badly formed. Hence the teaching role of the church assumes that humanity needs guidance. As Article 14 of the declaration on religious liberty asserts, "in forming their consciences the faithful must pay careful attention to the sacred and certain teaching of the church. For the Catholic Church is by the will of Christ the teacher of truth."[34]

While making the distinction between infallible and noninfallible teaching, the church continued to insist that each authoritative issuance of the magisterium is binding on Catholics. That duty of acceptance—*obsequium animi religiosum*—is variously translated as "respectful readiness to accept," "deference," or "religious submission of mind." The phrase is used in Article 25 of the council's *Lumen Gentium,* which also instructs that the faithful are "obliged to submit to their bishops' decisions, made in the name of Christ, in matters of faith and morals, and to adhere to it with a ready and respectful allegiance of mind. This loyal submission of the will and the intellect must be given, in a special way, to the authentic teaching authority of the Roman Pontiff, even when he does not speak *ex cathedra.*"[35] Even so, that deference depends on a range of aspects, including a teaching's content, source, relationship to the Bible and church tradition, general acceptance, and constancy. "Because the matter is so complex, one cannot make any general statement about what precisely amounts to 'religious submission of mind,'" Dulles said.[36]

THE GROWTH OF CATHOLIC theological work in the university setting has complicated these demands of assent to the magisterium. On this matter, both the first and second Vatican councils were two-edged swords; they sought adherence to church teaching while unleashing the theologians to critical inquiry. At the First Vatican Council, the theologians were unbridled by the historic formulation of the church's understanding of revelation. Knowledge of God descends by revelation but can also be ascended to by natural knowledge. For the church fathers in their 1870 "Constitution on the Catholic Faith," supernatural and natural knowledge "are distinct in object."[37] This view of revelation opened the way for theologians to make their vocation an experimental science. And yet as in the nineteenth century, theology remained subordinate to the magisterium. Theology was relegated to the science of the abstract, though admittedly the idea of magisterium was abstract as well. The hierarchy still maintained the practical hold on church policy while the pastoral practice of the priest remained the most concrete reality.

The great council of 1962–65 pushed back the frontier of critical, intellectual inquiry still further. "It is clear that Vatican II . . . was more careful and reticent in dogmatic pronouncements, gave more scope to 'dialogue' within the Church, and allowed the different theological currents to be expressed in a less inhibited manner," Rahner said.[38]

The dialogue aimed outward as well, for the council acknowledged the church's inextricable dependence on the secular world. "The church has always had the duty of scrutinizing the signs of the times," the council said in *Gaudium et Spes*.[39] The council asserted that there is autonomy in earthly affairs, created things, culture, and science. Moreover, Catholic theology now recognized the freedom and dignity of persons and the role of the laity. As did Vatican I, the Vatican II declaration on divine revelation asserted that God could be known through the natural creation. Unlike past formulations, it gave more attention to the changing and existential nature of knowledge. The council recognized that the human race "substitutes a dynamic and more evolutionary concept of nature for a static one."[40]

The result, some say, was a change in the very assumptions of theology. "No longer is theology understood in the light of a science seeking certitude based on a deductive methodology," Curran has said. "Interpretation of the sources of revelation and of the teaching of the hierarchical magisterium in the light of the signs of the times is theology's function."[41] The theologian's work will never be done because, other than a "saving encounter" with God by faith, knowledge of God will remain imperfect. To the degree that knowledge of God is conditioned by the language and symbols of a particular time, the next age will demand that those outward vestiges be peeled away.

Considering what this suggests for academia, American Catholic educators sought foundations in council documents for a new autonomy in their institutions. "Only in freedom [can] man direct himself towards what is good," the pastoral constitution said. "The people of our time prize freedom very highly and strive eagerly for it. In this they are right. . . . But that which is truly freedom is an exceptional sign of the image of God in man."[42] Furthermore, the council's declaration on religious liberty had an unspoken implication for Catholic educators and theologians—academic freedom in Catholic colleges and universities.

The modern movement for academic freedom began in nineteenth century Germany, where the distinction was made between *lernfreiheit,* the freedom of students to learn, and *lehrfreiheit,* the freedom of inquiry and teaching by professors. Though such formal distinctions did not arise as early in America, the same issues played out in the second half of the nineteenth century as science, especially the Darwinian variety, clashed with religious authority in American institutions of higher learning. American college graduates who sought advanced study in Germany—some eight thousand from 1870 to 1900—brought the convictions of academic freedom back to American shores by the 1890s. From then until the First World War, "a good proportion of the leaders and targets in academic freedom cases had studied in Germany," Walter P. Metzger said.[43] The American notion of academic freedom, which became formalized in 1915, took on its own character. The student aspect was de-emphasized. Professors went further than the German practice by declaring their autonomy even in external affiliations, such as political groups, making extramural activity the basis of most academic freedom disputes even today. But as in the German tradition, the American professors' right to this autonomy hinged on academic competence.[44]

The protection of academic freedom was important because of the way many American universities were founded—paid for by the great robber barons of the late nineteenth century. That list was long, to include Johns Hopkins, Vanderbilt, Columbia, and the University of Chicago. Scholars needed freedom from the political views behind the great endowments. They also needed freedom from each new regime of university president and trustees, who often stood for the social, political, or business interests of the day.

The first organizational clout behind academic freedom came from the American Association of University Professors (AAUP), formed in 1915.[45] At the founding, a committee on academic freedom and tenure produced "A Declaration of Principles." A 1925 meeting called by the American Council on Education also produced a statement on academic freedom and tenure, endorsed by the AAUP and the Association of American Colleges, of which The Catholic University of America was a member. By 1940 a streamlined document, "Statement of Principles on Academic Freedom and Tenure," superseded them all. From that position the AAUP expanded policies in other areas, such as a 1958 statement on procedural standards in faculty dismissal proceedings and, in 1976, recommendations of institutional regulations on academic freedom and tenure.

In the view of the professorial establishment, Catholic higher education was not up to secular standards. The AAUP's 1915 statement said that if a church establishes a college as an instrument of propaganda, that school is not a university. However, the statement noted that such institutions are rare and dwindling. The 1940 statement had recognized this problem and carried over from 1925 a "limitations clause" to protect the interests of a professor. "Limitations of academic freedom because of religious or other aims of the institution should be clearly stated in writing at the time of the appointment," the clause said.[46] Efforts in the 1980s to rescind the clause faced the AAUP and others in higher education with a dilemma: Do they want to be the ones who finally write off church-related institutions?

Before the 1960s, educators inside and outside the Catholic tradition said academic freedom could not be compatible with Catholic institutions of higher learning. According to an old dictum, a Catholic university is a contradiction in terms. The secularist Sidney Hook wrote in 1953, "There is no academic freedom in Catholic colleges."[47] Some Catholic educators did not necessarily find the charge offensive. "The lowliest child who has completed his penny catechism knows more about the meaning of this . . . universe than the assembled faculty of some of our universities," the Jesuit Hunter Guthrie said in his inaugural address as president of Georgetown University in 1949. In his commencement address the next year Guthrie took on academic freedom as a "sacred fetish."[48] There were very few studies on academic freedom and Catholic institutions before the 1950s, and the two major ones produced in that decade argued for limits.

Catholic scholarly organizations in the 1960s began to endorse the 1940 academic freedom statement of the secular universities. Only three hundred of the AAUP's fifteen thousand membership in 1940 came from Catholic institutions, but Catholic involvement would grow. Faculty members at Catholic universities began to call in support from the AAUP in disputes. Though the association has censured a medical school at St. Louis University, it did not begin to intervene regularly until 1962, censuring Catholic institutions that violated academic freedom or rights of tenure. In 1965 the National Catholic Education Association Bulletin published an educator's call for acceptance of full academic freedom at Catholic institutions. More articles, for and against, appeared in Catholic journals. At a symposium at the University of Notre Dame in 1966 speakers extolled academic freedom.[49] A dissertation at Catholic University in 1969 made the case for full academic freedom even in Catholic theology, a position that had been rejected in a 1958 dissertation.

The two major battles for academic freedom in Catholic institutions took place in the 1960s at Catholic University—the Curran affair—and at the University of Dayton. At Dayton, professors accused each other of public dissent from church teaching. The conflict led to the archbishop's intervention and finally the resignation of the original accusers, a sort of Curran case in reverse.

Defenders of the modern American system of Catholic universities argued for "influence" rather than "control" and called anything juridical legalistic. They said Catholic identity and truth is assured by the exercise of moral authority rather than canonical authority. Beginning in the early 1970s the exchanges between American Catholic educators and the Vatican showed this concern. While the hierarchical magisterium might issue a public warning in an extreme case of theological dissent, a 1971 report by the educators said there can be "no question of juridical intervention in the institutional affairs of the university itself."[50] In 1976, the educators complained again that the Congregation for Catholic Education spoke as if the university were "an arm of the church." Language such as "juridical relationship" and "canonical establishment" was contrary to views of Vatican II, they insisted. "Freedom from outside constraints is the very breath of life for a college and university."[51]

WHATEVER THE PROFESSIONAL or economic benefits of claiming institutional autonomy—from accreditation to government funding—within the church a legitimate critique responded to the new elevation of academic freedom. Some commentators asked how a university could be a privileged part of the Catholic community and not be bound by some obligations. Those duties would have to be defined somehow in canonical law or in juridic relationship to the church.

On the philosophic level, academic freedom was called a misnomer; only the human will is free, whereas the mind is constrained by the truth. When a secular accrediting agency defines academic freedom it is in effect defining that truth—a form of control on free inquiry. The logical conclusion is that all academic freedom must exist in a context; it does not exist in a pure abstract form. Those who believe it does, critics added, are under the spell of Kant's philosophy of pure reason. Nor is academic freedom neutral when it is championed by a certain group or organization. The parallel has been made with the limits on human rights: No one can shout fire in a theater and claim free speech. For the magisterium, then, academic freedom has its limits in the Catholic context. "True academic freedom must be seen in relation to the finality of the academic enterprise which looks to the total truth of the human person," John Paul II said in 1979.[52]

At its inception, academic freedom was championed primarily by natural and social scientists. These were the so-called "Intellectuals" associated with the new German universities and dedicated to scientific positivism. With these origins academic freedom easily took an ideological character, becoming a quasireligion in competition with the old order of religious knowledge. For good reason it gained widespread acceptance. As a simple rhetorical concept it appealed to the human desire for liberty and truth. Serving the pragmatic interest of professors, who wished for total exemption from restraint, it became the basis of a brotherhood. It came to be "equated not only with free intellectual inquiry, but an ethic of human relations and an ideal of personal fulfillment," historian Richard Hofstadter said.[53]

The privileges of today's academics mirror the medieval church's control of the conventions of knowledge and learning, according to historian Philip Gleason. In the Middle Ages the "benefit of clergy" allowed them both exemptions and special rights. That benefit is now afforded to professors, and on the assertion of academic freedom they use it well to their advantage, Gleason said. "Their analysis of the concept and their prescription as to its application can hardly avoid assuming a quality of advocacy rather than cool scientific analysis."[54]

As an alternative belief system, that is, a "religion of the Enlightenment, academic freedom had no better advocate than John Dewey, the American educator. The title of his 1934 book, *A Common Faith,* was speaking about knowledge not about religion. "There is such a thing as faith in intelligence becoming religious in quality—a fact that perhaps explains the effort of some religionists to disparage the possibility of intelligence as force," he said. "They properly feel such faith to be a dangerous rival."[55] But as the heyday of Dewey passed, some of the secular scrutiny of Catholic institutions was lifted. The scholarly world began to admit that even its research, once called pure and objective, nevertheless reflected some value judgments, indeed biases.

"Virtually every philosopher or writer on higher education in modern times has affirmed this theme: there is no such thing as 'value-free' thought or research," educator Page Smith said. "Those who act sincerely on such a premise deceive the world and, more dangerously, themselves."[56]

This type of assertion would be well heeded by Catholic scholars, theologians, or educators, who erect the protective shield of academic freedom with no value context, suggested Monsignor George A. Kelly, a Catholic educator and a founder of the conservative Fellowship of Catholic Scholars. "Absolute commitment to absolute noncommitment," he said, "is no less a restriction on academic freedom than a faith commitment and indeed may be less honest because the serious observer is hard pressed to discover real-life examples of the totally uncommitted man."[57]

With this contest between the claims of religion and science as a backdrop, a variety of propositions were put forth to solve the tension between the university and the magisterium. In one view the university should be seen as the church learning, while the magisterium is the church teaching. In the 1970s the dean of Catholic educators, Theodore M. Hesburgh of Notre Dame University, explained the interaction this way: "Theology in the Catholic university must enjoy the same freedom and autonomy as any other university subject because, otherwise, it will not be accepted as a university discipline and without its vital presence, in free dialogue with all other university disciplines, the university will never really be Catholic."[58]

Another solution is the secular one—make pluralism the mode of theological education and research. But for Hesburgh, Curran and others, a university called Catholic should make Roman Catholic theology its focus. Curran asserts that even when Catholic theology is at a university's core, there would be no need for the magisterium to violate academic freedom. In a 1988 *Texas Law Review* article, Curran proposed three safeguards against theological mistakes. First is theological debate; second is the right of the hierarchy to declare a teaching wrong, though it would not intervene in the academy; third is a judgment of competence. "Academic peers would rightly judge incompetent a Catholic theologian who does not believe in Jesus or does not accept a role for the pope in the church," Curran said.[59]

Peer review, however, raises another problem. In the Curran example, for instance, the majority of professors in the academy would say belief in Jesus or the pope have nothing to do with academic competence, theological or otherwise. Indeed, Curran has pointed out that some fellow scholars find his view of academic freedom rather constrained. James Annarelli of St. John's University said academic freedom can give no quarter to presuppositions that are narrowly Catholic but must be more widely accessible. Lonnie D. Kliever, a theologian at Southern Methodist University, said any element of fidelity to a belief undermines full academic freedom.[60]

Even among Catholic academics who share some common presuppositions and a note of fidelity, there may be no guarantees in peer review. Theologians are reluctant to criticize each other, Karl Rahner observed soon after Vatican II. "It is a false politeness and collegiality when theologians are too concerned to take pains to be 'indulgent' with one another," Rahner said. "The indisputable decline in theological criticism is to be deplored in this respect, and it is an extremely dangerous situation."[61]

NOTHING TESTED THE role of the magisterium in the modern church more than the debate over the issue of artificial contraception. The 1968 encyclical *Humanae Vitae,* which retained the ban on birth control, drew every sector of the church into the debate and precipitated a never-before-seen public dissent. The core issue was whether faith and morals had equal weight under the magisterium.

Stationed in universities, a few theologians were seeking changes in that pairing, held over since Vatican I. They said the magisterium confused the infallible teaching of faith and dogma and the noninfallible principles of living a Christian life called morals. These theologians saw it as their task to separate the two, especially in an effort to free the fields of moral theology and ecclesiology from dogmatic constraints.

The debate continued unabated through 1990, when two new Vatican documents asserted again the unity of all church teaching in faith and morals. First, a draft for a new universal catechism was released for review by the world's bishops. A group of American theologians held a symposium on the draft and came to the conclusion that it lacked a distinction between what was core infallible belief and what was not; church beliefs from the smallest ritual to the dogma of Christ's divinity were given equal importance, they said in their critique.[62]

Several months later came the *Instruction on the Ecclesial Vocation of the Theologian,* which gave equal weight to church assertions on faith and on morals. "What concerns morality can also be the object of the authentic magisterium," and the competence of the magisterium "also extends to that which concerns the natural law," the *Instruction* said. "It is a doctrine of faith that these moral norms can be infallibly taught by the magisterium."[63]

The modern debate over the place of morals under the magisterium goes back to the contraception question as it was raised before Vatican II. John Paul XXIII established a Commission for the Study of Problems of Population and Family, which was expanded to forty members under Paul VI.[64] The commission's original mandate seemed to be to determine the morality of the birth control pill, but the panel began to see its role as lifting the church's condemnation of contraception. In that dramatic period, commission documents were leaked to the press and speculation abounded. "The existence and momentum of the commission led many to believe that Paul VI would come to find some forms of contraception compatible with the Catholic view of marriage," professor Janet E. Smith said.[65] Numerous books and articles appeared supporting a liberal position. Finally, the papal commission documents were leaked to the liberal Catholic papers, the *National Catholic Reporter* and the *Tablet* in England, in 1966. The majority of the commission, according to the reports, had voted in favor of changing the church teaching. The leak of the private documents was considered an effort to force Paul VI to issue an encyclical. He finally did, but its unbending condemnation of all contraception created an uproar.

As a result, theologians now dealt head on with the question of how the pope determines something to be true, especially if he ignores trusted experts he asked for advice. A growing number of theologians concluded that the authority of ordinary papal teaching is only as strong as the arguments presented in that teaching. This conclusion signaled a modern split between those who deemed themselves "experts" by virtue of their free inquiry and those who wielded pastoral authority based on papal appointment.

In all these ways, *Humanae Vitae* was a watershed. By comparison, Hans Küng's dissent from an infallible doctrine such as the primacy of the pope or teaching office of the bishops did not create such an outpouring. Neither did Schillebeeckx's subtle distinction over the humanity of Christ. It was in the area of moral theology that both the dissent and the popular outpouring broke the back of the magisterium.

FOUR

Moral Theology

In its academic form, moral theology can be the practice of cool reason, working out human equations of action, circumstance, and motivation like a problem in geometry. But in life it touches the nerves. "The only thing that ultimately stirs people up is in the field of morality," Charles Curran said in 1967. "And I think it is because I am in this field that my views became such a matter of concern."[1] Almost twenty years later Cardinal Joseph Ratzinger attested to the continued volatility of the subject. "Today the sphere of moral theology has become the main locus of the tension between the magisterium and theologians, especially because here the consequences are most immediately perceptible," the cardinal said.[2]

In many ways, the practical and theoretical struggle between authority and freedom is most vivid in the modern development of Catholic moral theology.

Now filled with complexity and diversity, the field of moral theology began with a simple desire of the early church: to discern rightness of action in all areas of life. Age-old Christian concerns about religious obligations, sexual practice, marriage, abortion, lying, and killing became its object of study. Today, these questions have been joined by the issues of artificial contraception and medical technologies that can create, extend, or terminate life.

The point of controversy in the Catholic Church today is not the issue of what moral theology should address. The topics have changed with time but for both Ratzinger and Curran no moral issue is out of bounds for the church. Instead, sharp differences arise over the method and theory by which a topic is addressed. Two different methods, worked from different theological assumptions, can end up describing the same action as morally right or morally wrong. When proposed as church teachings, these conclusions are what, in Curran's words, "stirs people up."

The two broadest views in moral theology today, one represented by Ratzinger's "official teaching" of the church and the other by the "new" moral theologians, are not easy to simplify. Both say that there are unchanging moral absolutes. Both also say the human situation, in history and moral circumstances, changes, raising ever new moral choices. The two views differ by their emphasis and thus by their practical result.

The official teaching of the church stresses that moral absolutes are binding and true, promising human fulfillment for all people in all times. This assumption derives from Catholicism's venerable theology of natural law, a cosmic principle defining the order, nature, purpose, and ends of all existence. Its norms are known by reason, through the Ten Commandments, and in the revelation of Scripture. Detractors have called this the "classicist" view, suspending man as an abstraction in time like a fly in amber. But that is a caricature, said moral theology professor William May, a member of Pope John Paul II's International Theological Commission. While there are absolute norms, he said, "It is, of course, true that morality is to some extent relative to contingent social and historical reality."[3]

By contrast, the view of the "new moral theology" admits to some form of unchanging absolute but does not make such absolutes primary in judging morality. Those absolutes are, in the key word of the new moral theology, a "transcendental" aspect of human nature.

"The transcendental approach attends to the structures of the human knowing process itself," theologian Richard McBrien said. "Truth, including moral truth, exists not in the mind's grasp of reality itself but in the meaning the mind gives to reality. Our meanings can change in such basic realities as community, family, or the state. This is not to say that there is nothing objective 'out there' upon which we impose our meaning. The transcendental approach rejects both naive realism and idealism."[4]

As a result, transcendent norms or ideals may be seen as moral lighthouses, but the final judge of morality is the context of a complex and changing world. The Ten Commandments apply most of the time, but not always. In this view natural law's claim to certitude is obsolete; a view argued by noting that Vatican II's "Pastoral Constitution on the Church in the Modern World" (*Gaudium et Spes*) used the term natural law only three times. A stereotype projected on the thinking of Catholics of this transcendental stripe is "moral relativism," an extreme found in liberal Protestantism but not common in the new Catholic approach.

These are the two views that Ratzinger refers to when he speaks of a tension between the magisterium and the theologians, for the majority of Western theologians adhere to the second view's emphasis on historic change. Even then, drawing a clean line between the magisterium and the theologians is problematic; they both use the same sources of authority to argue their case. The way moral theologians use Thomas Aquinas is instructive. Curran, who takes a moderate course in the new moral theology, evokes Aquinas's *Summa Theologiae* to draw this conclusion: "Thomas admitted that although the first principles of the natural law were always the same, the proper conclusions of these principles can admit of exceptions because of the complexity of the situation in diverse elements entering into the final decision. The more one descends into particulars, the greater is the possibility of exceptions because of the complexity of the situation."[5] Theologians who emphasize the primacy of historical context also rely on Aquinas's phrase *natura humana mutabilis est*—human nature is changeable.

Another favorite reference in Aquinas for the new moral theologians is an apparent assertion that the Ten Commandments are not absolutely binding. "The precepts of the Decalogue," Aquinas said, "as to the essence of justice they contain, are unchangeable; but as to any determination of application to individual actions—for instance that this or that is murder, theft, or adultery, or not—in this point they admit change."[6] And so, such absolute norms as characterized by the Decalogue are "valid only for the most part," said Josef Fuchs, one of this century's major critics of the old natural law theology of the church.[7]

Traditional moral theologians, contesting the view of Fuchs and Curran as being "revisionist," would hold that some moral norms are without exception. Again, Aquinas is a source: "The natural law is altogether unchangeable in its first principles."[8] Those unchangeable absolutes can be apprehended by human reason and common sense, reinforced when there is confusion or doubt by negative norms as well—the Ten Commandments. And hence Aquinas said unequivocally in regard to one example of human action, "One ought not commit adultery for the sake of any good whatsoever."[9]

The moral theology of Charles Curran, though it has unique aspects, contains the main characteristics of the new moral theology. That trend is widespread enough that Curran has rightly said he is in the mainstream. "From an intellectual perspective, I am not a radical," he said. "How can one who emphasizes tension and complexity be a radical?"[10] In departing from the traditional moral theology, Curran first asserts that historic change undermines absolute norms. "Moral norms in my judgment are not the primary, or the only, or the most important concern of moral teaching and moral theology," Curran said. "Moral teaching deals with general perspectives, values, attitudes, and dispositions, as well as norms. Values, attitudes, and dispositions are much more important and far-reaching for the moral life than are specific norms."[11] This concern for the "wholeness" of a person and the "totality" of a moral choice also characterizes the new approach. And with no easily accessible absolute at hand, the greater good, even if it is achieved by a lesser evil, is the norm of morality. That good is chosen by the person and hence this view has been called the "preference principle" or "proportionalism." It derives from the fact, Curran said, that "morality is intrinsic and not extrinsic."[12]

John Paul and Ratzinger would balk at the idea that absolute moral norms could be compromised. But they also would agree with much that the new approach has done for renewing moral theology. Indeed, John Paul himself was a student of the same school of phenomenology—the new field of descriptive psychology—and personalism—the emphasis on human experience—from which thinkers like Fuchs and Bernard Häring sprung. The young Polish priest Karol Wojtyla completed his dissertation, "On the Possibility of Grounding Catholic Ethics on the System of Max Scheler," from 1952–58. Scheler, a German phenomenologist, was a major influence as well on Curran's mentor, Häring. With such similar influences, not to mention their common work in the Catholic tradition, there was still one wedge powerful enough to separate them: the nature of moral norms. Though both Wojtyla and Häring worked out of phenomenology and personalism, one believed persons cannot reshape the truth of a moral norm while the other believed the opposite. In Ratzinger's words, the disengagement from absolute moral norms produced "an exaggerated personalism." This "led some theologians to reject the internal order, the language of nature, leaving to sexuality, conjugal included, the sole point of reference in the will of the person."[13]

In practical terms, the difference today between the church magisterium and the new moral theology comes down to a negative principle, what is called the "absolute negative norm": There are some acts that can never be moral. "Deliberately killing the innocent, having intercourse with someone other than one's spouse (i.e. adultery), making babies by *in vitro* fertilization or by artificial insemination, and using contraception are examples of types of actions specified by norms of this kind," theologian William May said.[14]

The new moral theologians recognize these absolute norms, even as negative absolutes, but call them "formal norms." These static "abstractions" are not the big issue. For the new theologians the critical question becomes, for example, "What constitutes deliberately killing the innocent?" Here, moral theologians enter the realm they call "material norms," a far more ambiguous area conditioned by all manner of shifting intentions, circumstances, and consequences. Working from this level, Curran said that under certain circumstances the range of actions that the church unequivocally condemns based on negative norms can be potentially moral: Abortion, divorce, premarital sex, homosexual acts, masturbation, artificial birth control, sterilization, and euthanasia.

Catholic dissent from official church moral teachings has grown, but in retrospect it is hard to know where this divergence began. Did the new moral theology persuade a Catholic population to follow its lights? Or were today's Catholics already defying authority and going their own way, with the new theologians simply following along? Whatever the case, a polarity has emerged in which the subtlety and merits of moral arguments between natural law and personalism have been lost to most Catholics. Natural law has become a code word for tradition and authority. The new moral theology styles itself as "development," but in many ways it means a blank check for freedom.

Although this debate is personified today in the Curran case, its roots are in the past. The church has experienced stormy seas more than once as it has traveled between authority and freedom in search of moral absolutes.

FROM ITS EARLIEST instructions on morality, Christianity assumed the existence of an objective moral order.[15] Such an order was already recognized in the ancient world. Hellenistic philosophers found it in nature or in the Platonic "ideas" above. The church fathers discovered it in the will of God as stated in Scripture. Like church doctrine, moral teaching was influenced on all flanks: Jewish ethics, the contemplative approach of Platonism, the virtues of Stoicism. But these were subsumed into the central moral principle of Christ's agape love, or *caritas*.

Some of the church's earliest documents are moral treatises, often quite literal in guidance. The "Didache," or "two ways," gave moral instruction. Clement I set down a Christian's day with details about meals, prayers, care of the body, sexual life, and social activities. Many of the virtues he listed were derived from Aristotle's Nicomachean Ethics. Underpinnings of reason for Christian morality were adopted from Rome's orator Cicero and poet Virgil. Saint Ambrose patterned his *On Duties* almost exactly after Cicero's work of the same name.

Since these patristic times, much attention was devoted to sexual sins. For the church fathers, the *porneia*, or sexual behavior, listed in the New Testament books of Matthew, Acts, and Corinthians became a penitential concern. The emphasis lasted for centuries. In 1975 the Congregation for the Doctrine of the Faith declared, "The moral order of sexuality embraces such important values of human life that every direct violation of that order is objectively serious."[16]

The "negative" approach to sexuality has been linked to Saint Augustine of Hippo, who brought moral thought in the early church to maturity. Though he wrote no specific treatise on the subject, it surfaced in references scattered through some one hundred books, two hundred letters, and five hundred sermons he left behind. There was a positive contribution nevertheless, for beginning with Augustine and carried on through to Aquinas, the moral enterprise was seen in the categories of four cardinal virtues united in charity. Moreover, Augustine's commentary on *Genesis* defined the "threefold good" of marriage as "offspring," "fidelity," and "indivisibility," a view sustained by Aquinas and modern popes.

Augustine expressed his pessimism about human nature most starkly in his *Confessions.* Incomplete and internally riven, he said, man longs for a fulfillment that is satisfied only in God. Finding God is the supreme human good. And in seeking that final end, he said, "We must use this world, not enjoy it."[17] The first modern papal encyclical on family, marriage, and sexuality showed that Augustine's influence remained great in the twentieth century. The opening words of the 1930 *Casti Connubii* were "Of chaste marriage," the dominant theme of the document.

Through the centuries church practice came to be dominated by individual confession, followed later by the legal application of moral norms. Private penance, an oral confession of sins, was spread by the old British missionaries, instilling across the church of the early Middle Ages a focus on individual moral issues rather than corporate ones. The practice was extended in penitential books, detailed lists of sins with a corresponding penance. Following the work of Gratian, the Italian monk who founded canon law in 1140, the church took a legal approach to sins and marriage. The Fourth Lateran Council of 1215 declared that confession to a priest was required at least once a year by all mature laity. "It must be made to the priest as the physician of the soul, and include all 'deadly' sins—the catalogue of which was now much larger than in the early church," historian Williston Walker noted.[18]

FROM THE YEAR 700 to 1100 the decrees of popes, councils, and bishops were the vehicles of moral instruction, as not a single theological work on morals appeared.[19] And although the term *theologia moralis*—moral theology—was first used in about 1160, it was not a distinct science apart from theology and did not become one until the end of the sixteenth century. By the twelfth century, however, the first great crisis was upon the theology of moral action. Peter Abelard, the turbulent French scholastic, presented the first full-blown emphasis on the subjective view of morality. Abelard's ethics argued that a person's intention—not his act—determines the moral good or evil of an action. The novelty of Abelard's approach, historian Gordon Leff said, "lay in transforming morality from a supernatural to a personal matter; in an age of objective criteria, Abelard turned to subjective values."[20] The supreme subjective moral value, however, was to please God; the worst was to despise God. To illustrate the extremes of the subjective stance, Abelard suggested that even those who killed Christ or executed martyrs, if they thought they were doing God's will or had "no contempt for God," acted morally. "We cannot say that they have sinned in this," Abelard said.[21] He readily admitted, however, that men frequently are deceived in what God's will is.

Abelard sought to take the subjective intention, which had been a focus of Augustine's reflections, and expand it across the whole range of ethical actions. As a result, the discussion became concerned with the attitude of man rather than the nature of his deeds.

This was a beginning point for Thomas Aquinas's reflections on moral action. He added other criteria to Abelard's argument for intention. In addition to the motivation of a person, Aquinas said the circumstances of an act and the material out of which it is fashioned, the "object," should be considered. For an action to be good it had to satisfy the definition of goodness in these three areas, which Aquinas said could be determined by using reason, the laws of nature, and divine revelation in Scripture. In this balancing of the subjective and objective, nature and grace, Aquinas established a criteria that still endures. Commentaries on the *Summa Theologiae,* which addressed the moral life in its second part, became the basis for the distinct discipline of moral theology two hundred years later.

The next great crisis in moral and theological thought came as a challenge to Aquinas's assumption about an objective moral order in which all things have natures, which prescribe a thing's purpose and ends. For the English Franciscan William of Ockham, however, this was rationalist nonsense.[22] Do such natures really exist, or are they just ideas to help categorize the world in human language? he asked. In the Franciscan's view, good is what God orders and evil is what God forbids. With "Ockham's razor"—a product of later followers—the cobwebs of reason and natural law were cut away to expose the stark encounter of a free God and a free man. Only God was absolute because the laws of nature could be changed by his will. All moral good comes from man's free obedience to God's law.

By the late Middle Ages, the clear debate within moral reasoning was over the subjective and the objective and how the two meld. It came down to a conflict between realism, also called Thomism and scholasticism, and the subjective approach of nominalism. Nominalism collapsed the cathedral-like structure of scholasticism. That theoretical split gave momentum to a political one, for early Protestant thought drew on the precepts of nominalism and its twin, fideism. Within Catholicism, nominalism also gave rise to new trends. One was the emphasis on the subjectivity of moral action. Another was a moral legalism in which God's will was legislated for persons in manuals of right and wrong.

In his own day, Charles Curran grappled with the legacy of this split. Curran came out in opposition to moral legalism, yet he drew on the tradition of moral subjectivity. He rejected the traditional application of Thomistic natural law, though he retained the language of that philosophical system. Curran's choices prompted one Catholic critic to assert that his views were "more Protestant than Catholic"[23]

A few centuries after the medieval era, the very idea of moral absolutes—whether in God's will or in nature—was challenged. Before that modern relativism was born, however, the application of moral theology permeated the institutional Catholic Church.

MORAL THEOLOGY AS a practical discipline had it origins in the Catholic Church's effort to counter the Protestant Reformation and reform its own internal life. A revival of Thomism had begun in the 1400s and would later flourish particularly in Spanish universities. Spanish Dominican and Jesuit theologians combined an interest in Aquinas with a taste for the concreteness of nominalism. The outcome was the juridical approach to moral theology that would be secured at the Council of Trent, ending in 1563.

The Spaniards were the midwives for this new and practical moral science. They moved the great theoretical commentaries on the *Summa Theologiae* toward practical and pastoral application by publishing in 1600 the *Institutiones morales,* the work of the Jesuit Juan Azor in Rome. Trent had fixed the norms for the sacrament of penance, requiring confession for grave sins once a year, and this manual was its embodiment. To train clergy in the exactitude of moral science, the council shifted theological education from the universities to a new church institution, the seminary. There, students learned from the much-imitated *Institutiones,* which addressed conscience, human acts, sin and law, and studied particular cases in relation to commandments of God, the church, sacraments, and censures. The different religious orders developed manuals, each usually with three volumes, as the basis for moral instruction, hearing confession, and giving penances.

This legalistic approach to judging the sinfulness of particular actions accentuated the role of conscience in a new way. Since the mid-fifth century, the principal meaning of conscience was consciousness of one's bad behavior. For the Spanish moral theologians, however, the question for the conscience was: "What am I to do when I am not sure what to do?" They sought a rule that would help the conscience find escape from doubt in the face of so many moral precepts and propositions. A school of thought called "probabilism" emerged. The modern rendition of the word "probable" is "provable" or "arguable." Hence, a range of moral dilemmas could be addressed with a variety of good arguments. This thesis was first expressed by the Spanish Dominican Bartolomeo de Medina in 1577. "If an opinion is probable . . . it is permissible to adopt it, even if the opposite be more probable," he said in his *Commentary* on Aquinas. A probable opinion, he added, is one "stated by wise men and confirmed by very good arguments."[24]

"Probabilism" was a legalistic solution to the moral choices in the sixteenth century, and its basic principle lasted down to the Vatican Council of 1870. Probabilism spawned a new breed of priest, a sort of lawyer advocate who helped troubled souls escape conviction in the divine court. Criticized as a theory that propagated abuse, probabilism sparked two centuries of conflict involving the papacy, rival religious orders, and sectarian movements.

Probabilists had created lists of thousands of courses of action, all with an argument. Some moralists became renowned for what they offered. One was called the "Lamb of God" because he took away all the sins of the world and another was dubbed the "Prince of Laxists." To counter the extreme of laxism, a new rigorist approach to morality arose, led by the Dutch Bishop Cornelius Jansen, founder of the Jansenist movement. Jansen revived Augustine's pessimism about sin just as its sting was being taken away by probabilist confessors. Popes also intervened. Alexander VII (1665) and Innocent XI (1679) condemned more than one hundred laxist propositions. They included such assertions as:

"It is permitted to kill another to defend not only one's property but also one's expectations; It is not breaking a fast to eat little but often; It is licit to procure abortion before the foetus is animated, in order to prevent discovery leading to death or loss of reputation; No one is obliged under pain of mortal sin to restore a large sum, however great, which was stolen in installments; The church's commandment to hear Mass is satisfied by hearing two halves of it, or even four quarters, said simultaneously by different priests."[25]

Alexander VIII (1690) condemned both laxist and rigorist theses. The Vatican, however, stayed out of the dispute between the probabilist and its subsequent opposition views.

The first assault on probabilism came from the Dominicans in 1656 with "probabiliarism," which urged doing what seemed more likely to be right, or "more probable." The Jesuits tended to stick with the original probabilism. A stricter reaction came in what has been called "saferism" or "tutiorism." It argued for the safest course, preferably obedience to a moral or church law.

Finally, the most durable solution was argued in "equaprobabilism." In this view, a choice could be made between the two best alternatives, one inclined toward the law and the other toward liberty. In all these cases, a legalistic approach was employed. It was no surprise, then, that the founder of equaprobabilism was an Italian lawyer, Alphonsus of Liguori, who was also a great reviver of the belief in Hell. His *Theologia Moralis* was published in seven successive editions and depicted sound opinions removed from the extremes. In 1732 Alphonsus founded the Redemptorist order. Beatified as Saint Alphonsus in 1813 and made a doctor of the church in 1871, he was declared patron saint of confessors and moral theologians by Pope Pius XII in 1950.

Next to Alphonsus, the Spanish Jesuit Francisco Suarez probably had the most lasting influence on future moral theology. Suarez's work in the sixteenth and seventeenth centuries made law, responded to by free will, the supreme norm of rightness. Authentic laws, he said, are derived from divine authority and are "the act of a just and right will" from a superior to inferior.

From these fountainheads of probabilism and "legalism" came a tradition that Charles Curran both adopted and rejected. Suarez's work, which was subtle enough to allow exceptions to law for intrinsic reasons, nevertheless caused him to be portrayed in grim stereotype as the stern father confessor wielding authority through laws alone. He has become the object of rebellion and the perfect foil for the new moral theologians. Overturning the extrinsic legacy of Suarez, Curran frequently gives an intrinsic example: Something is not good because it is commanded, it is commanded because it is good. More significant for Curran, however, is the legacy of probabilism and its art of moral argument, a skill called casuistry. The practice goes back to the Roman orator Cicero, but its legacy has a direct line to Curran. Two centuries after the moderate casuist Alphonsus founded the Redemptorist order, it produced the influential moral theologian Bernard Häring, Curran's mentor.

Few theologians would wish to be called casuists today. The vilification of casuistry by the French mathematician Blaise Pascal in the mid-seventeenth century lingers on. Pascal was a part of the Jansenist movement and its call for piety and strict morality. Jansenists took deadly aim at the Jesuits, adept masters of casuistry who were the main confessors for social elites. "One single casuist can make up new moral rules according to his taste, and dispose as he wishes of all that concern moral behavior," Pascal protested.[26] Thanks largely to his literary tour de force, casuistry suffers a perpetually bad reputation. *Webster's* dictionary calls it "subtle but misleading or false reasoning."

Yet casuistry remains one of two basic approaches in moral theology, closely akin to the "new" school. "Even today Christian moral theologians are troubled by the problems of linking a faith that includes moral imperatives of paradoxical sublimity with the incessant demands of a rough and mean world," a major study of casuistry said. "Some resolve the problem by dwelling in a realm of ideal generalizations and exhortations; others plunge into the welter of practical life attempting to cut and shape their ideals to fit its fragmented demands."[27] Like the high era of probabilism, today's revival of casuistry follows the latter pattern. Indeed, Curran has been described as one of its last great practitioners.

AFTER THE SIXTEENTH century the world shared two Christian views, the Roman Catholic and the Protestant, and hence two foundations for Christian morality. Both would have implications for culture. As history would show, Catholic culture combined its moral outlook with an emphasis on authority and order. The new Protestant cultures took a different tack to human nature and morals and to that added freedom, which gave rise to notions of social liberty but also to checks and balances on power because of sin.

These directions had theological roots. For the Catholic theology of Trent, sin had not destroyed the human relationship to God. In a word, natural drives still were considered good in themselves. John Paul II may be strict, but he knows the pleasures of a good wine while vacationing in the mountains, a type of moral knowledge that is taboo to a Baptist preacher. The preacher's spiritual ancestors, the Protestant reformers, tended to believe human nature had been made totally depraved by original sin. Under these circumstance, only God's grace builds the relationship and makes human action good.

While Catholicism focused on each sin, as in confession, Protestantism tried to make the whole sinful nature of man right with God by faith, followed by avoidance of temptation.

"Catholicism can be radically ascetic, but it is not puritan in ordinary life," the Protestant theologian Paul Tillich has observed. A group of Protestants from the northern and eastern sections of Germany went down to Catholic Bavaria, Tillich recounts in a story. There, the country seemed to have a gaiety lacking in the religious and moral climate in the Protestant areas. "The difference had a basis in doctrine," he said.[28] As a backdrop for the modern debate on moral theology in North America, the distinction remains an important one.

Protestant hegemony in the United States until the 1950s placed a certain Puritan restraint on Catholicism. But as pluralism broke that hold, the latent Catholic optimism about human nature went public. Today's American Catholics are more liberal than Protestants on moral issues. While seventy-two percent of American Catholics believed premarital sex was morally wrong in 1969, by 1985 that had dropped to only thirty-three percent, according to Gallup polls. The general population in the same period went from sixty-eight percent disapproval to thirty-nine percent disapproval. A 1989 Gallup poll gauged Catholic students at secular universities similarly. Seventy-five percent of Catholic students thought premarital sexual relations were not wrong, while the average for students was sixty-nine percent. Most students approved of "trial marriages," but Catholics were higher than average in acceptance of abortion and divorce.[29] There have been two other interpretations for this trend. As a former minority in the United States, Catholics are a more tolerant religious group—and this would extend to moral behavior.[30] In the view of sociologist-priest Andrew Greeley, after *Humanae Vitae* Catholics are rebelling against church meddling in their sexual lives.[31]

Ratzinger attributed the moral liberalism of the West, including among Catholics, to economic factors. The moral crisis in Catholicism is largely a product of the developed world, he said: "Economic liberalism creates its exact counterpart, permissivism, on the moral plane." Accordingly, "It becomes difficult, if not altogether impossible, to present Catholic morality as reasonable," he said. The result, he added, is that "not a few" Catholic moral theologians have aligned with the dominant moral culture.[32]

Coming from his Catholic heritage, Ratzinger was of the view that in matters religious and moral a culture of authority best suited human ends. That was a view long established in Catholic history but one resisted now by secular Western culture. Yet it was welcomed in the traditional cultures of the developing nations, where authority and the supernatural still were viewed as one. As an American Catholic, Curran was moved to argue from his cultural experience, and that was an argument for freedom.

WITH THE TWENTIETH century the perennial confidence in absolutes was finally shaken. Preceding that undoing was a philosophical shift of almost glacial proportions. It began during the late nineteenth century, when a cosmology of fixed and objective absolutes was challenged by a cosmology of historic change and subjective reality. Much of it, inside and outside the Catholic Church, came from Germany.

The German Protestant theologian Frederick Schleiermacher redefined modern Protestantism, which he believed was weighed down by dogma and enervated by rationalism. Religious and moral truth were found in "inward emotions and dispositions." Such subjectivism had already been known in the Christian tradition, from Abelard to the mystics. Bernard of Clairvaux in the twelfth century had said, "As a man I speak of Him [Christ] as a Man to men." Bernard spoke of a transcendent reference point in the religious experience. By contrast Schleiermacher had a different version of inwardness, one that tended to turn from a transcendent Christ to the self: "As a man I speak to you of the sacred mysteries of humanity . . . of the innermost springs of my own being."[33] A step was being taken from the supernatural to the humanistic, a step that represented modernity.

Another philosopher of the age who was to have an abiding impact on future thought was Frederick Nietzsche, who died in 1900. A classical scholar, Nietzsche diagnosed the dilemma of modern man: Rationalism, historicism, and dogma had all been undermined by their own precepts. Seeing the abyss ahead, Nietzsche said the sole escape was in the "the will to power," by which he meant a creative mastery over life. His "superman" created "values." Man, Nietzsche said, is the "valuing animal." In his study of modern American higher education, *The Closing of the American Mind,* Allan Bloom traced contemporary subjectivism to a fast and loose use of Nietzsche's insight. The result, Bloom said, is that self-created values are given the highest praise while the pursuit of moral absolutes in reason or in nature is ignored. Commitment to and caring about these values, whatever they might be—and here enters the moral relativism—has replaced the quest for knowledge of truth itself, he said.[34]

The notion of absolutes was also rocked by modern physics, which has proposed that reality is a process. The views of phenomenology and empiricism argued that only experience, not revealed precepts, could be true. Catholic theologians would hence begin to rely on psychology and sociology to understand moral science. From American shores came an individualistic brand of personalism. A generation of Catholics, including John Paul II, was influenced by such communitarian personalists as the Frenchman Emmanuel Mounier. The rise in Europe of existentialism—the view that man is totally free and responsible for his acts—also showed its mark on Catholic thought. All of this, with its focus on the experience of persons, was overlaid by a still more dramatic change in the modern world view, the rise of historicism. In this approach, all truths recorded in history were conditioned by their time and place.

These two trends, subjectivism and historicism, posed a new challenge to Catholic thought. They hit at the classic precepts about the natural and supernatural aspects of persons and the belief that unchanging truth exists even as history and universe are in flux. In the generation of theologians that led up to Vatican II, two solutions were being offered to challenge this new world view. The neoscholasticism that dominated Roman theology, and was represented by the Curia at the Vatican council, answered the modern dilemma within the framework of traditional natural law. This answer rejected the new models proposed by modern European philosophy.

The "progressive" solutions that did adopt a new approach came out of France, Germany, and North America. The German Jesuit Karl Rahner was at the forefront of this break with scholasticism. He probably had the largest impact on the next generation of theologians and moral theology.

Some commentators find Rahner, who addressed mainstream Catholic issues of dogma, liturgy, ecclesiology, and theology, influenced by the existentialism of Heidegger and the German idealism of Hegel, who saw history as a dialectical process. Rahner's intellectual heirs have credited him with solving the dualism in Catholic thought prompted by scholasticism, replacing it with a more integrated model of the relationship between the supernatural and physical, between nature and grace. Rahner, who was extremely theoretical, said that natural law and history should be understood by what is "transcendental" to them. For persons and for history absolutes existed as transcendental norms, to be found in the consciousness of man, a realm of ideals, hopes, and desires given by God and sought concretely in the historical world.

On this basis, Rahner displaced law as the guiding light of man with the aspiration toward good. The person is able to judge good and evil by a "moral instinct of faith." The transcendental even superseded doctrinal confession—Rahner thus spoke of the world's "anonymous Christians." What the transcendental principle does for Catholic theology is allow it to recognize historical and personal change without sliding into relativism; the transcendental norms became anchors that once were provided by the absolute norms of natural law theory.

The Canadian theologian Bernard Lonergan built upon Rahner's work by becoming his practical-minded counterpart. Lonergan developed an intellectual method to identify what is transcendental in the real empirical objects of a culture or a time in history. Together, Rahner and Lonergan laid the foundations for the broadest school of moral theology today, sometimes called transcendental Thomism. Historical-mindedness was a term used by Lonergan, who characterized the old natural law theory as the "classicist" view that believes "man as such, precisely because he is an abstraction, also is unchanging." To understand God in human reality, Lonergan said, the historical-minded view is preferable. Through it, "one can apprehend mankind as a concrete aggregation developing over time, where the locus of development and, so to speak, the synthetic bond is the emergence, expansion, differentiation, dialectic of meaning and of meaningful [human] performance."[35]

In the face of this, Ratzinger has criticized what he believes to be a rampant historicism. "If everything is only a culturally and historically conditioned role, and not a natural specificity inscribed in the depth of being, even motherhood is a mere accidental function," he said.[36] Curran, however, counts Lonergan as one of three major influences on his own work.

The new historical approach had a major impact on moral theology. The emphasis went from universals to concrete situations in judging the morality of particular acts. Norms for morality were found inductively by beginning with the particular. No longer was there assumed to be a universal norm from which all behavior could be reasoned deductively. There were absolute norms in the new moral theology, but they were more like ideals. They are "exhortations rather than norms in the strict sense," moral theologian Josef Fuchs said.[37] Such "transcendental" norms would include: "One must always act in conformity with love of God and neighbor" and "One must always act in accord with right reason."[38]

The next logical step in this way of thinking was to say that human acts are morally neutral until placed in a concrete situation. All potential acts are therefore "premoral"—neither right nor wrong in themselves. Without an absolute norm that said some acts are always wrong while others are always good, the morality of an act was determined by its result. This gave rise to "proportionalism," a widespread school of thought in moral theology that said a moral decision is good as long as the positive values outweigh the negative values. From proportionalism arose a variation called consequentialism; it judges the morality of an act by its short-range and long-range effect. And who is to judge what is the greater good? For the new moral theology, the informed person is to make that decision, an idea that smacks of relativism to the more traditional moral theologian.

These arguments, also called the "preference principle" or the "principle of proportionate good," found a benchmark expression in the 1967 majority report of the papal commission which narrowly approved artificial contraception. (Pope Paul VI, of course, disagreed with the report and declared the opposite in *Humanae Vitae*). Killing is contrary to right reason "unless there is a question of a good of a higher order," one part of the majority report said. Elsewhere it said, "Infertile conjugal acts [by contraception] constitute a totality with fertile acts and have a single moral specification, namely, fostering of love responsibly towards generous fecundity." Although the report did not deny moral absolutes, according to an analysis by May, its form of reasoning allowed absolutes to be eclipsed by pursuit of a human "totality" or "a good of a higher order."[39]

Coinciding with this new application of proportionality and consequence was a revival of casuistry. It emerged in the 1960s, not because of philosophical changes but as a result of "the challenge to authority and expertise."[40] As the moral consensus of society was upset, the methods of casuist reasoning were well suited to new and complex moral dilemmas. It was a concrete method for concrete problems. The weighing and analyzing of moral choices was derived from casuistry's past heritage, but now the subjects were medical and business ethics, public policy, law, and war.

OVERALL, MORAL THEOLOGY has become more optimistic in the past generation. The roots of that optimism can be traced to nineteenth century Germany. Theologians at the University of Tübingen, which also launched the theological attack on papal infallibility, said moral theology springs from the ideal of Christ, not the Ten Commandments. Moral theologians elsewhere began to reject the science of penance handed down by Alphonsus and Suarez. In the mid-1900s a neo-Thomistic renewal in France, with Jacques Maritain and his Thomist personalism at the center, emphasized the ethical category of good in natural law theory.

New approaches to marriage were evidence of the more positive view. In the 1930s and 1940s some Catholic theologians challenged as one-sided the view that marriage's only divine purpose was procreation. Working from the personalist philosophy, they said that canon law's treatment of marriage as the means to procreation overlooked its essence: love, creativity, and happiness. These fruits of the relationship now were considered as equally important as procreation.

The theological work that most represented these developments was the 1954 tome *The Law of Christ* by Bernard Häring, who was trained in the Tübingen School. Häring, considered the most influential moral theologian of his time, added a new emphasis to the use of Scripture—especially the Sermon on the Mount—in moral theology while retaining the traditional lists of virtues and sins found in the old manuals. Häring, not unlike John Paul II, was influenced by the phenomenology of Max Scheler. Scheler was concerned about immediate relationships with, and perception of, objects. In those encounters the person intuitively, by insight, knows eternal values. These values are absolutes, and yet in human experience they are relative because people perceive the values from their different perspectives. What gives any object value is love, by which the object "attains the ideal state of value intrinsic to its nature," Scheler said.

Based on this and other influences, the central theme in Häring's 1,146-page volume, translated from German into fifteen languages, was the primacy of the relationship with Christ. "Christ's moral code is religious in its very essence," he said. Religion is the free human response to the living God, a "dialogue" that makes man truly responsible. Other moral virtues, in the form of human actions, do not have God as their direct object. Thus to Häring, the highest morality is the religious response to God.[41] His view was a form of what would be called the "fundamental moral option," in which persons are made not by the sum total of their acts but by their fundamental choice for or against the Creator.

Some practitioners of the new moral theology have taken that view to an extreme. It has not gone unchallenged.

"They even claim that a person can at times freely choose to do what he or she believes to be gravely immoral—for instance, to have intercourse with the 'wrong' person or to kill an innocent human being without proportionate reason—and still remain, in the core of his or her being, a morally good person," May said. "In short, for revisionists, the everyday deeds we choose to do in exercising our 'categorical' freedom of choice 'horizontally' in our daily relationships are of a fundamentally different moral character from the option we make . . . deep within our being in our 'transcendental' relationship with God." To the contrary, May said, "we make ourselves to be the kind of person were are in and through the actions we freely choose to do." And herein lies the importance of moral absolutes: They "show us what love *cannot* mean," May said.[42]

BEGINNING HIS EXPLORATION of moral theology in the 1950s, Curran was influenced greatly by Häring, his direct instructor, and by the work of Lonergan. From one he received the existential and scriptural view and from the other an appreciation of historical consciousness and the person as subject, the center of things. Curran has described his own stance in moral theology as broader than most, taking into account all aspects of Christian reality—creation, sin, incarnation, redemption, and resurrection destiny—when faced with a moral problem.

But Curran is most set apart from his fellow theologians by his absorption of Protestant ethics, which are more pessimistic about sin in the world than is Catholicism. This ecumenism of thought led to Curran's election in 1971 as the first Catholic president of the Protestant-dominated Society of Christian Ethics. In referring to his moral realism, Curran has noted that he dissented from the natural law methodology employed by Pope John XXIII's encyclical, *Pacem in Terris*. It showed, he said, "the penchant for a too one-sidedly optimistic understanding."[43] Curran said that he, like Ratzinger, also has criticized the overly optimistic outlook of Vatican II.

To distance himself from tendencies toward relativism in Protestant thought, Curran issued critiques of Joseph Fletcher, the liberal Protestant advocate of "situation ethics," a utilitarianism with happiness as the goal. Yet Curran's thought retains a distinctly Protestant emphasis: human freedom in God's grace. The monk Martin Luther decided that walking to the altar on his knees or paying indulgences did not make him one iota better in God's eyes. Curran, too, has doubted that works or actions are the principal evidence of faith or morality. Protestant influence reached Curran through the works of Lutheran scholar H. Richard Niebuhr, the Reformed ethicist James Gustafson, a student of Niebuhr's, and the conservative Methodist ethicist Paul Ramsey. The three shared the Protestant notions of God as other, the centrality of sin and grace, and, most important to Curran, the complexity of defining "the good" in the human situation.

Mixing this moral realism of Protestantism with Catholic naturalism and rationality, Curran fashioned his own two unique contributions to Catholic moral theology. The first was his "theology of compromise."[44] As a moral agent, a person exists in a sin-soaked environment, lowering Christian expectations for human behavior and changing the rules by which morality is measured. In the intractable situations of the fallen world, persons must compromise and choose the lesser of evils. "Sometimes the presence of sin in the world will force one to do something which, if there were no sin present, should not be done," Curran explained.[45] So, for example, it is better—and hence moral—for a homosexual person to have a commitment to one partner than to practice promiscuity. In another case, if a financial burden related to a marriage can destroy a loving relationship between a man and woman, then cohabitation without marriage can be a moral choice.

Complementing the theology of compromise is Curran's view of the give and take of all things with a person as the subject. An individual choice is made with many considerations, theological and environmental. Hence, he proposes for Catholic moral theology a model of "relationality-responsibility," a theme developed in Niebuhr's 1963 work, *The Responsible Self*—that personal choice affects society.[46] With an emphasis on freedom and conscience, the person is "the subject and agent in the midst of multiple relationships with God, nature, world, and self," Curran said. The morality of a life is determined as it grows in multiple relationships in community. Once that life comprehends Christian ideals of virtue, then moral judgments can be made on concrete actions. In past moral theology, Curran said, actions were the first and only consideration.

Curran's critique has focused on a use of natural law theory which he calls "physicalism" or "biologism." In his dissent from the church's teaching against artificial contraception, Curran argued that *Humane Vitae* advocated physicalism. In other words, the physical act of intercourse was made absolute. "The natural law basis for such a position absolutizes the physical and biological at the expense of the total person," Curran said. That distinction, he said, has always been made on the question of killing; killing is a physical act and murder is a moral act. So for Curran, "Natural law itself is not primarily the given natural or biological order but right reason. In the name of right reason, one can and should interfere with physical and biological structures."[47] On a similar basis, Curran has criticized a range of church teachings regarding sexual and medical ethics in which he believes physicalism appears.

Ratzinger may have been thinking of this charge when he said the contrary: "To respect biology is to respect God himself, hence to safeguard his creatures."[48]

Ratzinger has claimed that because the moral teachings of the church are considered unreasonable in the permissive West, moral theologians are fighting for their credibility. "Consequently they set out on a search for theories and systems that allow compromises between Catholicism and current conceptions," he said.[49] They are left with a choice, he said, "between opposing modern society and opposing the magisterium."[50]

Much of that choice, as evidenced by the career of Charles Curran, was being made in the theology departments of hundreds of American Catholic colleges and universities.

FIVE

Catholic Higher Education

American Catholic students choose a university or college today no differently than their peers. Their concerns are cost, reputation, academic standing, location, size, and certain campus intangibles—all of which have nothing necessarily to do with religion. It was not always that way.

For more than a century after the founding of Catholic higher education in the United States in 1789, its three prime motives—training of priests, protection and propagation of the faith, and character formation of youth—sprang from religion. Similar motives prompted the rise of Catholic women's colleges beginning in 1896. All Catholic schools were "preoccupied with preserving tenets of the faith and with teaching policies ensuring the allegiance of Catholic people to the Church," historian Edward J. Power said.[1] Learning has long been a product of Catholic culture. But unlike today, academic achievement, let alone specialized training for employment, was not the original priority.

Two centuries after the first academy was established in the United States, Catholic higher education has largely been a success. Of the nation's 1,600 independent institutions, about half are church-related, with Catholic institutions—some 230 colleges and universities, which includes 14 "research universities"—forming the largest denominational bloc.

This history of Catholic education can be seen as an evolution from authority toward freedom, a conflict between the two, and finally an uneasy but real equilibrium. Catholic colleges and universities in America had to flirt with freedom and come again to realize the significance of some form of authority to retain something distinctly "Catholic."

Thus, the third century of American Catholic higher education opens with internal and external challenges that some say make a crisis. Internally, the struggle is for purpose and identity, the very raison d'etre for having Catholic educational institutions. At one time it was essential for Catholics, an ethnic and religious minority, to prove their contribution to American society. One Catholic educator asked in 1957, "Where are the Catholic Salks, Oppenheimers, Einsteins?"[2] The answer came in political form—the 1960 election of John F. Kennedy as the first Catholic president. By this time a growing number of Catholics had passed through higher education and entered professional fields. With the education and assimilation of Catholics accomplished, the average Catholic institution was forced, once again, to attempt to define itself in terms of religious personality.

One dramatic facet of this identity "crisis" was the Vatican's action to curtail the teaching of Charles Curran at The Catholic University of America. The dispute highlighted anew all sides of the identity question. The wider Catholic education community struggled once again with how to balance authority and freedom. In practical terms, the question was how the Vatican distinguishes between ecclesiastical schools or departments, in which it has some jurisdiction, and those schools and departments that are nonecclesiastical. There was alarm, but many Catholic educators argued that the Curran affair had limited implications for Catholic education in general. Curran, an American academic and priest, taught in a one-of-a-kind university with special ecclesiastical schools that are, in effect, licensed by the Vatican to give church-approved degrees in sacred sciences. For the alarmed educators, however, there was a rub. The Vatican ruling allowed the university's board of trustees and the local archbishop to bar Curran from teaching Catholic theology even in the nonecclesiastical departments. Authority, in this view, had tipped the scales against freedom.

Catholic identity, as an internal dilemma, manifests itself externally in the question of truth in advertising. To survive financially, can today's Catholic institutions assure the contributing Catholic population that they are preserving something uniquely Catholic? While being persuasively Catholic, the institutions must also convince secular education and government of their autonomy from church control. Too close a tie could hurt academic accreditation by secular agencies. It also could trigger lawsuits by critics who see government grants as money going to the church.

All of private education, of which Catholic colleges are part, has been rolled back by an expanding public sector. After the Second World War, enrollment in American higher education was about evenly divided between the private and public, but the latter now is eighty percent. Private institutions enrolled about 2.8 million of the nation's 12.5 million college and university students in 1987. That same year Catholic institutions enrolled fewer than five percent of all students in higher education. Catholic colleges and universities comprise fewer than ten percent of all institutions of higher learning.

To endure these modern challenges, Catholic institutions have diversified their approaches to both identity and financial survival. They are motivated to endure, "despite the pressures and severe problems," because "The principal strength of Catholic higher learning has now shifted to the United States," according to a 1976 report by American Catholic educators.[3] The nation's roughly six hundred thousand students in Catholic colleges and universities are half the entire world enrollment in such institutions.

Today's diversity of approaches ranges from an emphasis on authority to one on freedom, with a mixture in between. While not necessarily "pontifical," the colleges most aligned with church authority operate almost exclusively for Catholics. Larger universities, such as Fordham and Notre Dame, are pluralistic Catholic—steeped in a Catholic heritage but catering to students of all religious backgrounds. Others have gone entirely secular, claiming a Catholic heritage, but only in the sense of a "mission" in education. Some experts suggest Catholic institutions are no longer needed. For them, the mission has been accomplished; the nation's immigrants are educated and in the mainstream. Even the new immigrants, millions of Hispanics making up a fourth of the American church, do not justify turning back the clock. For in this view, university-style academic freedom is incompatible with Catholic religion; it requires a complete separation of freedom from authority. An alternative in this vein would be a Catholic "presence" at secular schools, such as a Newman Center for students or an endowed chair of Catholic studies.[4]

Before fourteen months of his pontificate had passed, John Paul II had addressed the question of Catholic identity in three major actions. His first encyclical, *Redemptor Hominis,* in March 1979 defined—among other things—the values of Christian humanism that he said should infuse education.[5] He contrasted these with the false or partial forms of humanism such as technology, scientism, economics, biology, or psychology.

The next month the pope set out to codify the nature of ecclesiastical higher education, following on the plan of Paul VI, pontiff from 1963–78. He did so by promulgating the apostolic constitution *Sapientia Christiana,* which set forth the conditions to govern the teaching of sacred sciences in ecclesiastical faculties at universities.[6] The 1979 document required Catholic institutions to submit statutes based on the new laws and regulations to the Congregation for Catholic Education in Rome for approval. Under these new local statutes, professors teaching faith and morals must receive a canonical mission from the chancellor. To acquire tenure, a faculty member needs a declaration of *nihil obstat*—"nothing stands in the way"—from the Holy See. The statutes stressed that teachers are to carry on their work in full communion with the magisterium.

Finally came John Paul's address to Catholic educators in the United States at Catholic University in October 1979. He outlined a three-part mission of the university. A Catholic university, he said, should aim for the highest research in "all aspects of nature and man," prepare youth capable of making a "personal synthesis between faith and culture" and able "to bear witness to their faith before the world." It was to establish among the faculty and students a "community where sincere commitment to scientific research and study goes together with a deep commitment to Christian living."[7]

From that time forward, the question of identity and purpose for the modern Catholic college or university entered a new phase in the American debate. Despite the papal initiatives, which would finally include an apostolic constitution in 1990, the answer for all the dilemmas of Catholic higher education were not entirely clear.

What is elusive in the present, however, is sometimes clear in the past. Catholic educators can look there for a sharp identity in their religious tradition and even some solutions to the clash of authority and freedom.

The university, or *studium generale,* traces its origins to the flowering of the high Middle Ages in eleventh century Europe. It was then that the church provided Western civilization with its great patrimony of the liberal arts, Christian humanism, and the scholarly vocation. In the Middle Ages, the task of the university was to reconcile Christian belief with the philosophy and literature of Greece and Rome. Today its task is to reconcile faith with the findings of the social and physical sciences. This effort to harmonize religious truth with secular knowledge has gone on for centuries.[8]

EARLY CHRISTIAN EDUCATION was pioneered by Greek church fathers who sought to make the Christian view of the universe compatible with Greek thought. Clement of Alexandria and Origen, who argued Christianity was the culmination of Hellenistic culture, established schools known around the Mediterranean. Saint Augustine and Saint Jerome endorsed Christian use of secular schools, but only if pagan literature and rhetoric served Christian life. Toleration of Christians in the Roman Empire during the fourth century allowed Roman education and new catechetical schools to flourish side by side. With the four centuries of tumult that accompanied the decline of the Roman Empire, Christian monasteries maintained the momentum of education.

The most significant schools were those founded by the bishops, usually attached to the cathedral. Considered a bridge, these schools were successors to the old Roman system and precursors to modern grammar-school education. The court of Charlemagne, the Frankish leader who became Roman emperor in 800, was the great magnet for pioneers of educational progress. The German city of Aachen became its center. Alarmed at the grammatical ignorance in Latin of churchmen and functionaries, Charlemagne enforced education for clergy throughout his empire, in effect founding medieval education. In the terms of Charlemagne's chief scholar, Alcuin of Britain, the court was an "academy." A library was formed, texts and books were copied, and a discipline was prescribed for other centers of learning in the empire.

Outside Aachen a few seats of culture also existed, in northern France, Germany and Italy, where archbishops sponsored schools or missionaries built them to standard. The breakup of the Carolingian Empire under Charlemagne's grandsons, followed by Viking raids, ended that brief renaissance of learning. What did survive was the focus on grammar and the works of the classical authors.

Christian Europe's educational renaissance would come in the twelfth century as a number of factors converged. Medieval society was being organized around new monarchies, and the cities were reanimated and structured as large communal enclaves. Through trade, and by the Crusades, continental Europe developed contacts with the East and the Moors in Spain, further stimulating intellectual life. Arabic renderings of Aristotle and related commentaries, lost to the West, were translated into Latin. Finally, an increasingly centralized papacy, begun under Gregory VII around 1100, made standards for church instruction uniform.

In cities, the development of royal administrations offered employment opportunities to educated clergy. Schools for notaries, rhetoric, and law increased in importance. These schools were organized under a collegiate church or cathedral. Schools for secular subjects were directed by an archdeacon, chancellor, cantor, or cleric with an academic title, such as *scholasticus,* assisted by one or more other masters.

The success of these urban schools made it necessary in the mid-twelfth century to define the teaching function clearly. Religious authority accredited those schools that qualified, a stamp of approval that centuries later would come from a secular authority. Only those provided with the *licencia docendi,* conferred by the bishop or, more often, by the *scholasticus,* could teach. Teaching with such a license was limited to the city or diocese, where clerical leaders held supervision. Papal concerns about accrediting such teachers were met when the Lateran Council of 1179 made the license requirement universal.

Early conflicts over the principles of authority and freedom changed the shape of education. Indeed, pursuit of academic freedom was a political matter from the university's birth. "In the thirteenth century masters and learners fled the interference of merchants, bankers, and feudal lords to seek from bishops the protection of their freedom, and then the patronage of popes against bishops," professor George A. Kelly noted.[9] Such disagreements with local religious or civil leaders prompted education centers to seek independent status, leading to the *studium generale*. Shifting away from cathedral authority, the schools came under masters holding special licenses, ones exceeding those of mere teachers. These licenses, granted by a pope, emperor, or king, gave the master mobility and the right to confer degrees.

The next stage was for certain centers of learning to claim they had more than local standing. Their claims were backed by reputation but also attracted the backing of eager patrons—again, a pope or emperor. Hence, from about 1292 onward the *studium generale* was understood to be a licensed center established under a papal or imperial bull. Oxford University in England and some noted centers in Spain, however, never sought the decree but rose by sheer reputation.

The word *universitas* was used originally to describe guilds of students and teachers brought together by particular topics or a certain trade. A broader use appeared by the latter part of the fourteenth century to mean the entire community of teachers and scholars corporately sanctioned by ecclesiastical or civil authority. The term "college" arose to describe smaller groups, often bound by national language, focus of study, or as a circle of masters who conferred degrees, at the university.

Bologna in Italy was the site of the first real university. But the University of Paris, formed between 1150 and 1170, became the model for other schools from the thirteenth to fifteenth centuries. Oxford was begun by English students returning from Paris about 1167. With papal support, Paris became the center of orthodox theological teaching. In 1231 Gregory IX, in the bull *Parens Scientiarum,* or "Mother of Learning," gave the university self-regulation and freedom to modify its constitution. This pope realized that autonomy provided a unique stimulus to learning. The fully developed university at Paris divided into four faculties, the three superior ones being theology, canon law, and medicine.

By 1200 the university movement was well underway, as historian Christopher Dawson showed in a colorful passage: "Paris and Bologna were thronged with crowds of students from every part of

Christendom, and the Bohemian life of the needy and turbulent scholars had already become a favorite subject for poets and satirists. This new class was no longer contented with the patient scholarship and strict discipline of the cathedral schools as represented by Chartres. It was an intellectual proletariat of needy and ambitious students, contemptuous of the past, impatient of restraint, following the fashionable teacher and doctrine of the moment."[10]

Throughout the universities, two bodies of educational material became standardized. The liberal arts curriculum, or *trivium,* included grammar, rhetoric, and logic. The *quadrivium* focused on geometry, arithmetic, music, and astronomy. Philosophy was a separate discipline, with its four branches. Each of the major universities developed a particular emphasis. While Paris became a center of scholasticism, derived from the *trivium,* the University of Chartres emphasized the *quadrivium,* the closest thing to science as we know it today. Stimulated by the Greco-Arabic translations of Euclid, Ptolemy, Hippocrates, and other Hellenistic scholars, Chartres's scholars attempted to Christianize Greek cosmology, explain Genesis according to physics, and rediscover nature. Italian schools became renowned in canon and civil law, owing to increased conflicts of church and secular authority and by the discovery of the *Corpus Juris Civilis,* the sixth century Roman code of Emperor Justinian. Medieval princes turned to this law code to legitimize their politics, as did the papacy.

Through this wide array of subjects students naturally began to specialize, both by taste and associations with certain teachers who had become masters in a field. A natural byproduct was the rise of rivalries between schools of thought and methods. Before long there were two or three rival chairs on most subjects.

At the University of Paris, for example, a sort of union dispute arose in the 1250s between the masters of theology and the friars, whose new religious orders had gained patronage from the papacy. These Franciscans and Dominicans, ousted temporarily, were reinstated in university chairs as the pope took the administrative upper hand. This university debate, in fact, fanned the first major scholarly discussion on the extent of papal authority.[11]

Realism and nominalism clashed at the medieval schools. It was one of a few precedents for the modern-day dual between Curran's new moral theology and the traditional approach. Weary from the endless abstract debate between realists and nominalists, some Italian universities subordinated logic to rhetoric. Scholars turned to ancient literature, laying the ground work for an educational revolution—the Renaissance. Before long, the modern concepts of freedom would overshadow the long-established claims of authority.

PROPELLED BY THE Renaissance and the Reformation, the individual moved into the foreground of education, just as the Roman Catholic Church lost its comprehensive hold on European politics and culture—and hence on the nature of universities. A combination of the "new learning" of humanism and science and the jolt of the Reformation planted the seeds of academic freedom. But they did not bloom quickly, for the Reformation in fact produced confessional schools, and the University of Paris still censured books until the 1620s.

The need for political peace through religious toleration grew, however, and finally the Enlightenment drove the great wedge between the university and church authority. "Academic freedom and religious freedom have one root in common; both are based upon freedom of conscience," historian Richard Hofstadter said of the period.[12] Along with the Enlightenment's rights of man came the notion of a liberal education, premised on the right of intellectual freedom.

These were the issues that John Henry Newman, the English convert and future cardinal, grappled with in the mid-1800s in his *The Idea of a University*. The work captures the modern struggle over Catholic identity in university education, making Newman's reflections still a beginning point for modern Catholic educators. Newman's main argument has been described thus: Liberal education should not inculcate virtue or teach a vocation but rather train the student to have a philosophical "habit of mind."[13] Modern educators call this Newman's emphasis on "university," with "Catholic" being a modifier. Newman distinguished between a church and a university, saying it is neither a convent nor seminary, but a place to fit men of the world for the world. "The formation of soul and character he would leave to the home and to the church," a commentator said of Newman.[14]

Yet another of Newman's views has been spotlighted in the last of *Idea of a University's* nine "discourses." There, Newman argued for a direct jurisdiction of the church in the university, not a mere influence. Indeed, in a skeptical age Newman was drawn away from Anglicanism by Catholicism's unique lure, authority. "If the Catholic faith is true, a university cannot exist externally to the Catholic pale," he said. "Hence, a direct and active jurisdiction of the church over it and in it is necessary, lest it should become the rival of the church with the community at large in those theological matters which to the church is exclusively committed." Science and literature left to themselves, Newman said, become hostile to religion, largely because liberal knowledge tends to impress modern man with philosophical theory instead of revelation, "making us our centre, and our minds the measure of all things."[15]

For the next century, the Roman Catholic Church mistrusted what the secular universities stood for. Afraid of license and heterodoxy, the church through the mid-1900s opposed all modern freedoms: of worship, press, conscience—and teaching. At the end of the nineteenth century Pope Leo XIII condemned such liberties. When Pope John XXIII outlined the ideal social order in 1961, it contained charity, truth, and justice but still lacked liberty—an element added two years later in his *Pacem in Terris*.

Protestants, who had nurtured ideas of liberty since the sixteenth century, saw the modern university differently. Their leading schools in Europe, once used to train personnel for the church and the state, began to throw off ecclesiastical control. The new direction began in Germany, where one major university stopped teaching Latin in 1693 and another began teaching history in 1736. In 1809 the University of Berlin broke entirely from the past by emphasizing philosophy, science, research, and graduate education. Later in that century the modern educational ideas of academic freedom, research, and specialization were firmly in place. As a University of Berlin professor said in 1902, "It is no longer, as formerly, the function of the university teacher to hand down a body of truth established by authorities, but to search after scientific knowledge by investigation, and to teach hearers to do the same."[16]

It was under these prevailing circumstances that the Catholic Church developed, in the manner of medieval practice, the "canonical mission." Born of the secularization of universities and schools in

Germany in 1848, the license was the church's way to protect the domain of religious instruction in state-run institutions.

After the turn of the century, this means of regulating approved church teachings on faith and morals was applied even to institutions that continued to be church-related. It was a means for authority to make its claim in an environment of freedom. And it was a claim dramatically tested when the Vatican stripped Curran of his canonical mission.

ROMAN CATHOLICS IN THE colonial United States, though few in number and faced with some discrimination, could partake of the revival of higher education after the Revolutionary War. The religious freedom clauses of the U.S. Constitution were their gateway. The first Catholic bishop in America, John Carroll of Baltimore, appointed in 1790, made education a priority. Before his elevation he founded an academy, today's Georgetown University, in 1789. Many of its first teachers were French priests fleeing the anticlerical French Revolution. Georgetown's opening was the start of Catholic higher learning in the United States, and it came at a time when only seventeen colleges existed in the nation. The emergence of Catholic higher education in the United States parallels the nation's educational development but lags behind chronologically.[17] Protestant-founded American colleges secularized at the end of the nineteenth century, becoming hybrids that joined the English model of a four-year college with the German focus on departments, research, and specialization.

Steeped in the continental tradition, American Catholic educators followed a different pattern. They drew partly on European patterns of religious authority. They perpetuated a six to seven–year college that included preparatory years equivalent to high school. St. Louis University in 1880, for example, was the first school to experiment with a four-year curriculum. Notre Dame did not drop the preparatory years until the 1920s, and the complete break for Catholic institutions in general did not come until the 1940s. Some other aspects of the European tradition endured through the 1960s. The strong presidency reflected continental secondary education, reinforced by the clerical tradition. Clerical governance was a tradition not ended anywhere in United States Catholic higher education until

1967, when it was dropped at the Universities of St. Louis and Notre Dame. The notion of a classical liberal education also endured, epitomized by the *ratio studiorum,* developed by the Jesuits in 1599. This curriculum embraced humanistic, philosophical, and theological studies.

Immigration, which dramatically increased the number of Catholics and changed the character of their communities, was a prime mover in the development of Catholic institutions. The peak years of immigration for Irish and Germans were 1851 and 1882. As a result, between 1860 and 1920 no fewer than 156 Catholic institutions were established, adding to those founded since 1786. Women's colleges came late in the immigration period. Notre Dame of Maryland was the first, formed in 1896 and followed in the next decade by eighteen others; by 1955 there were one hundred sixteen Catholic women's colleges. The religious orders became the engines of higher education. Also because of immigration, the Catholic college became a place to preserve ethnic and religious traditions, rather than a vehicle for assimilation. Most Catholic immigrant groups founded separate colleges and seminaries to help create their own elites.

A century after Georgetown's opening, Catholic University was founded in 1889 as the first graduate-level institution related to the Catholic Church. Though created by the American bishops for the advanced training of clergy and given a so-called "charter" by the papacy, it reflected the German, research-type institution while still retaining continental structures. It was the first Catholic institution to straddle two worlds, the religious and the scientific.

COMING INTO THE twentieth century, some, such as Englishman Thomas Macaulay, had great hopes that education would save democracy itself. H.G. Wells went further: He said education would save mankind. Modern history, he said, was "the race between education and catastrophe."[18] With a similar anticipation, the United States federal government quadrupled its spending on education between 1910 and 1930 from $426.25 million to $2.3 billion. Spending on higher education jumped to $1 billion. Illiteracy fell during that period from 7.7 percent to 4.3 percent.[19]

Catholic education, alert to the general trend, reorganized itself from about 1900 until after the First World War. But the Catholic "system" faced a proliferation problem, epitomized by a dictum of Boston Archbishop William O'Connell: "No Catholic community can be content without a Catholic college."[20] As the decades passed, the Catholic education landscape became one of disparate schools founded arbitrarily by religious orders and dioceses. The challenge was to unite and standardize. This began in the Association of Catholic Colleges, which first met in 1899 and five years later merged with the organization representing parochial schools and seminaries. The (National) Catholic Educational Association was born. It broke the isolation of Catholic institutions and undertook to standardize four-year colleges. The accreditation system was forcing all education to go this way, and by the 1920s a uniform credit-hour and elective system touched every institution, Catholic and secular. By these criteria the Catholic Educational Association issued an approved list of fifty-two Catholic colleges in 1918. All of them surrendered some of their focus on classical education, with its unified study of humanities, literature, and philosophy, to incorporate the elective system and modern teaching methods.

Assimilation, however, was not painless. Traditional Catholic education was "religious, literary, humanistic in spirit, synthetic in vision, rigid in approach, liberal in aim and elitist in social orientation," historian Philip Gleason explained. Now it faced a new American system that was "secular, scientific, technical in spirit, particularized in vision, flexible in approach, vocational in aim and democratic in social structure."[21]

After the First World War, enrollment in Catholic colleges rose threefold to some 102,000 students and by 1940 the figure was 162,000. There was a general optimism as well that Catholicism, mixed with reason and education, had the answer to modern man's material and spiritual needs. Hence, in 1929 Catholic University professor Fulton J. Sheen urged teachers to "educate for a Catholic Renaissance."[22] The association of colleges and universities declared in 1935, "The Catholic college will not be content with presenting Catholicism as a creed, a code, or a cult. Catholicism must be seen as a culture." Graduates would understand the whole sweep of Western civilization and "will have seen before them not merely the facts of the natural order but those in the supernatural order also, those facts which give meaning and coherence to life."[23]

Such practical aims were put on hold with the onset of the Second World War. But if those years of death and destruction shaded the previous idealism of Catholic educators and clergy, the war's end brightened prospects for the institutions themselves. Near universal military service led to near universal education via the GI Bill of Rights in 1944. In 1940, fourteen percent of young Americans were going to college; by 1955 the rate had risen to twenty-five percent and by 1965 to about forty percent. Enrollment in Catholic institutions rose to 293,000 in 1948 and 384,526 in 1965. Students at Catholic institutions in 1961 were three times more likely than their professors to be the sons or daughters of a college educated man.

More education meant more free thinking, with its inevitable outcome. These Catholics no longer gave automatic deference to church authority.

A PHILOSOPHY OF EDUCATION also took hold in the postwar period, and it was adopted by Catholics as they entered mainstream America from their ethnic or urban enclaves. Its optimism overwhelmed, historian Paul Johnson said. "In the 1950s the myth that education was the miracle cure for society emerged stronger than ever," he said.[24] Higher education, a leading economist claimed in 1962, fueled nearly half of America's growth from 1930 to 1960.[25] "What the railway did for the second half of the last century and the automobile for the first half of this century, may be done for the second half of this century by the knowledge industry," Clark Kerr, president of the University of California at Berkeley, said in his 1963 Godkin Lecture at Harvard. "That is, to serve as the focal point for national growth."[26]

Catholic educators increasingly shared this optimistic vision, and it began with a short period of Catholic self-criticism. The self-flagellation was not entirely new. It was evoked briefly by a 1934 study that said only six departments at all Catholic universities—five at Catholic University and one at Notre Dame—were capable of offering adequate doctoral programs. Catholic historian John Tracy Ellis stirred the contemporary debate in 1955 with his speech, "American Catholics and the Intellectual Life," made to the Catholic Commission on Intellectual and Cultural Affairs, a small group of restless Catholic intellectuals. He, among others, pointed out the lack of a Catholic intellectual tradition in the United States, criticizing the "overemphasis which some authorities of the church's education system in the United States have given to the school as an agency for moral development" instead of "intellectual development."[27]

Then in 1960 a major study of graduate education caused new embarrassment. No Catholic university was rated among the top twenty-two in the study, although five were among the next rung of twenty-five. The same study noted only Catholic University as conferring enough doctoral degrees—at least one percent of the national total—to be called a full-fledged university. Catholic institutions conferred only 3.14 percent of the 104,139 doctorates from all universities between 1955 and 1964.[28]

As Catholic schools reassessed their goals, most American Catholics were drawn to the secular universities. It was part and parcel of Catholic assimilation, based on improved social status and the growth of public-sector education. Two out of three Catholic college students were found on secular campuses during the 1963 school year. That put only 366,000 of 1.07 million Catholic students in Catholic institutions.

In this buoyant postwar setting, Catholic higher education faced three challenges. The first was to maintain its identity as it competed with the prevailing direction of education. Second was the encounter with the cultural upheavals of the 1960s. And finally there arose the question of economic survival, an import of the 1970s.

IN THE SPIRIT OF the Second Vatican Council of 1962–65, which re-examined the relationship between religious truth and secular knowledge, Catholic universities sought a modern Catholic identity by becoming more friendly with the "world." In the United States, the stage had been set in a 1961 address by Notre Dame president Theodore M. Hesburgh, who described the role of Catholic higher education as "mediation."[29] Vatican II's "Pastoral Constitution of the Church in the Modern World" (*Gaudium et Spes*) said in 1965 that the church "carries the responsibility of reading the signs of the times." It recognized the "autonomy of earthly affairs," specifically warning that Christians can slip into attitudes "derived from a shortsighted view of the rightful autonomy of science." Clergy and laity alike are due "a lawful freedom of inquiry, of thought, and of expression, tempered by humility and courage in whatever branch of study they have specialized.'[30]

Catholic educators, like the theologians and churchmen who debated at the council, became divided between those with a classical view of education and those who saw the world and its knowledge in flux. Authority and freedom were in a face-off. As the 1960s approached, those who believed in change and wanted freedom seemed to have reality on their side. With the dramatic growth of Catholic schools, increasing numbers of lay professors and administrators were called upon, causing a dilution of the clerical character of past tradition. In 1958, for example, eighty percent of the faculties of six fairly representative medium-size to large-size Catholic institutions were composed of laymen. Moreover, after the mid-1950s faculties began to play more of a role in policies on academic freedom, appointments, salaries, curricular changes, admission practices, academic standards—and tenure.

The introduction of tenure gave yet-unknown protection to Catholic professors probing in areas potentially unpopular with the Catholic powers. But such safe haven, some have argued, brought to Catholic institutions the same abuses known in secular academies. Tenure became a form of financial job security that superceded all other matters of principle. According to some critics, it eased the way for departments to become strongholds of current "orthodoxies" that brooked neither new thinking nor revival of older schools of thought. "What faculty needed and deserved to have was review procedures that protected them from arbitrary actions by administrators or trustees," educator Page Smith said about the history of tenure. "What they got was much more: a degree of security unequaled by any other profession and difficult to justify in abstract terms."[31]

Beginning in 1968, the governance of Catholic colleges and universities began to change from entirely clerical trustee boards to mixed or lay boards. Educators in the 1960s saw the primary purpose of universities as intellectual development, not maintenance of a church culture on campus or the moral guidance of students. Accordingly, some Catholic universities liberalized campus hours, converted to coeducational dorms, and spoke of themselves as being "under Catholic auspices" or having a Catholic "presence." Many campus ministers became psychological counselors rather than pastors. Mass became optional or was revised to appeal to youth. Academic clergy on campus longed to be indistinguishable from laity and stopped wearing their collars.

Catholic universities decreased their requirements in theology and philosophy, and those courses also changed in character. A 1989 study of course offerings pointed up "the substantial degree to which Roman Catholicism fails to represent its own central perspectives adequately in the religious and theological curricula of its institutions."[32] The study of the religion departments of Catholic University, Notre Dame, and St. John's University (New York) categorized three approaches in the religion courses. Category 1 argued the case for Catholic doctrine, ecclesiology, apologetics, and moral teaching. Category 3 based the study of religion on secular disciplines such as psychology, sociology, anthropology, and comparative religion. Category 2 was a mixture. Between 1955 and 1965 at the three schools, there were 355 category 1 courses and 15 category 3. In the final decade of the study, 1975 to 1985, category 1 dropped to 135 courses and Category 3 soared to 1,135.

The figures reflected a broader trend that gnawed at the fabric of the classic idea of a liberal education with its core studies united by one educational vision. Like their secular counterparts, Catholic schools had to offer students more and more courses, giving them specialized tracks of study in academic communities united only by a credit-hour system of bureaucracy.

Ironically, contemporary Catholic colleges and universities focused on professions and specialization rather than liberal arts. A tradition of professional departments began early in Catholic higher education. In recent decades it has become widespread. The professional bent was first seen in the School of Medicine of St. Louis University, founded in 1836. That was followed by the Georgetown University Medical School, founded in 1851. At Notre Dame, the law school was established in 1869, and civil engineering was introduced in 1873. Catholic University began engineering courses in 1897. Studies show that most students in recent decades have sought degrees in public administration, accounting, business and business administration, engineering and other preprofessional programs. Indeed, Catholic universities and colleges have succeeded better in the sciences than in the humanities. They also send more students to professional schools than to arts and sciences graduate schools.[33]

Catholic education officials have described their institutions in recent years as diverse but bound by common characteristics. They are chartered by the state with tax-free status and are under private control. Catholic identity and commitment is infused through the departments of religion, Catholic administrators and faculty members, and reflection on church teachings. Last, the goal of each school is to create responsible persons for the church and the world. Still, Catholic identity remains a pressing concern. "A Catholic school without an identity does not become neutral: it comes under the influence of the current community ideology, or nationalism, or secularism, or faddism," educator Harold A. Buetow said.[34]

Since medieval times that identity had been guaranteed by the intervening role of the bishop, an idea that has not faded. As the pope reminded in 1990, "Even when they do not enter directly into internal governance of the university, bishops 'should not be seen as external agents but as participants in the life of the Catholic university.'"[35] It was authority's check on freedom, a balance desired by many after the experience of the 1960s.

THE CULTURAL AND SOCIAL ferment of that decade affected the largest-ever student population in United States history. In 1966, there were nearly 6 million college students, an increase of 2.25 million over the number enrolled in 1960. This was partly due to the bounding birth rate, which had grown from 2.8 million in 1946 to 4 million the next year. Catholic higher education also experienced this increase in enrollment, and this at a time when it was struggling to be a part of constructive change without capitulating on the principles of its tradition.

Faculty at swiftly growing Catholic institutions expected new rights and freedoms to keep pace as well. When they didn't, tension often mounted. The faculty dispute, strike, and firings at St. John's University in 1967 followed a decade during which the student body doubled to thirteen thousand. "The crisis and revolt are directly related to this incredible rapid expansion," two St. John's educators recalled.[36] For students everywhere, the expansion decade of the

1960s was a time of experimentation, dissent, and the exaltation of personal happiness, often to the point of license, a trend that affected sexual, religious, and artistic life.

Walter Lippmann said in 1966 that universities had replaced churches and government as sources in the quest for "a good life in a good society."[37] In the battle of ideas that followed, Catholic institutions also became centers in the contest for culture, and for the source of faith and morals. The new moral guidebooks included such works as Charles Reich's *The Greening of America,* which held out a third consciousness for the generation, and Herbert Marcuse's *One Dimensional Man,* which promised sexual liberation in a post-capitalist civilization. As in Marcuse's work, reconstructed forms of Marx and Freud were used by others to explain 1960s man and his society, with rock music playing in the background. Classical philosophical frameworks took a beating. The dominant academic ideologies of the 1960s were British-American analytic philosophy, liberal economics, and remnants of logical positivism. Religion brooked "Death of God" theology, the "secular city," and the behavioral psychology of B.F. Skinner.

There was a price to pay for having too much freedom as the authority of church teaching diminished. Catholics entering colleges and universities were hard pressed to synthesize their faith with the alien ideas they confronted. That inability stemmed from "the galloping religious illiteracy among youth and the tendency of many current religion programs to be thin on content," according to Buetow.[38]

Student dissent was a main component of the 1960s campus culture. And for a Catholic institution, where the top-down governance had prevailed in both religion and education, the release had a special, if sometimes adolescent, satisfaction. At Catholic institutions, "Everything was a little less violent, less extreme and less overtly hedonistic and secular," according to Edmund Pellegrino, a past president of Catholic University. "But there was a decided drift toward adaptation to the trends that characterize secular institutions."[39]

The first signs of radical student interest in social and political issues appeared in 1958. Sit-in protests began in San Francisco against the House Un-American Activities Committee in 1960. To follow were campus protests against matters of university discipline, university training corps, loyalty affidavits, and fraternity and sorority discrimination. Welcomed first as a sign of "maturity" and "awareness," student activism turned violent. During "Freedom Summer" in 1964 at Berkeley, students faced off with riot police. In their first mass showing, some 25,000 students converged on Washington in 1965 to protest the Vietnam War. Between 1966 and 1967 more campuses were radicalized. "The 'campus riot' became part of the college culture, as university presidents compromised, surrendered or abdicated," Johnson said.[40]

The National Student Association claimed there were 221 demonstrations at universities in America during 1968. While social issues were attached, the sheer act of rejecting authority in the name of freedom had a thrill that student leaders openly admitted. A symbol of that was the clash at Columbia University, where the Students for a Democratic Society, or SDS, took over the administration offices on April 23. Reflecting back on how such episodes of revolt affected professors, the president of the Modern Languages Association lamented in 1971, "The young go into the profession with dread; the old can scarcely wait for retirement; and those of the middle years yearn for sabbaticals."[41]

Universities in general had raised expectations that were not met. In his 1987 study of higher education, *The Closing of the American Mind,* Allan Bloom said that higher education lost its timeless, internal compass.[42] It sought to be relevant to the most pressing social issues. The same has been said of Catholic higher education, and critics cite Curran as one of many accomplices. Indeed, how does education combine the timeless with the contemporary? Some in education gave up on that quest. Enamored of the 1960s trend, these professors and students decided education was not relevant at all. They dropped out. At the other pole, senior faculties felt overwhelmed and usually went along with the "reforms" even when they disagreed with them.

IN THE MID–1970s a financial and morale crisis began in education, both secular and Catholic. Spending on education was lavish between 1960 and 1975, when the number of American colleges and universities grew from 2,040 to 3,055. Then recession and general disillusionment caused the student population to plummet. The number of college men in the 1960s was forty-four percent of the eligible population, but that dropped to thirty-four percent by 1974, contradicting optimistic predictions of a decade earlier. While the end of the baby boom was one factor, a loss of confidence in education as an economic and social benefit was another.

Even with an estimated 1.5 million to 2 million living alumni in 1976, the nation's 250 Catholic colleges and universities, with a combined enrollment of 425,000 students, were hurting. The growth of less expensive public education was a factor, as was the erosion of their "living endowment" of service contributed by clergy and sisters.

"Catholic institutions, colleges and universities are obliged to seek funds from sources other than constantly escalating tuitions," Catholic educators said in 1976. "Because of our public service, we feel government has an obligation to help." In fact, they said, without state aid to Catholic colleges and universities "The vast majority of them may not survive."[43] Federal, state, and local funding to all private higher education in the United States rose from $1.7 billion in 1970 to $7.1 billion in 1986, though that rate of increased funding did not match the rate of increase in the cost of private education. In 1986 more than half a billion dollars in government money went to Catholic colleges and universities, with seventy percent of all students relying on some assistance.

Access to federal funding has become complicated by a history of legal challenges. So far these have only stripped support from Catholic elementary and secondary education. Public funding of Catholic higher education has survived court challenges, but many would argue that it stands on thin ice. The most important Supreme Court decision affecting church-related colleges and universities was *Tipton vs. Richardson* in 1971, decided by a margin of 5–4. The court ruled that the Higher Education Facilities Act, which provides grants and loans for building and construction, did not violate the no-establishment-of-religion-clause in the United States Constitution by helping church-related institutions.[44] Two other cases that reached the Supreme Court in 1973 and 1976 contested these benefits to Catholic institutions, though unsuccessfully.

To withstand such constitutional challenges, Catholic institutions have sought to prove their autonomy. That process toward becoming independent from Rome began years before the legal challenges arose. In 1949 Pope Pius XII initiated an International Federation of Catholic Universities. While its affinity with Vatican policy continues, by 1964 the federation had functional autonomy. Its 1968 triennial meeting aimed to define the Catholic university's modern role. In the time before the gathering took place in Kinshasa, Congo, regional members began formulating their concepts.

North American educators met in Wisconsin in July 1967 and issued a "declaration of independence" that emphasized autonomy and academic freedom. It was signed by the twenty-six university administrators and officials who gathered, and the document's name took on the local flavor of their retreat—the Land O'Lakes Statement.[45]

Yet a division of views continued among the church's education elite. Vatican officials and other proponents of a "pre-Vatican II ecclesiology" sought church jurisdiction in the schools. Educators who championed autonomy and academic freedom believed that it was not allowed under the "new ecclesiology" of Vatican II. The Land O'Lakes Statement followed the "new" lights. Yet it had minimal impact on the meeting in Africa; the Kinshasa document did not even mention the term "academic freedom."

With a desire to form its own guidelines, the Holy See invited world educators to bring their findings to Rome the next year, 1969. North American ideas had slowly leavened the world group. The educators who met in Rome did not produce bold results, but the assertion of autonomy, if ambiguous, had increased. The subtitle of their nuanced "Rome Statement" was illustrative: "The Catholic University and Aggiornamento."[46] Even this was too bold for the Vatican's Congregation for Catholic Education. It rejected the report and in 1970 issued a traditional set of guidelines.

Yet the dialogue remained open and friendly, allowing the federation to move forward on its own—especially its North American members. They wrote more reports urging autonomy and academic freedom until their efforts bore some fruit in November 1972. The congregation again invited federation delegates to Rome, and the outcome was a firmer bid for the modern university. The delegates' resulting document, "The Catholic University in the Modern World," claimed that autonomy and loyalty, academic freedom and orthodoxy, could coexist.[47] The statement was daring enough that it was not issued in the name of the federation, but rather by an ad hoc congress. Even this declaration, however, did not matched the pluck of the Land O'Lakes Statement.

The 1972 "modern world" statement set out four ways institutions keep their Catholic character without needing ecclesiastical intervention: Christian inspiration; reflection on Catholic faith; fidelity to church teaching; and an institutional commitment to service. "All universities that realize these fundamental conditions are Catholic universities, whether canonically erected or not," it said.[48]

With praise for its general thrust, the congregation said it nevertheless considered the statement "valid but needing improvement."[49] Head of the congregation, Cardinal Gabriel Marie Garrone, said the statement failed to be explicit on university statutes that commit to "Catholic" character and on internal mechanisms to regulate faith, morality, and discipline. American Catholic educators recall that a period of limbo followed, during which they remained unclear on what the congregation was expecting. To obviate the need for these types of juridical arrangements, the educators formed a committee with the American bishops to exchange facts about their two realities and create informal lines of communication. Meanwhile, institutional autonomy was still the educators' official line.

Then, in 1975 came a Vatican proposal for a new "academic law" for ecclesiastical institutions and departments. This was the kernel of what became the apostolic constitution *Sapientia Christiana,* promulgated in 1979. The proposal was circulated for comment to all university presidents, whether they oversaw an ecclesiastical entity or not. "This new constitution created a certain amount of confusion among the leaders of Catholic higher education," recalled Sister Alice Gallin, the executive director of the Association of Catholic Colleges and Universities. "Why were we being consulted on ecclesiastical faculties?"[50] Once again the American educators drafted a response. "We can only say that juridical, canonical, statutory relationships which would infringe upon proper institutional autonomy are not in keeping with our circumstances, and would make no contribution to our effort to maintain and strengthen Catholic higher education and its service to the American culture."[51] Despite its ostensibly narrow focus—only university departments that gave Vatican-approved degrees—the apostolic constitution troubled many educators when it was issued, Gallin said. "Fear swept through the Catholic higher education community that such an approach might ultimately be intended for Catholic colleges and universities, not only ecclesiastical faculties."[52]

The Catholic educators became concerned again as a new Code of Canon Law was being slated for promulgation in the church in 1983. It contained new canons on Catholic higher education. Vigilant as ever, a delegation of the educators went to Rome in March 1982 to consult with the pope. They objected to certain canons as they stood. One canon said, "No university may bear the name 'Catholic university' unless it has been erected by the Apostolic See or by the Conference of Bishops."[53] This canon and a few others finally were modified or deleted. In the end, the key university canons were 808, which limited the use of "Catholic university" in an institution's title, and 812, which said the bishop must give university teachers of faith and morals a "mandate." That broader term replaced the original term "canonical mission," already found in *Sapientia Christiana*.

By the time Curran became the first test case of a dissenting theologian with a canonical mission, the educators had one more Vatican initiative with which to deal. It was the 1985 "Proposed Schema for a Pontifical Document on Catholic Universities."[54] For all the pope had said and promulgated on the subject, he still had not issued a global apostolic constitution on higher education. He had a desire to "flesh out" the 1983 Code of Canon Law, and the draft was the beginning point.

Still unresolved the month before Curran and Catholic University went to trial, the consultations on the schema continued as yet another contest between autonomy and control. "While much has happened between 1968 and 1988 these are still the fundamental areas of disagreement between the universities and the congregation," Gallin said at that time.[55] When the pope did speak in 1990, his apostolic constitution was called a workable agreement.

Even if that agreement had been reached sooner, it would not have quelled the turmoil over Curran at Catholic University. The conflict between authority and freedom had been building up for too long.

SIX

The Catholic University of America

Founded by bishops and given a papal charter, The Catholic University of America was established in the grand ecclesiastical tradition. Since the flowering of Catholic institutions in twelfth century Europe, the teaching and juridical authority of the Vatican had been intimately involved, through its bishops, in higher learning.

Although the debate in America over academic freedom and Catholic identity has a uniquely modern quality, the degree of tumult is the same as in the past. The medieval universities of Paris and Bologna were the confluence for conflicts between the concepts of realism and nominalism, the politics of religious orders and bishops, and the claims of faith and humanism, and the same is true of Catholic colleges in the United States.

Catholic University's prominence in the early stages of American higher education made it a natural forum for the struggle between authority and freedom. It was the arena for many of the American church's stormiest debates. In its first century, the cast of characters included nine popes, five archbishops, twelve rectors (the last three called presidents), and a host of free-thinking scholars.[1]

With this perspective in mind, Catholic Church historian John Tracy Ellis told an audience at Catholic University in summer 1986 that the "fuss" over Charles Curran was not new. "The university has been woefully abused by the church hierarchy at times," he said, taking a neutral position on the as-yet-unsettled Curran case. "There have been episodes of the kind that have done it great harm." But apart from the isolated abuses of "ecclesiastical intrigues," he said, "there is a built-in tension that will never be settled, a tension between ecclesiastical authority on the one hand and academic research on the other. From the perspective of history, it's a built-in tension. It has come again and again."[2]

Each incident raised the lament that Catholic University was losing its credibility. Yet in the patient eye of history its core has changed little. The constant, according to documents, administrators, and trustees, is the university's "special relationship" with the Holy See. As a living institution, however, it has an outer form that grows and changes. During its first fifteen years Catholic University provided only graduate-level education, and in 1978 it still drew seventy percent graduate students. That emphasis on graduate education continues, but only in head count—in the fall of 1988 there were 3,246 undergraduates and 3,774 post-baccalaureates. The trend has been toward a greater percentage of part-time students at the graduate level while, at the same time, that part-time segment has been decreasing in number. As a result, historian C. Joseph Nuesse noted, "The university's student profile now resembles more than ever before what would be regarded as the typical American institution, in which the undergraduate component would be considered to be the heart of the university."[3]

While the university began with the purpose of educating clergy, clerical enrollment has declined along with religious vocations in general. As recently as 1964, when the university's enrollment was six thousand, at least one in three students was either a priest, seminarian, brother, or sister. Now religious make up only about six percent of the student body.

The most dramatic change in the school's history came in 1968, when it acquired new bylaws that abolished clerical control of its board of trustees, stipulating that no more than half of the board could be clergy. Despite its special ties with Rome, Catholic University was among the first three Catholic Church-related institutions in America to share governance with nonclergy. That ended an earlier era of unhampered access by the hierarchy. Since then, however, the mercurial question of how to balance authority and freedom has continued.

Despite its autonomous board of trustees, the university is still "pontifical" based on its papal charter and the three "ecclesiastical" divisions, which issue Vatican-recognized degrees. These degrees, as well as civil degrees, are granted by the departments of theology and canon law in the school of religious studies, and by the school of philosophy. Even with the bylaw changes, the role of the church remains integral. The question is how to create an arrangement where, in the words of Pope John Paul II, the bishops are not "external agents."[4] And that applies to the spirit of the entire university, which is composed mostly of its autonomous schools: arts and sciences, engineering and architecture, law, library and information science, music, nursing, and social services.

Since the disposition of Curran's case, his supporters have said that the balance has been irreparably harmed and authority has swallowed up freedom. The university has formulated it differently, of course. The institution says it has every right to respond to the "influence" of the church, which it did in the Curran case, but as an autonomous institution it continues to resist outright "control" by Rome or any other authority.[5]

THE ESTABLISHMENT of a national Catholic university met resistance from the beginning.[6] Soon after Curran's Irish ancestors settled on American shores, the university became an engagement point in the contest between authority and freedom. That was characterized by the tension between European ways and American ways. It was born of a mood that gave rise in the 1880s and 1890s to the "Americanist" movement and its attendant controversy.

Influenced by American individualism, pragmatism, and the emphasis on inner spiritual authority, "The Americanists raised the possibility of legitimate divergence from European models of church order," historian James Hennesey said.[7] The idea of a national Catholic university, despite objections in some quarters, was initiated by Peoria's Archbishop John L. Spalding, who presided at the 1884 Third Plenary Council of Baltimore. Some of the nation's seventy-two bishops and many German Catholics opposed it, siding with Rome's concern over an exaggerated Americanism in the church. For similar reasons, the Jesuits and some in the Catholic press voiced opposition. Nevertheless, Spalding won over the majority by using the carrot of Catholic progress and assimilation. So long as the bishops "look rather to the multiplying of schools and seminaries than to the creation of a real university," he said, the progress of American Catholics would be "slow and uncertain."[8] Catholic University would be put at the center of the "Americanist" crisis, which finally evoked an anti-Americanist papal encyclical in 1899. Because of these struggles the fledgling university "was almost crippled at the outset," historian Philip Gleason said.[9]

Symbolically, an Americanist was chosen in 1886 to be the first rector. Spalding had declined the post, and so Richmond Bishop John J. Keane was selected. He was rector for a decade. Keane was an indirect spiritual heir of Isaac Thomas Hecker, founder in 1858 of the first American religious order, the Missionary Society of St. Paul the Apostle, or Paulists. Translation of Hecker's biography in France in the 1890s had caught Rome's attention and spurred the Vatican assault on Americanism. Logically, the Paulists were the first religious order to establish a center near the university. About seventy years later there were eighty-seven houses of study for religious orders in a neighborhood now dubbed "Little Rome." The Paulists contributed nine of the forty-six students in the first class of Catholic University, the largest bloc from a religious order.

Bolstered by an endowment of $300,000 from Mary Gwendoline Caldwell, a twenty-one-year-old Rhode Island heiress, the bishops allowed a committee to formulate plans for the university and chose its name. In principle, the plenary council called for a university in which "all the letters and sciences, both sacred and profane, could be taught."[10] In 1885 Pope Leo XIII sent private approval of the project and in 1887 gave his endorsement in a letter to Cardinal James Gibbons, archbishop of Baltimore. Over time, that endorsement, together with a similar one two years later, was said to constitute the "papal charter."

The bishops' committee located sixty-five acres of land three miles from the center of Washington and purchased it for $29,500. Though not yet built, Catholic University was given its "certification of incorporation" by Congress—because the District of Columbia had no sovereignty—under District laws on April 19, 1887. The university government was vested in a seventeen-member board of trustees composed of the cardinals and other archbishops; the chancellor, who is archbishop of Washington (or of Baltimore before 1947); the rector; and a number of elected bishops, priests, and laymen. In the eyes of civil law, the seventeen clergy-trustees as a group became the owners of the institution.

Though it was not realized at the time, the effort to resolve the tension between authority and freedom in this unique Catholic institution had crashed on the shoals of secular legality. Almost a century later, when the university ended clerical control in 1968, the archbishop of Baltimore's lawyer made a sobering assertion: The first civil charter from Congress made no provisions for church control, hence the clerical board had been illegal all the while.

The pope approved the university's statutes and on March 7, 1889, issued his apostolic letter, *Magni Nobis gaudii,* much as Pope Gregory IX had done in 1213 to recognize the University of Paris. At the time, only nine other institutions outside the city of Rome had that honor. Catholic University was fated to be a convenient milestone in American Catholic history. It opened ceremoniously on November 13, 1889, in concert with the first centenary of the American hierarchy.

Graduate-level institutions in America were in their infancy as the bishops put their own flagship on the sea of higher learning. The Johns Hopkins University, the first school to commit itself to research as well as learning, opened in 1876. Such institutions adopted the research model of the nineteenth century Prussian university, and Catholic University, in its own way, did the same. By 1900, it was one of fourteen American institutions offering academic doctorates. Its dual personality, which, according to most accounts, vowed to combine academic autonomy with allegiance to the magisterium of the hierarchical church, would last through the century. From its founding, Catholic University had secular claims as well. For one, it was the only American institution that professed to offer graduate studies exclusively. It also was the only Catholic institution to be a founding member of the Association of American Universities, an exclusive circle that includes only fifty-four schools.

In the 1890s, amid the nation's 125 Catholic colleges—which overshadowed 30 or so Catholic seminaries—Catholic University alone boasted graduate studies. The university began with ten faculty members, two being Sulpicians brothers, two Paulist priests, and five European-born clerical scholars. The tenth, a layman, taught English.

Classes were held in a single building, Caldwell Hall, which today houses the school of religious studies. For twenty-one years as a professor there, Curran lived and taught in that original building. The university did not earn the honor of being the nation's only Catholic graduate institution entirely by its own merit. In those politicized times, Jesuit educators at the century-old Georgetown University a few miles across town had developed a graduate program but scrapped it. Jesuit superiors who gave the order in Rome sought to avoid the appearance of competing with the American bishops' university.

Catholic University soon realized, however, that there was limited demand for its novel offering. Few priests came to the university for graduate work—most still went abroad for that, and only some who wanted to attend were eligible. In Catholic University's first class of forty-six students, thirty-six came from twenty-one dioceses. Baltimore contributed the most—four students. Steps were taken to expand the clientele as financial pressures mounted. In 1895, under what Keane named the "faculties for the laity," the schools of philosophy and social sciences were established, with law and technology included in the curriculum.

Finances for the school were drawn entirely from student fees, gifts, and a meager investment income—the initial large endowments had been spent on land and buildings. By 1903, when the third rector was appointed, the school faced a financial crisis. With support of the chancellor, Cardinal Gibbons, the rector asked Pope Pius X to issue a public authorization to begin annual collections to aid the school. Those collections continue until today, and have provided a measure of popular Catholic support during times of controversy—such as Curran's—and times of stability. The first year's collection, however, was not enough to save the school from bankruptcy in 1904. Cardinal Gibbons appealed to the hierarchy for help and established the "Cardinal's Fund." But donations came to only $136,200 in the next six years, despite a debt that reached $876,000.

After it became evident that there were not enough students interested or eligible for graduate studies at Catholic University, undergraduates were admitted—a solution to both the financial crisis and the growing need in the Catholic community for educators, nurses, and social workers. With all resources combined, the university finally covered its early losses. After 1909, when Bishop Thomas J. Shahan began his twenty-year term as rector, the urge to build had strongly returned. Several buildings that define the campus today were erected, and work began on the nation's largest Catholic church, the Shrine of the Immaculate Conception. Its cornerstone was laid in 1920. Though the university stood in its great shadow, the shrine was built independently over fifty years by the bishops and the contributions of lay Catholics and fraternal orders. It stood as a reminder that church authority gazed down benignly but firmly on a campus that symbolized youth and freedom.

A RAIN STORM pelted the university grounds the day in March 1888 when hundreds of people, including Cardinal Gibbons and President Grover Cleveland, gathered under American banners to lay the cornerstone of Caldwell Hall. Like a portent, the storm would symbolize struggles in the university's early years which produced its first two Curran-style affairs. The Americanist fight of the 1890s and modernist crisis in the next decade showed that both parties, the Americans and the Romans, could use censorship as a tool. In 1895, six years after the university opened, theologian Joseph Schroeder got caught in the Americanist cross fire. Liberal bishops on the university board of trustees resented the scholar's loyalty to the Vatican and wanted the German monsignor out. "Schroeder's chief offense was his public opposition to these 'Americanist' prelates who deemed him too conservative," historian James Hitchcock said. Schroeder's opponents "exulted" that his expulsion showed the power of the American bishops.[11]

Not too many years later, as a result of the modernist spillover from Europe, another professor became an issue. Conflicts over modernism had arisen in France, where some leading theologians promoted higher criticism of the Bible and early Christianity. Modernism was not an American dispute, but it echoed on New World shores, at least enough to get some professors in trouble. A Dutch biblical scholar and priest, Henry Poels, resigned from the university in 1909 when he came under pressure from the Vatican for his critical approach to biblical studies. Some of the nation's top bishops, led by Cardinal Gibbons, defended Poels but finally acquiesced to the Holy

See. Other Bible scholars were also scrutinized from upon high for their higher criticism.[12]

John A. Ryan, a priest who was recognized in 1906 as the leading Catholic socioeconomic theoretician in that progressive age of legislation and labor, also ended up at the university. By 1924, when a constitutional amendment for federal regulation of child labor was sent to the states, Ryan was working with labor activists as a publicist to Catholic communities. For one, the archbishop of Boston complained to the university chancellor about Ryan's "socialistic" and "radical" support of such state intervention in the family. Bishop James H. Ryan, who was rector from 1928 to 1935, also was considered a progressive, leading some bishops to work successfully for his removal.[13]

With no mass media to call attention to these theological quarrels, they did not produce the kind of front-page public controversies known today. There was more publicity over the issue of admitting women, which some newspapers early in the century reported as imminent. The administration said that such an important decision should not be made hastily: "It has not been considered by the Board of Directors, and nothing will be done except as they decide."[14] Women were admitted in 1928. In another area, the university also served as a laboratory to create the American church's social agenda. University sociologist William Kirby was architect in 1910 of the National Conference of Catholic Charities. The university had become what Gleason calls "the principal channel through which the methods and spirit of modern university work were diffused into the world of Catholic higher education."[15]

FOLLOWING THE NATIONAL trend in America's postwar higher education, Catholic university underwent a total reorganization at the start of the 1930s. The college and graduate school of arts and sciences were established, as were the schools of engineering and architecture. By custom, Catholic University was, and still is, called a "pontifical" university, and its nucleus continued to be its school of sacred sciences. Its programs gave rise to a school of canon law in 1923 and, by 1932, a seminary department and religion department. Distinct schools of sacred theology and philosophy were established in 1937, thus defining thereafter the three main "pontifical faculties": theology, canon law, and philosophy.

The restructuring came as Pope Pius XI, concerned about clarifying the "academic law" for Catholic colleges and universities, promulgated his apostolic constitution *Deus scientiarum Dominus* in 1931. At the time, the church and its clergy were in firm control of Catholic higher education. In the mix of authority and freedom, authority was dominant by consensus, not legal definitions.

As a result hardly anyone debated the difference between "pontifical" or "ecclesiastical" institutions and ordinary Catholic colleges. The 1917 Code of Canon Law did not clearly separate the two, although ecclesiastical colleges were given some special canons to abide by. Pius XI's *Deus scientiarum Dominus,* likewise, did not make a clear distinction. What was clear, however, was that a professor teaching sacred sciences in an ecclesiastical faculty received his appointment from the local bishop. Indeed, the requirement of such an appointment was clear enough to Catholic University that it revised its statutes for its ecclesiastical schools, maintaining the necessity of a "canonical mission" to teach. The university adopted the new statutes in 1937, and they ostensibly stayed in force through 1964, when they were reprinted in the faculty handbook—a year before Curran began teaching theology at Catholic University.

After the Second World War, Catholic University experienced a boom, filling it to capacity for the first time. By 1964 there were 4,115 full-time students and 1,935 part-time. The faculty numbered 437 full-time members, as well as 128 lecturers and 106 graduate assistants. Catholic faculties and administrators across the country were whispering about the need for change, in education and in the church, and had been since the mid-1950s.

Though a conservative institution, Catholic University seemed to be a breeding ground for new controversies. In 1954, for example, Jesuit theologian John Courtney Murray gave a lecture saying that the watchdog of orthodoxy in the Vatican, Cardinal Alfredo Ottaviani, did not hold the same progressive views on church and state as Pope Pius XII. Murray subsequently was required to submit writings to his superior in Rome before publication. After Vatican II, however, he was vindicated as the author of modern Catholic views on religious freedom. In a similar vein, church historian John Tracy Ellis was in his twenty-first year teaching at Catholic University when in 1955 he criticized the American church leadership for allowing intellectual mediocrity to flourish among Catholics.

Those who were eager to change the situation at Catholic University tended to personify their obstacle in Irish-born Monsignor William McDonald, the rector since 1957. McDonald, who later became auxiliary bishop in Washington as well, ran the university with a firm and orthodox hand. Some perceived his concern for preservation of proper tradition as a hindrance to free inquiry. McDonald was of the old and classical school; freedom was attained by adherence to a system of truth found in Catholic thought and discipline. But the times had brought the new notions of freedom to the Catholic University's door, in effect beating it down.

In 1959 McDonald vetoed as "imprudent" a proposed biology department symposium on evolution and Christian theology that had been organized to mark the Charles Darwin centennial. He refused to approve a university sociologist's request for a Ford Foundation grant to study "family size preference of American Catholic college girls." The topic, he said, was "too controversial." In 1962, a professor of scripture, Edward F. Siegman, was ousted for reasons of health despite a vote of protest by the sacred theology faculty; Siegman was a purveyor of modern biblical criticism. Finally, the leadership of the Second Vatican Council asked the university's canon law department to make a list of obsolete church laws for the council's guidance. It was prepared, but McDonald did not send it, to the consternation of some in the American hierarchy.[16]

Parochial until now, the simmering disputes went public—via the media—in March 1963. University officials decided to exclude four progressive theologians from a Lenten week lecture series on campus. Providing a forum for Murray, Gustave Weigel, Hans Küng, and Godfrey Diekmann might make Catholic University appear to be taking sides—the liberal one in particular—since Vatican II was in session until September, university officials said. In an uproar over the "speaker ban," more than 200 of the university's 350 faculty members appealed to the trustees. "For nearly a decade, this type of suppression has been going on constantly at this university," Ellis charged at the time.[17]

Before this flap occurred, members of the school of arts and sciences had formed a committee to investigate complaints against McDonald. The impulse for freedom, not finding an outlet, had risen against authority in a new way. A series of hearings over a year and a half produced a report in 1963. It said that the rector tended to control the academic senate, and that representation was uneven from the different schools, with a preponderance of clergy.

A mood was emerging in the Catholic universities across the country, culminating in 1966 in the first serious conference on academic freedom, held at the University of Notre Dame. In the next year, what became the Land O'Lakes Statement, a declaration of academic independence, was drafted. On the rising tide, a group of Catholic University professors felt confident enough to confront Archbishop Patrick O'Boyle, chancellor of the university. During a 1967 visit they stated their concern about academic freedom. To their surprise, the cardinal said something was already being done. After decades of glacial movement at the university, what would take place in the next two years seemed like an earthquake.

UNLIKE A MILITARY institution, with its precise rules and regulations, Catholic University was far more pliable; it was organized around a statement of purpose that was then given flesh by a governing structure and bylaws. In this respect, Catholic University was no different from other universities and colleges, all of which prefer to err in the direction of freedom and flexibility. However, the one facet of Catholic University that made it different—its status as a pontifical institution—made fundamental changes problematic.

The story of how Catholic University evolved from a tone of authority to a spirit of freedom is told by the arcane documents that define the institution. Behind that paperwork is a range of human encounters, decisions, and struggles that sprang up within the campus and were enhanced by interventions of the Holy See. This process was at a high pitch between 1967 and 1981. The university created a new statement of aims, revised its bylaws, and formed new canonical statutes for the ecclesiastical faculties. Indeed, this was *the* decade of change at Catholic University and the time when Curran and a host of others, on both sides of the aisle, struggled for the university's soul.

As a feat of drama the mass walkout for Charles Curran in April

1967 made the push for change visible. But the prompting had already been underway for several months from various quarters. Before the Curran strike, the trustees had established a Survey and Objectives Committee. When the ad hoc Faculty Assembly met with O'Boyle the day after Curran's rehire, its members were asked to work jointly with the committee on proposed changes in the institution. They met about once a week through the spring and summer of 1967.

These meetings led to a formal process for reevaluation of the university's statement of aims, which is set forth in its official handbooks as the guiding philosophy. The revision sought to present in the best possible light the two purposes of the institution: Catholic commitment on the one hand and the promise of academic freedom on the other. Given the apparent tension between the two, especially in regard to the study of faith and morals, the 250-word statement of aims was not agreed upon without a fight. University faculty, the academic senate, the board of trustees, and finally the Vatican all had a hand in it.

When the board of trustees adopted the final version on July 26, 1968, the two claims were intact. The demands of both authority and freedom had been met in this conception of the university's character, and each had its code words in the document. In freedom's interest, the statement said, "The only constraint upon truth is truth itself." That was followed up with: "As a member of the American Academic Community, it [Catholic University] accepts the standards and procedures of American institutions."[18]

Those clauses would have implied the maximum extent of academic freedom except for another one, added at the request of some bishops and the Holy See that contained the code words for authority. The clause said the university would remain "faithful to the Christian message as it comes through the church."[19] That phrase was not in the original 1968 version approved by the academic senate, and its arrival in the final version revealed the hand of the hierarchy.

In the future, both advocates of academic freedom and those who upheld church influence would cite this document to support their concerns. Whatever the interpretation, the university's 1970 self-evaluation report for its regional accrediting agency, the Middle States Association of Colleges and Schools, described the statement of aims as "the most carefully considered, widely promulgated, generally accepted, and authoritative formulation of the nature and goals of the university."[20] However, the statement of aims printed in the evaluation did not include the crucial qualifying phrase: "faithful to the Christian message as it comes through the church."

THE STATEMENT OF AIMS was formulated in 1968 as an internal effort to reconcile authority and freedom. There were outside pressures on Catholic University as well. These came from its accrediting agency, Middle States, a secular authority that demanded educational freedom within institutions it approved.

This particular intervention by Middle States began a year earlier, in the summer of 1967. Five reviewers from the Philadelphia-based accrediting agency made a routine visit. The university had hoped accreditation would be renewed with a minimal review. But Middle States officials in its Commission on Institutions of Higher Education decided a full self-study followed by a visitation was necessary. With an eye to the school's autonomy, the Middle States officials worried about statements such as this in the university statutes: "Full jurisdiction over the university rests with the hierarchy of the United States."[21] This and other built-in aspects of Catholic University gave the Vatican control through its power to appoint the chancellor and rector and change the bylaws. Already the federal government had recognized this, and for years it had threatened to require the rector to sign a statement saying he did not work for a foreign government. Federal money was thus provided, but for church and state reasons only to the nonecclesiastical departments.

To meet Middle States's concerns, the board of trustees, who were all clergy, appointed a committee under Cardinal Lawrence Shehan of Baltimore to redraft the bylaws. In the words of the committee's lawyer at the time, "The threat of losing accreditation is a real one."[22] Most of the work was done in Baltimore by Shehan and Frank Gallagher, his archdiocesan lawyer. In an April 1968 letter to Shehan, Gallagher outlined what he believed to be the acute problem, one he had to drive home to the American hierarchy: "It is incorrect to say the bishops own the university. The civil corporation owns the university and the trustees act not for the bishops of the United States but for the corporation itself. When Congress conferred a charter on the seventeen original incorporators, it did not say that the incorporators were trustees for the Catholic Church. The original incorporators and their successors may and have, in fact, been Catholic bishops but this does not place ownership in the Catholic Church." Hence, Gallagher said, "the statutes [bylaws] of the university are, in my opinion, in conflict with the charter when [the bylaws say] 'full jurisdiction over the university rests with the hierarchy of the United States.'"[23]

This frank representation, carried by Shehan to the cardinals and bishops who made up the board of trustees, paved the way for a change in bylaws. Without the change, counsel warned, Catholic University could lose its accreditation, not to mention its federal funding in student aid, construction loans, or research support.

In its final form, the new set of bylaws expanded the board to forty-two members, with an equal number of clergy and lay representatives. Half of the clergy were bishops, and the others were priests. The trustees, in turn, were allowed to elect the university president, who could be a layman, and amend the bylaws. A key concern in debate over the bylaws was the role of the chancellor. Some had recommended, though unsuccessfully, that instead of the local bishop, the chancellor be the president of the National Conference of Catholic Bishops, a three-year post.

In the final version, the bylaws said the chancellor was a liaison between the university and the Holy See. Thus, by implication his only special role was tied to the ecclesiastical faculties. Here was a concrete example of the shift from authority to freedom. Others called it a slide, for thereafter they viewed the archbishop's role as mainly honorific. At the next graduation, for example, the university president awarded the civil degrees and the chancellor awarded degrees in the ecclesiastical program. Before, in full church regalia, the chancellor had awarded them all.

A new word was heard among faculty members and some administrators: "depontificalization." In their eyes, the purpose of the bylaw revision was to remove the Holy See's control over the university, putting Catholic University in accord with American university practices. From the opposite side, a Vatican official questioning American representatives about the change coined another term, asking if it meant a "deconfessionalization" of Catholic University.[24]

Whatever the case, the university had taken a major step in forming an autonomous structure. Secular educators looking on from the outside were enthusiastic at the historic break Catholic University had made. "I have just heard, I hope correctly, that the authorities in Rome have released their hold on the university and have made it possible for the trustees to function as they should," a letter from Middle States official F. Taylor Jones, head of its higher education commission, said to the new university president, Clarence Walton. "This is immensely helpful. Congratulations to you and your colleagues for the new freedom it gives you."[25] Walton replied, saying it was indeed a "historic decision" for Catholic University.[26]

Although the new bylaws said the academic senate was "the immediate policy determining board," nothing it did had legal force unless the university president or board gave approval. This melding of presidential authority and faculty freedom was strained, for neither wished to be a rubber stamp for the other. Yet the faculty was aware of its new gains. Urged on by advocates in the religion department, its leaders worked to secure permanently the rights of academic freedom. In 1969 the academic senate passed a resolution saying that there were no "arbitrary and extrinsic constraints, be they civil or ecclesiastical" on academic freedom. The statement echoed the Land O'Lakes Statement of two years earlier. Another rallying point was the 1969 report of the university's Marlowe committee, which concluded that Curran and the nineteen other professors on the theology faculty had acted with academic propriety when they publicly opposed the 1968 papal encyclical, *Humanae Vitae*. By all counts, it seemed—and most believed—that academic freedom had won the day.

But the task of defining what these new bylaws really meant was not finished yet. There were those, such as O'Boyle, who wanted to reinstate the role of the chancellor after the bylaws weakened the post. The chancellor, an archbishop, was the only church official related to the university able to speak on orthodoxy. Backed by Rome, O'Boyle sought to reinstate the archbishop's influence. Catholic University was about to revise its statutes for the pontifical schools, and he would ensure that they upheld the chancellor's customary rights and duties.

CATHOLIC HIGHER EDUCATION had, of course, received new international attention during Vatican II. Though the council did not set forth new canons for institutions of higher learning, its document on the subject, *Gravissimum educationis,* called for improvements in both its relevance to the modern world and its ability to uphold Catholic identity. In the wake of this call, the Vatican moved to update the church's "academic law," something laid out in modern times by the 1931 *Deus scientiarum Dominus.*[27] In short, the seat of authority wanted to assure its foothold in a domain increasingly ruled by freedom.

As Catholic institutions in the West were increasingly influenced by the secular standards of surrounding society, the Holy See wanted to clarify where it laid its claim—the so-called ecclesiastical faculties or schools. Technically, this included very few Catholic institutions, those formed by a diocese or founded by bishops, which was Catholic University's uniqueness in the United States. At Vatican pace, however, the modernizing of *Deus scientiarum Dominus* could require several years. So the Holy See took an interim measure. In 1968 it issued *Normae Quaedam,* a set of temporary, or experimental, guidelines.[28] These retained the content of *Deus scientiarum Dominus* but added the new concerns of Vatican II.

On the contentious issue of the canonical mission, *Normae Quaedam* became another battleground for those seeking release from ecclesiastical control and those desiring to preserve it. The document provided the norms under which Catholic colleges and universities could form special statutes for pontifical schools. As in all other changes, the special statutes drafted by Catholic University needed final approval from the Holy See. For the time being, *Normae Quaedam* seemed to promise a liberalizing effect. Its strongest assertion for authority was that professors "do not act as teachers in their own name, especially in the case of the sacred disciplines, but in virtue of the mission which they have received from the magisterium."[29] Rather than using the 1931 term "canonical mission," *Normae Quaedam* simply said faculty must have a "mission," which advocates of increased academic freedom—such as Curran—would interpret to mean nothing more formal than being "in full communion with the church."[30] Those who interpreted "mission" liberally took the next step by saying a bishop was not required to give it or take it away.

The special statutes were the generally conservative hierarchy's last chance to maintain explicit control of an institution it called Catholic. That, too, was the Vatican's concern. During the revision process, the point was made bluntly by Cardinal Gabriel Garrone, prefect of the Congregation for Catholic Education in Rome. In a November 1969 letter the French prelate advised O'Boyle: "In order to protect the university from the danger of unorthodox teaching in doctrinal matters, we recommend the inclusion in all contracts of the faculty members in the ecclesiastical schools an agreement on the part of the teacher that he will teach authentic Catholic doctrine as such and his failure to do so shall constitute grounds for dismissal."[31] It was a radical suggestion for the time, even though not too many years earlier such faculty members had been required at the start of each school year to gather and make a solemn verbal profession of faith. Garrone's advice was not followed.

The notion of a canonical mission was suspended in uncertainty. The university's 1969 special statutes did not use the term, and from 1937 to at least 1981 the "canonical mission" was not formally given; that is, there was no document signed or ceremony held. Later, the university's lawyer claimed that it was given "implicitly": It was done without discussion or paperwork and was an institutional assumption. So assumed was it that the term was hardly used; it probably was unknown to the average faculty member or administrator. After an eleventh-hour amendment in December 1969, the special statutes provided: "The rights and duties of the chancellor shall be in accord with the provisions of the norms of the Holy See."[32] At best, "rights and duties" implied powers to give a canonical mission.

At the board's February 17, 1970, executive committee meeting, university president Walton announced that the special statutes had been approved by the Vatican. But still, the statutes received only temporary consent. "We, the Holy See, have decided to withhold our immediate and official approval," a letter from Garrone to Shehan said.[33] Instead, the statutes were approved on a five-year basis, giving the Vatican the chance to observe what the new organization at Catholic University might bring.

POPE PAUL VI'S DEATH in 1978 cut short his plan to promulgate a new papal constitution on the ecclesiastical dimension of Catholic education, setting forth an "academic law" for the world church. The short reign of Pope John Paul I further delayed its issuance. The task finally fell to John Paul II. Under the title *Sapientia Christiana,* the Polish professor-turned-pope released it to the world a few months after his election.

Theologians at Catholic University recoiled, for it made plain they were being required to have a canonical mission to teach. Since 1975, Catholic educators in the United States had also resisted the papal constitution, worried that its intended focus on ecclesiastical faculties might blur and bleed into the civil departments. At Catholic University, the document's arrival provoked "a great uproar in the department of theology,"[34] Curran recalled. Despite the opposition, Catholic University implemented the requirement by creating another new document—the Canonical Statutes for the Ecclesiastical Faculties.

The professors affected by the "canonical statutes" were, to some degree, scattered across Catholic University. Since 1973 most religious studies had been merged by an action of the academic senate into a new and enlarged school of religious studies. The umbrella school, the senate argued, would provide continuity in scholarship, coordination of academic work, a lure to new professorial blood, new programs, and improvement in undergraduate religious instruction and ministerial studies. The school contained two ecclesiastical faculties, the department of theology and the department of canon law. The school of philosophy was the third ecclesiastical faculty. But the school of religious studies had other departments with no ecclesiastical status, such as religion and religious education, church history, and biblical studies. Under one roof, in effect, the school trained students seeking Vatican-approved degrees and those seeking diplomas with no special standing in the church—civil degrees. In fact, in the last few years of Curran's teaching two-thirds of the students in the department of theology sought civil degrees.

To draft the canonical statutes, a council of the ecclesiastical faculties was formed, of which Curran was a part. Canon law expert Frederick McManus, a twenty-year veteran and vice-provost at the university, chaired the council. The discussion on the statutes raised a flurry of different opinions, especially regarding the canonical mission. The advocates of freedom used the credo that canon law is meant to find the least restrictive way to govern, and thus they found much leeway in the church's law book. In McManus's view, the insertion of the term "canonical mission" into the new canonical statutes amounted to a "reintroduction of something that had lapsed a generation or more before."[35] At least it had lapsed as a formal designation. At worst, the 1931 requirement of *Deus scientiarum Dominus,* adopted at Catholic University in its 1937 statutes, had become completely impotent. Curran would argue in trial that a letter written by university president William J. Byron referred to an "introduction" of the requirement. Cardinal James A. Hickey, who became archbishop of Washington and chancellor in 1980, assumed the mission was given implicitly, not through formal paperwork.

Clearly, the question of whether the canonical mission had died or merely lay dormant was not resolved to everyone's satisfaction. The debate would erupt in the Curran affair six years later. But since 1981, the new statutes had been explicit: "The chancellor grants the canonical mission to teach in the name of the Church." What is more, the chancellor may "withdraw the mission . . . only for the most serious reasons and after providing information regarding specific charges and proofs."[36] Opponents of the requirement worked successfully to put a buffer phrase about academic freedom in the statutes, hoping this would protect them if the mission requirement were invoked.

For Catholic University, the 1981 canonical statutes were the clearest prescription yet on who needed what commission to teach and in which schools of the university. Faculty members teaching Catholic faith and morals in the pontifical schools, which had become known as the "ecclesiastical faculties," needed the canonical mission. But those faculties were not governed in their entirety by the statutes. "These faculties," the statutes said in the first paragraph, "are not exclusively ecclesiastical. They also have other academic programs which do not have canonical effects and to which the statutes do not apply."[37] In the case of a dispute, the statutes provided for faculty review and a right of representation before the board. Still, the chancellor had the right to remove the canonical mission if the board of trustees agreed the action was warranted by "most serious reasons."[38] With Vatican approval, Catholic University's canonical statutes were adopted in 1981. They were inserted in the faculty handbook and passed again, with revisions, by the board of trustees in 1984, although the Vatican never approved that version.

In August 1982 Curran received a copy of the canonical statutes in the campus mail. By then the Vatican's investigation of his writings, begun in 1966, had been known to him since 1979. In that same year, as a member of the department of theology and representative on the academic senate, he had fought the canonical mission requirement. He knew it had passed anyway. Yet he clung to the belief that he neither needed a canonical mission nor could have one imposed on him by the statutes.

Though bound to church authority by priestly obedience, Curran thought he was afforded a unique freedom as an academic. He also thought that freedom was a greater component of Catholicism than authority. Now, seeing the statutes in published form, he decided to state his belief formally to the vice provost.

"Since my contract with permanent tenure with the university antedates these statutes," his letter said, "I want to confirm in writing that my contractual relationships with the university are in no way governed by these new canonical statutes."[39] He asked that his declaration be put in his permanent file. He hoped it would protect him if the worst would come. He did not have to wait long to find out.

PART THREE

The Trial

SEVEN

From Campus to Court

Nearly twenty years had passed since Charles Curran had been the subject of a special hearing at The Catholic University of America. But in the fall of 1986 he had a strong sense of deja vu. What differed, he believed, were the stakes; they were higher now for both him and the Vatican. No less than the Holy See had declared him no longer "suitable nor eligible to exercise the function of a professor of Catholic theology."

That ruling, however, had not come out of the blue, for he had been corresponding with Vatican authorities on the matter for seven years. Perhaps in that time some compromise could have been reached between Curran's bid for freedom and the Vatican's bid for authority. Instead, they had charted a collision course.

Under the canonical statutes, a professor facing withdrawal of his canonical mission is entitled to a hearing by his faculty peers. Curran asked for it, and by April an ad hoc faculty committee had been formed. The committee's mandate, given by the chancellor, was to hold hearings and then advise the trustees on whether the Holy See's decision constituted "a most serious reason" to withdraw Curran's canonical mission, which licensed him to teach in the name of the church.

Since October 1985, when the Vatican's Cardinal Joseph Ratzinger had warned Curran to recant or face discipline, both the university and Curran had seen a showdown ahead. A few months later, Curran began to write *Faithful Dissent,* his documented account of the investigation. University president William J. Byron, who had foreseen the rise of a stormy debate on academic freedom, also began to put his positions down in early 1986. He drafted a "discussion paper" as a forum for him and Archbishop James A. Hickey, chancellor of the university, to sort out any differences in their opinions. Their vantage points naturally differed; Hickey was a "prince of the church," Byron a university president. But the time was coming when they would need to speak publicly with one voice. Out of practical concern, both parties also turned to legal counsel.[1]

Catholic University's first legal adviser was Steven Frankino, the dean of Catholic University Law School and university counsel. In October, when Curran invoked his right to a faculty hearing, the university sought outside counsel as well. Curran had legal resources to draw on from his past. During the 1968 dissent over *Humanae Vitae,* one of the dissenting professors in the theology department had solicited the assistance of his brother, a corporate lawyer in a large New York firm. Along with Curran, professor Robert Hunt was among the twenty faculty members whose dissent had triggered the hearings, and John Hunt of Cravath Swaine & Moore had acted as their lawyer. In the intervening years all those professors had left Catholic University; Curran had remained and kept in touch with the Hunt brothers. John Hunt was ready to help Curran as before.

The lawyers for both sides first talked about the ground rules of the faculty hearing, something vaguely outlined in the faculty handbook. This was the job of Frankino for the university and Paul Saunders at Cravath. Saunders, a senior litigator at the firm, had returned home from the Labor Day weekend to find a memo on his desk asking if he would like to work on the Curran case. He had read about Curran in the *New York Times* but was not directly familiar with the events of 1968 or the details of the new dispute. It took only a few days before he understood the vast implications, especially if the case were to go to court.

Between September 1986 and April 1987, the month the faculty committee began its work, Frankino, Saunders, and Hunt built the hearing's framework. Meanwhile, Byron corresponded with the patriarch of Washington lawyers, Edward Bennett Williams, himself a product of Catholic schools and colleges. Williams was one of the foremost trial lawyers of his time, and his firm, Williams & Connolly, played a major role in the capital. Few people of prominence did not at one time or another turn to him for advice. A sports' lover, he had bought the Baltimore Orioles and was president of the Washington Redskins. Williams, who would die of cancer in two years, took a special interest in the Curran case and agreed to represent the university. Though involved at the early stages, Williams assigned Kevin Baine, a partner in the firm, the lead role from the beginning.

Curran's suspension in January 1987 added another layer to the legal concerns of his case. Citing breach of contract, Curran sued the university on February 28. Baine filed a response in the Superior Court of the District of Columbia, arguing that the court had no jurisdiction in the matter. The lawsuit dramatically changed the association between Saunders and Baine; once advisers, now they were adversaries in litigation. But they agreed to put the litigation on hold until the university hearings, which might produce a reconciliation, came to a close.

The members of the faculty committee, seven senior professors from seven different schools, were in a difficult position. They had known Curran for a long time, and now they had to pass judgment on him. When their hearings opened in May 1987, two forces would be at work in their decision. All of them knew well that the Vatican had authority over matters of Catholic religious teachings. The withdrawal of Curran's canonical mission, which they assumed existed, seemed inevitable. But the big question was what would happen to Curran; as a tenured professor he had certain employment and financial guarantees.

The faculty committee had retained the law firm of Hogan & Hartson, whose lawyer Jack Arness served as the moderator of the faculty hearings. In procedure if not in spirit, the hearings were very much like a trial, with Arness sitting alongside the committee members and counsel representing each party. The committee heard testimony in May. Baine and Saunders gave opening statements for the parties they represented. The faculty committee called three witnesses and then the lawyers called others. Saunders requested that the committee call Hickey. But Baine opposed that as inappropriate. Hickey had to make a decision after hearing the board's recommendation to him; he could not be both judge and witness. The committee agreed with Baine. Byron was called, but both the committee and Baine limited the questions Saunders could put to him. The university, knowing the case could go to trial, to a degree was opting for the normal defense tactic of saying no more than it had to. Baine asserted that the committee's mandate was limited to deciding one thing: Does the Vatican letter on Curran's suitability to teach Catholic theology constitute "most serious reasons?"

The faculty hearing evoked some candid testimony, especially from the plain-spoken Curran and Byron. Yes, Curran said, his lawsuit did cause scandal to the church. "But I think it would give much more scandal if I were not to say what I believe on these issues."

When his turn came, Byron said it was so unlikely that the Vatican would revoke Catholic University's pontifical standing that the odds were akin to having every student who crossed the street from one particular campus dorm hit by a car that day. "It is possible, but the probability level on that one is so low, it really doesn't justify consideration."

For Saunders, as counsel for Curran, the more that was said on the record in the hearings the better. Saunders's primary concern, which he voiced to the faculty committee and wanted to probe with Byron, was what it meant for Curran to lose his canonical mission. Nine months into the case, Saunders became confident of one impression: Few if any faculty members or administrators were absolutely clear about the meaning of "canonical mission" or the effect of losing it. Did losing it mean a limit on Curran's teaching? Did it undermine his tenure? Baine said the university had not yet addressed that—it preferred to take the process a step at a time. But Saunders's question got to the heart of the dilemma facing the faculty committee. If the committee recommended that there was "serious reason" to withdraw the canonical mission, where would that leave Charles Curran, their peer and colleague?

Finally, they acted on principle but also from faculty instinct. "If the canonical mission is withdrawn, the rightful autonomy of the university, and the tenure rights of Professor Curran as understood in the American academic tradition, must be safeguarded," the report said. "The withdrawal of the canonical mission, accordingly, cannot be allowed to abrogate Professor Curran's right to teach in the field of his academic competence."[2] At a gut level, they found it just plain hard to sanction someone in their close-knit academic fraternity, a trait common to all academe.

THE COMMITTEE'S OCTOBER report concluded that Curran's canonical mission could be withdrawn, but only if he remained tenured in his field of competence, "namely as a professor in the area of moral theology and/or ethics."

This ruling, however, won the committee no friends on either side. Curran was dissatisfied that the report legitimated the Vatican's reach into the theology department. In considering the canonical statutes' dual commitment to authority and freedom, his faculty confreres, Curran believed, had sided with authority. Hickey liked the report even less; the committee had given him more advice than he had asked for. He sent the report back, saying he accepted its ruling that "serious reasons" existed to withdraw Curran's canonical mission but that its other recommendation "exceeded its mandate" and was gratuitous.[3] The committee stuck to its guns.

With his comments attached, Hickey sent the report along to the board of trustees. Technically, the faculty committee had broadened the issue for the board by talking about where and what Curran could teach. The board took this to mean that it must decide not only on the canonical mission but also on Curran's teaching status at the university. Baine informed Saunders that unless Curran objected, the board was likely to take on both issues. The question of where Curran could teach would have come up inevitably, but now it was taking center stage.

Despite some willingness to address the Curran dispute publicly, Catholic University and the church hierarchy wanted to avoid any implication that academic freedom was being diminished. During the Christmas period of 1987, Baine accompanied Hickey and Byron to Rome, where they held consultations with Vatican officials, including the prefect of the Congregation for Catholic Education, Cardinal William Baum.[4] All the legal implications were being considered. Back in Washington, public opinion was a concern as well. For now the public perceived Curran's disciplining as a parochial matter, involving only three very specific pontifical schools at the entire university. The chancellor and university hoped that perception would continue.

As the lawsuit languished in superior court, the board of trustees met with Curran and his counsel on January 16, 1988. Afterward the board adopted a resolution supporting Hickey. For the first time the board discussed limits on Curran's teaching. But under the canonical statutes, the board could not issue a definitive ruling on the canonical mission without referring the matter back to the faculty committee, as required by due process. The board said it agreed that the Vatican's directive constituted "the most serious reasons." The board was not ready to say what teaching limits would be put on Curran. But as winter gave way to spring, the next development in superior court pushed it closer to a decision.

On April 5, 1988, Judge Bruce D. Beaudin denied the university's motion to dismiss Curran's lawsuit. The case had come to Beaudin in the Civil II division of the Superior Court of the District of Columbia through a scheduling system that put different phases of a case in the hands of different judges. "This court finds the university's position without merit," ruled Beaudin, a former seminarian and graduate of Georgetown University Law School. "The university is a body incorporated under the laws of the District and derives its power to confer academic degrees from a license granted by the District of Columbia Educational Licensure Commission . . . Professor Curran has properly turned to this court."[5] The next day Curran issued a press release saying the lawsuit would resolve whether Catholic University was indeed a mainstream institution with "academic freedom and constitutional autonomy."

Under this cloud the board of trustees took its next action on April 12; it formally removed Curran's canonical mission. Hickey later said that it was inconceivable that the trustees "could simply join in what was really the defiance on the part of Father Curran with respect to the decision."[6] However, withdrawal of the canonical mission did "not remove Father Curran's tenure with the university," the board said.[7] Its internal discussion did not dwell on how Curran's contractual rights were affected. Some of the trustees presumably would have liked to fire him right then, but it was never seriously discussed. Instead, the trustees authorized a three-man committee—Hickey, Byron, and Cardinal Joseph Bernardin of Chicago—to look for an alternative teaching post for Curran because he could no longer teach Catholic theology in the name of the church. Wherever the teaching slot might be, however, the board decided to set a condition—in some form Curran had to accept the Vatican ruling. Hickey told the board that he believed Curran should sign a statement accepting the Vatican ruling, to be made public. "I felt that that would be of assistance in repairing some of the harm that has been done by his teaching," Hickey said later.[8] Eventually, though, Hickey, Bernardin, and Byron said they agreed that a less formal assent was adequate.

Since December of 1987 Hickey and Bernardin had been discussing Curran's teaching status. Their task was to define how Curran could teach in his area of competency without teaching Catholic theology as such. Bernardin felt Curran could teach certain subjects that were "theological or ethical in nature" and be consistent with the Vatican declaration. "There is not a clear distinction between theology and ethics," Bernardin said later.[9] He would agree with Byron's formulation of two courses to be offered to Curran because their titles were on ethics. "On the basis of what I have heard," Bernardin wrote Hickey, "I think Father Curran is quite orthodox or even somewhat conservative in these areas."[10] Hickey agreed with the ethics part but did not want Curran touching theology.

The board's press release after its April meeting described creation of the triumvirate to negotiate with Curran. The mandate was to find "an alternative teaching assignment within an area of his professional competence." Yet prior to the April announcement, the lawyers were laying the groundwork for a teaching post. Already, Baine had discussed with Curran's lawyer, John Hunt, possible alternative teaching positions.They agreed on a basic framework: Curran would teach in the area of social ethics in the department of sociology. Before the April board meeting Baine had drafted a proposed settlement agreement. It set forth three conditions Curran would be required to meet to teach the two social ethics courses: Ecclesiastical degree students could not receive credit for the courses; Curran would dismiss the lawsuit and end all claims against the university; and he would sign a loyalty oath. "I will not teach Catholic theology at The Catholic University of America in the future," said the oath, which included his acceptance of the Vatican ruling.[11] Curran also was asked to state acceptance of canons 750 and 752 of the Code of Canon Law.

Baine, according to his account, read the document to Hunt over the phone, and here began a comedy of errors. Hunt did not agree with every provision, but he said the proposed agreement would be a constructive step forward, if the board approved it—which it did. When that happened, Baine again called Hunt and read him the board's press release, which Hunt conveyed to Curran. What Hunt did not do, apparently, was explain to Curran the nature of the conditions the university had set.[12]

The offer to negotiate an alternative teaching post struck a positive chord in Curran, who immediately released his own statement, gratified that the board "affirmed the fact that I am still a tenured professor at Catholic University."[13] Disappointed that the board had barred him from teaching in the department of theology, he noted that he already had offered to move out so long as he could continue to teach in his area of competence. What Curran did not know was that the board had also resolved that he would not teach anywhere in the school of religious studies. He did not know about the conditions until the next day, when Baine sent Curran's lawyers the draft agreement he had read over the phone.

Curran was aghast at what he read. Five days later, his lawyer responded that they were "extremely disappointed" by the proposed agreement, calling it "offensive and demeaning to Curran and violative of the principles of academic freedom."[14] They submitted a counterproposal. The most intense period of negotiations and rebuttals, private and public, between Curran and the university had begun. Baine proffered a revised settlement proposal April 29 that only required Curran to write a letter agreeing to be bound by the Ratzinger declaration and the obligations of the two canons. For Curran, this too was "wholly unacceptable."[15] He held a press conference to announce breakdown of the negotiations. Whether or not he had fully understood the university's offer when he made his "victory" statement, he now said the offer was "cynical" from the start.[16]

A week later on May 25, Byron wrote directly to Curran and again offered the two social ethics courses, now with specific titles: "Ethical Reflections on the Problems of War and Peace in Contemporary Society" and "Ethical Issues in Economic Life." Again there was a condition: "This proposal is premised upon acceptance of the Holy See's declaration that you are ineligible to teach Catholic theology." The ethics courses and any others in the future would "not be theology courses," Byron added.[17] He then asked Curran to meet with him, Hickey, and Bernardin. But for Curran there was a snag. "I have no competency in political science, economics or sociology," Curran wrote back. "Therefore I would necessarily, and obviously not secretly, teach those course from my perspective as a Catholic moral theologian." He repeated that he would not accept the Vatican declaration and protested the restriction on ecclesiastical degree students. Curran said it was inconvenient to meet, unless he had somehow misunderstood the offer "as having strings when it was not meant to." In that case, he said, he would rearrange his schedule.[18] Next day, Byron wrote that "the inconvenience for you of a meeting tomorrow here in Washington suggests that we should not meet now."[19]

In the next week the board of trustees lowered the final boom. Faced with Curran's uncompromising position, the university had a dilemma: How could it keep Curran from teaching theology in the nonecclesiastical faculties while preserving the appearance of academic freedom? To Bernardin, Curran had in effect said defiantly, "I am going to teach Catholic theology."[20] As Byron recalled, "So then the question arose, what's left open to us."[21] Baine and Byron finally decided to drop the big one, and they hit on a formula by which to act. On June 2 the trustees issued a resolution, without discussion or debate, barring Curran from teaching Catholic theology anywhere at the university. The trustees said the Vatican declaration was binding upon the university as a matter of canon law and religious conviction. To reject it would be "inconsistent with the university's special relationship with the Holy See, incompatible with the university's freely chosen Catholic character, and contrary to the obligation imposed on the university as a matter of canon law."[22] Baine said the board had the grounds to prescribe limits on Curran's teaching because the faculty committee, with no objections from Curran and his lawyer, had included the question of limits as part of the hearing process when it made recommendations to Hickey.

Byron informed Curran the next day, writing to say the ethics job was still on the table. But there were no illusions that he would accept its conditions. "I find it regrettable that you now regard the Holy See's definitive declaration to be binding on no one, including yourself," Byron said. He reminded Curran that the board viewed the Vatican declaration as limiting his teaching scope. "If you are not prepared to comply with that declaration at this university, then I am forced to concur with the option stated in your letter, namely, your intention to 'pursue a temporary teaching assignment elsewhere.'"[23]

Before this climax Curran had already seen the impasse and had decided to go public with the dispute, later drawing Byron onto the same track. They both offered opinion pieces to the *Washington Post*.[24] Curran's came out first on May 22, saying Catholic University had lost all vestiges of academic freedom. Byron told the board members on June 2 that he viewed it as "an attack" on the university, and he read them his rebuttal.[25] Published in the *Post* June 5, it said academic freedom has natural limits; in the case of Catholic theology that freedom has an "ecclesial limit," an idea that Byron had coined and that would be much debated in the next few years.

On June 9, Curran responded to Byron that he was sorry they had not worked out an agreement. "I regret you have not been able to offer me a position without unacceptable strings and conditions," he said. The board resolution and Byron's Op-Ed piece, he added, "have placed Catholic University outside the mainstream of American Catholic higher education."[26] Curran added the board's June 2 ruling to his list of contract violations and filed an amended complaint in superior court the next day. In July five Catholic University graduate students joined in, charging they were harmed by the prohibition on Curran's teaching.

The June 2 board resolution was enormously significant and played a large role in the trial to come. For Curran it was a last-ditch effort to displace him. The exercise undertaken to withdraw his canonical mission, in his view, was a charade. In a stroke the university had reversed its "depontificalization" and placed itself once again under canon law: Twenty years of hard-earned autonomy was lost. Viewing it through this lens, Curran and Saunders saw staggering implications for Catholic higher education. By allowing a Vatican directive to bar him from the entire university—even its secular departments—the institution had given up its autonomy, they believed. "Theoretically, what happened to me at Catholic University could happen at any Catholic institution," Curran said.[27] Some Catholic educators questioned whether such a broad threat arose from the Curran case. Only the future could tell. In his own court case, Curran would argue against Vatican intervention as if the autonomy of all Catholic academe depended on it.

BAINE AND SAUNDERS, with some thirty years of courtroom experience between them, had moved beyond the minor leagues. Their two high-powered law firms were known for playing hardball. They had played some themselves. As if a portent of this legal duel, their former high schools in Long Island had faced off for years as rivals in football.

Saunders, forty-eight, earned his law degree at Georgetown University in 1966 and served as a captain in the Judge Advocate General's Corps of the United States Army for four years. He joined Cravath Swaine & Moore in 1971 and in 1977 became a partner. He was part of the team that defended IBM in a thirteen-year antitrust suit brought by the Justice Department in 1969. The government dropped its case in January 1982. Saunders also was a team member, and finally lead defense counsel, in one of the most colorful libel suits in recent decades, *Ariel Sharon vs. Time, Inc.* Sharon, former defense minister of Israel, had filed a $50 million libel suit against *Time* for implicating him in a 1982 Beirut refugee camp massacre. In January 1985, after a nine-week trial in a New York federal court, the jury dismissed the case, slapping *Time's* hand for being careless in allowing false and defamatory information to get into print.

At age thirty-nine, Baine specialized at Williams & Connolly in First Amendment litigation, defending free speech and religious freedom. He had graduated from Princeton and the University of Pennsylvania Law School, joined the firm in 1976, and had half the years of courtroom experience Saunders had. But his year of clerking for Judge Edward Weinfeld, a prominent trial judge, and another year with Supreme Court Associate Justice Thurgood Marshall, had given him a good look at the judicial inner sanctum. On numerous occasions as a litigator he had beat back lawsuits against the news media, including two highly publicized libel suits against the *Washington Post* by President Richard Nixon's friend Bebe Rebozo and the president of Mobile Corporation, William Tavoulareas. He also had argued a protracted Freedom of Information Act case before the United States Supreme Court on behalf of CBS news. Baine's first work for Catholic institutions had been defending the rights of parochial school students to receive remedial education aid from the government through the parochial system, something challenged as an alleged establishment of religion. He was counsel to the National Conference of Catholic Bishops and its action arm, the United States Catholic Conference. In April 1988, when the Curran case was in limbo, Baine successfully defended the bishops in the final match of an eight-year lawsuit that sought to force the Treasury Department to strip the Catholic Church of its tax exemption.

Baine and Saunders were both cradle Catholics, reared in the church and attending its schools. Neither considered himself an avid student of theology. In fact, neither had read Curran's writings. Saunders's wife, Patricia, had completed her graduate studies in social work at Catholic University and contributed to the university's annual alumni appeal. Saunders himself was a member of the Knights of Malta, a religious fraternal order dedicated to charitable work. Baine was a board member of the John Carroll Society in Washington, an organization of Catholic lay professionals. In October 1989 he was chairman of the committee for the Red Mass at St. Matthew's Cathedral, attended annually by Supreme Court justices, cabinet members, congressmen, judges, and lawyers the Sunday before the Supreme Court term begins. But as lawyers Saunders and Baine knew well how to separate whatever they believed privately from the case they were litigating. What they brought to the case was a sense of who and what they were dealing with: a venerable and powerful institution, cherished beliefs, and parties warring over principle, not vanity. In their casual conversations early in the process, Baine and Saunders decided this case was "not going to be tried in the mud."[28]

The process of discovery for the lawsuit began with depositions, or interviews taken under oath by the lawyers, the first taking place in July. Baine deposed only Curran, while Saunders called several witnesses, including Hickey, Bernardin, Byron, and two lay members of the board of trustees. By now each legal team had up to three lawyers working on the case. And as the court filings began, the tone and strategy of each side became evident.

Baine sought to portray the case as an internal church matter, something the court should be very reluctant to infringe upon. So his briefs referred to the subject as "Father Curran." The legal papers liberally used Latin phrases, canonical terms, and citations of papal documents to build the university's case. In principle, Baine argued that the court had no business interfering in the dispute because of its religious nature.

Saunders entered the case aware of a tremendous hurdle he would have to clear: Even an objective observer, such as the judge himself, could not escape from seeing this as the quarrel of a rebellious priest with his superior. Saunders's challenge was to extract from that ecclesiastical drama another reality: the story of a professor and his civil contract with a university. To put that spin on the case, the legal papers on Curran's side called him "Professor Curran," stayed away from ecclesiastical jargon, and focused on the civic aspects of the university's constitution. Saunders argued that under its bylaws and its public accreditation, Catholic University had civil contract obligations with Curran no matter what the highest church authorities decided. Academic peer review alone could decide his worthiness as a professor. The court had a compelling interest to defend academic freedom, he argued, because it is the vulnerable essence of all universities.

Baine's and Saunders's positions were simple, diametric opposites, but the evidence was a morass of complexity. Saunders was heartened by Judge Beaudin's decision not to dismiss the case, and so he requested that the same judge hear it at trial. Baine did not object to that. Because of its complexity, however, both wanted it tried in the Civil I division of the superior court, meaning a single judge would handle it all the way through. Judge Frederick Weisberg, one of a few judges—among fifty on the court—with a schedule opening, was selected by internal court procedures. As the papers and motions were filed, he too realized the subtle nature of the dispute. In a rare accommodation to lawyers from both sides, he spent two casual sessions, three hours each, with Baine and Saunders together in the weeks just before trial to grasp the issues and arguments of the parties. It was something few judges have the time or interest to do.

Weisberg, forty-four, had been on the superior court bench since 1978. Nominated by President Jimmy Carter, he was a lawyer with the Public Defender Service, an agency of the D.C. government, before his judicial appointment. He was of short and solid build with short brown hair. A thoughtful man of Jewish background, the judge had a whimsical and sometimes self-effacing wit that matched his intellectual demeanor. He was known for his smooth running of trials, civil and criminal—and the emotional ones, too. A week before the Curran trial, he dismissed a complex church case in which former members of Evangel Temple, a large Pentecostal church in the city, had sued the ministers. They sought to recover money contributed under what they called a high-pressure building fund drive, charging fraud and willful emotional abuse. After hearing the case, Weisberg ruled in the church's favor, saying, "The plaintiff's evidence has won my heart, but not my head." Fraud, he said, had not been proven. "I have tremendous sympathy for what they've gone through," Weisberg said. "But this case, like any other, must be decided by the head, not the heart."[29] A head-heart challenge doubtless faced the judge soon again.

MID-DECEMBER BROUGHT scattered rain, not snow, to Washington. The sun's fleeting appearances did not dispel the chilly pall that fell over the capital during the eight days of trial. The small third-floor courtroom where Weisberg would preside seated about fifty spectators in addition to the lawyers and their clients. Most seats were filled on the opening day of trial, Wednesday, December 14, 1988, and would be in use through the end. Friends, well-wishers, and students of Curran's attended, as did observant Catholic University faculty members, administrators, and staff. Supporters of both sides were represented, revealing themselves when they shook their heads or whispered quietly during the testimony. Curran and the administrators whose university he was suing would linger during breaks and sometimes chat amiably throughout the trial. A representative of the American Association of University Professors, Jordan Kurland, sat through the entire proceedings.

For a contract dispute, an otherwise mundane affair in court, this case promised some color. Before the trial was over, Roman Catholic cardinals, priests, theologians, university presidents, and professors would occupy the witness stand. The atmosphere would at times become taut as the legal arguments from both sides delicately maneuvered past an exploration of the Roman Catholic religion itself, a practice that makes judges nervous regardless of the denomination involved. Bernardin was called to testify and spoke later of his initial aversion to seeing the church in court. Like others so sensitized, Bernardin was quickly reassured by Weisberg's handling of the case. "The competence of the court must be limited to those matters that have civil effect," Bernardin recalled later.[30] From the start, that was Judge Weisberg's task.†

The judge, as he repeated often, had only one question—with three parts—before him. What are the terms of the contract? Did the university breach it? If so, what is the proper remedy? What made *Curran vs. Catholic University* unusual was that no single contract, in the form of a document, existed. In effect, the contract was contained in the promises made in the faculty handbook and the annual appointment letter given a professor, which stated his terms, salary and benefits, combined with what Saunders called "a course of dealing." Both parties agreed that these formed the contract, of which the guarantee of academic freedom was a part. But they disagreed whether the contract, however defined, specifically guaranteed that Curran could continue teaching Catholic theology after the Holy See ruled him ineligible.

The District of Columbia already had a track record on faculty contract disputes. In a town with six universities, lawsuits by displaced professors were not uncommon, and in recent years these had set some precedents. In one 1987 case, *McConnell vs. Howard University*, the superior court had ruled "an employee handbook . . . defines the rights and obligations of the employee and the employer, and is a contract enforceable by the courts." Curran's case argued that by custom and practice he had a guarantee of academic freedom. This debate had court precedent, too, in another Howard University lawsuit. In 1988 the court ruled that when a party claims the contract is based on custom and practice it must establish "by clear and satisfactory evidence" that the custom and practice is "definite, uniform and well known."

---

† *The following narrative and testimony of the eight-day trial are taken verbatim from the official court transcript, and will not be cited for endnotes. The court documents are listed in the bibliography.*

JUDGE WEISBERG OPENED the proceedings by noting that the schedule was not ideal for anyone. He had jammed the case in before the Christmas holiday, and was uncertain whether they would have to come back afterward. Because of scheduling conflicts with some witnesses, this arrangement would slightly disrupt the order of testimony. In a textbook trial, the plaintiff calls witnesses first and the defense goes second. The morning opened with a motion for summary judgment—a request for a ruling without testimony—and the judge said it was preferable to have a day for that debate alone. Given the constraints, each side had a half hour.

The judge now began a practice that would characterize his role in the trial, one that indeed made the long testimony entertaining. Weisberg would ask a "what if" question in an attempt to push a legal position to greater clarity, if not sometimes speculation. He had such a question for Baine to help him get the argument for summary judgment going. Suppose, he said, the university and Curran had sat down and drafted a contract around 1970. Suppose the contract recognized his dissent of 1968 and stated that the school would defend Curran's academic freedom even if it meant defying the Vatican, with which it had special ties. If such a contract existed and was signed by all parties, the judge asked, "Would this case be here?"

This sharpened Baine's "free exercise of religion" argument, one of the elements of the defense case. Because religious freedom is equal in weight to contract rights, "This university has the inherent rights as a church-related institution to change its mind twenty years later," Baine said. Under the judge's scenario, he added, the university could renege on its written promise to defy the Vatican, but Curran could probably claim some damages. Baine turned to what he considered the real dispute over the contract. "Some of the documents that comprise the contract are themselves provisions of canon law and at that point you have to stop."

Baine described the actions of the Holy See over seven years and said the Curran case was extraordinary. "There have been theologians in the past who have been disciplined but never before has there been one who, after being disciplined, insisted upon the right to teach Catholic theology, indeed to teach it in an ecclesiastical faculty at a pontifical university in defiance of the Holy See. Never before has there been a theologian who has sought to ask the court to resolve that kind of dispute."

More than a contract case, he said, it was a question of whether the university gave up its right to follow its religious principles, drawn from canonical statutes and papal decrees. Baine rebutted Curran's claim that only two university documents bound him, the 1968 Manual of Information for the Faculty and a Manual of Appointments and Procedures. Curran, he said, claimed that nothing later than 1970 was enforceable against him that was not also favorable to him. "That position is absurd," Baine said. It would lead to different policies for each professor and a massive filing operation. "As of today there are two documents that we say govern this case," Baine said. These were the 1979 apostolic constitution *Sapientia Christiana* and the canonical statutes of 1981.

Was it not reasonable, Weisberg asked, for Curran to say, "I'll take my contract in 1970." Baine said the 1981 document gave Curran even more protection, especially the right to a hearing.

"We agree that Father Curran was not explicitly, formally given a canonical mission," Baine said. But that did not deny that such a requirement existed. Did Curran need a canonical mission, Baine asked rhetorically. "The documents are clear," he said in the affirmative. "And even if they weren't, the provisions of canon law and the university have made the determination that he needs a canonical mission."

Curran, who did not contest in court the Vatican's right to question his teachings, did challenge the university's right under his tenure to bar him from teaching Catholic theology in his former department of theology. Again, Baine warned that this involved an interpretation of canon law in the statutes and governance of the university. "Even if this were not a matter of canon law, I would say to the court that an institution has to have the ability to interpret its own statutes finally, and this court could not say . . . 'I think you have misread your own statutes.'"

Point by point, Baine hit Curran's claims. Curran's offer to teach only nonecclesiastical students, for example, placed a burden on the university to separate its programs, Baine said.

He invoked a United States Supreme Court ruling, often called the Serbian Orthodox case—*Serbian Eastern Orthodox Diocese vs. Milivojevich*—in which the court said the highest official body of a church is recognized as having the final authority to interpret laws of the church. Hence, Baine said, Curran could properly go to the Congregation for Catholic Education if he disputed an interpretation of the canonical statutes, which the congregation approved. "But I don't think he can come to this court instead of the congregation and ask this court to say that we were wrong," he said.

Finally, Baine said universities can promise displaced professors a good-faith effort to provide them another job, but that is generosity, not law. Stating Curran's position as, "'It's an absolute right to find me one and to give me a teaching position in the field of Catholic theology,'" Baine added, "There's nothing in the handbook that supports that."

In conclusion, Baine noted that money was not an issue in the case, which is uncommon in civil suits. "We think this is an unusual case because the only real issue in this case is whether or not the court will order Catholic University to let Father Curran stay on," he said.

WEISBERG NOW TURNED to Saunders, presenting him with a question to focus his argument that the case should go to trial. "What is the source of your claim that Father Curran has a right to teach theology somewhere else in the university?" Weisberg asked.

Saunders said his claim stemmed from the university's "course of dealing" with Curran, which Curran believed guaranteed academic freedom and the right to dissent publicly from certain church teachings. If the right could be ended simply by evoking the idea of a canonical mission, "That makes the rights illusory," he said. "It's not a right at all."

As evidence of that guarantee, Saunders said he would show that early in the Curran dispute Byron had taken a position identical to Curran's about the professor's right to academic freedom. The evidence, which would get its airing at trial, was an article, "Credentialed, Commissioned and Free," the final product of the paper Byron had written to begin discussions on academic freedom with Hickey. In the end, Byron changed some points in accord with Hickey's view. But in the first draft, Saunders said, Byron's "understanding of academic freedom in that context at that time was the same as ours. It's changed since then."

Reviewing the history, Saunders said, "Our view of the circumstances is somewhat different from Mr. Baine's," which he said proved that there were "disputes of material fact in this case."

"We say there was a contract that had essentially the same terms but was not a written, negotiated, all inclusive, single piece of paper. It was more a course of dealing but had exactly the same terms," he said. This could be understood by reviewing the events: Curran's rehiring in 1967, his dissent over *Humanae Vitae* in 1968, and the decision in 1969 to restructure the entire university, prompted by Middle States Association of College and Schools' concern over the inhibiting control of Rome. Saunders implied that Curran was being treated differently now than he had been in those years. Cardinal Patrick O'Boyle, the university's chancellor, may have wanted to fire the dissenting professors in 1968, but "what he did not do was to withdraw their canonical mission," Saunders said. "Why? Obviously because he didn't think they had one." All this, Saunders said, was proof of Catholic University's commitment to academic freedom—a guarantee that encompassed Charles Curran.

During Saunders's summary of past events Weisberg interrupted. "I have a hard time understanding why you think that has anything to do with Professor Curran's contract," he said.

Curran's 1970 tenure was built on those events, Saunders said. "If the university wanted to say in the statutes, you must have a canonical mission to teach, they certainly knew how to say that in plain, simple English words," he said.

"They did say it," Weisberg said.

"Not in 1969," Saunders said.

"They said it in 1937 and reprinted it in 1964," Weisberg said.

"But the requirement, whatever there was in 1937, fell into disuse. It was never used," Saunders said. For example, the demands in the 1937 bylaws that certain courses be taught in Latin or that professors be cleared by a *nihil obstat* were not followed. Also, the statement that the chancellor controls the whole university was changed in 1969, narrowed to include only ecclesiastical faculties.

The requirement for a canonical mission fell into disuse, he said. "Nobody ever got one."

"Or everybody got one but not on paper," Weisberg said.

Saunders said the argument about an implicit mission was "sort of the magic wand theory," in which it was called real for everyone because it was in someone's mind. He claimed that when the 1981 statutes were written Hickey knew that the canonical mission idea was in disuse and that the statutes reinstated it. Curran claimed the 1981 statutes were not retroactive. All that was a question of fact that was appropriately before the court, Saunders said.

Weisberg said it was difficult to conclude that everything the university might have said became part of a contractual policy.

Saunders agreed, but pressed to the essential dilemma. "If you are a university, you have to have academic freedom and institutional autonomy," he said. "If you don't, you may be something else. You may be a seminary. You may be a catechetical institute, but you are not a university."

Judge Weisberg said Curran certainly might be "disappointed" that the university did not have the academic freedom he thought it did when he contracted as a professor. "He can speak about that and scream and yell all he wants, but he can also leave."

Saunders said yes, but in this case Curran was saying, "I hold you to your word." Emphasizing that Curran's controversial positions were well known for twenty years, Saunders said, "There's nothing new in Professor Curran's writing."

"Academics have been accused of that from time to time," Weisberg interjected, drawing laughs—a hearty one from Curran.

Saunders continued the repartee. "We won't tell his publishers."

In other words, Saunders said, "The actions that are being taken against him are not taken because of some brand new heretical position that he took eighteen months ago." In Curran's case there was no accusation of incompetence in his field, and the university seemed to stand by its claim of twenty years earlier to be "a full modern American university in every sense of the word. Professor Curran took them at their word and he's entitled to rely on that," Saunders said in conclusion.

Baine, in a brief reply, contested some of Saunders's description of the institutional history and said Curran's expectations were unreasonable. In a sense, Baine said, Curran believed the university "is contractually obligated to join him in dissent from the Holy See's declaration."

After a break Baine saw that he had lost this first round. Weisberg returned to lament that he did not have more time to consider the motion fully, in which case he might have decided the opposite. He said that a summary judgment should be made only when there is very little merit to a case. "Applying that standard to this case, I have concluded that is not true of the dispute between these parties," he said. "The question of whether the contract does or does not incorporate canon law is not itself a question of canon law and must be decided according to neutral principles of contract law."

"The plaintiff has shown in opposition to the motion for summary judgment that there are genuine disputes between the parties that can within the constraints of the First Amendment be decided by the court, and, therefore, the motion for summary judgment must be denied."

The real trial would begin.

EIGHT

A Cardinal's View

James A. Hickey had occupied many seats of responsibility in his forty-two years as a priest. He had been director of the North American College in Rome and then bishop of Cleveland. As archbishop of Washington he was also chancellor of The Catholic University of America. But at age sixty-eight he was occupying a witness stand for the first time, and now he was a cardinal, elevated just seven months before the trial.

Hickey was the first witness under an agreement between Kevin Baine and Paul Saunders. Normally the plaintiff's witness would testify first. But the two lawyers, for reasons of their own, had worked out a change. Baine, representing the university, wanted to interrogate Hickey as his witness at the outset, putting before the judge the whole Charles Curran story from the church and university point of view. Of course, Saunders could cross-examine. Baine felt that Hickey's going first helped his case. Between such arrangements and the scheduling conflicts for various witnesses, the eight days of testimony were a hodgepodge. That would have been consequential in a jury trial, putting the logic of certain arguments at risk, but it was no problem in a trial by a judge. Judge Frederick Weisberg could jump into the middle of any testimony, as he often did, to clarify a point or push it further.

The morning Weisberg had ruled against Baine's summary judgment motion, he had told the lawyers he reserved the power to dismiss the case if, after the plaintiff rested his case, the burden of proof had not been met. Saunders agreed, saying the burden was indeed on him to convince the judge every step of the way.

Weisberg's ruling also had cleared the way for the lawsuit of the five graduate students, interveners in the Curran case, to continue. The students, who would rely on the same witnesses called by

Curran and the university, wanted to show that their academic freedom was inhibited by the action against Curran. The university had acted in bad faith, they also claimed, preventing them from completing their degrees because Curran had served as their academic adviser. Of the five interveners, one was near to completing a master's degree. Another had been at the school for fifteen years and was in a doctor of ministry program. The rest were at various stages in Ph.D. programs. All of the students at one time or another had had scholarships. Weisberg turned to Philip Malet, chief lawyer for the interveners. Giving an illustration, Weisberg said there had been cases where a university had run out of money or had closed a department, displacing a professor and disrupting the study of his students. Would those students have an argument for suing the school? And, he wondered, if the Vatican action on Curran was "a force beyond the university's control," was the university still liable? Malet answered that the university could have resisted the outside "force" and so was culpable.

Before Hickey took the stand to be sworn in, both sides made brief opening statements. The arguments over the summary judgment motion had exhausted their main points, so they introduced a few new twists.

Courtrooms in the Superior Court of the District of Columbia are sort of "theaters-in-the-round." Saunders and Baine were stationed almost next to each other at the same semicircular lawyers' table that faces the judge and witness stand. At each other's elbow, they could confer when necessary. They posed their questions to the witnesses from the same wooden rostrum in the center of the lawyers' table, surrendering it to each other with each examination and cross-examination.

The dark-haired Saunders cut a tall, slim figure, enhanced by his dark blue and gray suits. Talking with a faint Long Island accent, he spoke more slowly than Baine, as if to emphasize the methodical reasoning behind his questioning. Saunders began with an analogy. Harvard University, he said, has a chair of Catholic studies, and the president of the school has a right to say that a professor in that school does not teach in the name of the church. But it would not be acceptable for the pope to tell the school president to relieve the professor of his duties because the Vatican considered him unorthodox. Saunders said Catholic University officials confused those two roles. A distinction needs to be made between the theologian's roles in the church and in the academy, Saunders said.

It was Baine's turn. He contended that Saunders's analogy tried to separate theology from the church, a division Curran himself did not make. Baine was slightly shorter than Saunders but as trim, with sharp features, light brown hair, and distinct blue eyes. His presentations were rapid and, by the nature of his case, a little more to the point: Catholic University had had every right to do what it did, and the court must not intervene. To counter Saunders's analogy, he said that Curran did indeed believe he was primarily a theologian for the church. Quoting from Curran's book *Faithful Dissent* he said, "My theology is done primarily for the church. Some theologians will be properly classified as doing their theology for the academy but that is not my role. I decided to stay and do my theology at Catholic University because of the role it gave me in the life of the Catholic Church."

Weisberg said they were going a little afield; he did not see any confusion over the two roles a theologian could play. In time, however, the question became more complex than the judge anticipated.

HICKEY WAS CALLED to the stand to take the oath. This was a first for Weisberg, too. Sensitive to the law and religious freedom, he asked the cardinal awkwardly if it was proper for him to submit to taking the oath. The oath posed no problem, Hickey reassured the judge. As with all fifteen witnesses to come, Hickey began by answering questions about his background. Given his role in the hierarchy, he was asked about the structure and nature of the Roman Catholic Church. The cardinal, dressed in black suit and collar with the chain of his gold pectoral cross dropping into his side pocket, leaned forward and spoke in a relaxed manner. For now, under Baine's amicable questioning, he was among friends.

In the past, he said, the Congregation for the Doctrine of the Faith in Rome had disciplined theologians. Its actions could include declaring that someone was not a church theologian, requesting a wayward theologian to spend a period of reflection or, in more severe cases, excommunicating the offender. Under Canon 272, he testified, theologians and clergy were required to follow the directives of the Holy See: "Clerics are bound by a special obligation to show reverence and obedience to the supreme pontiff and to their own ordinary [bishop]."

The cardinal's testimony developed the position that the Vatican was well within its rights to take action against Curran. For one thing, Curran dissented as a teacher in an ecclesiastical faculty at a university chartered by the papacy, a pontifical university, Hickey said. "This university has responsibilities of the church in the United States that are special to it," Hickey said, reading from the faculty handbook. The apostolic constitutions governing the school, evidence showed, required the canonical mission.

"And do you grant that mission?" Baine asked.

"I grant that mission," Hickey said.

At Weisberg's request, Hickey explained that Catholic lay teachers on the ecclesiastical faculties also must be granted a canonical mission. "If they are not of our faith they receive a document which is called the *venia docendi,* permission to teach," Hickey said.

Weisberg wanted a better understanding of the obligations of the contracts in the ecclesiastical faculties. What if, he asked, the apostolic constitution denied lay teachers and non-Catholics a canonical mission, would Hickey have to fire them? Hickey said the question was too hypothetical, and too unlikely, for him to respond. Yet as unlikely as that hypothetical event was, it went to a core issue, and the question would arise again.

During the Second Vatican Council, Hickey had been a *peritus,* or expert adviser, to the Commission on Seminaries and Universities. "And so I sat in on the drafting of the document that had to do with Catholic universities," he said. The later document *Normae Quaedam,* in his view, required fidelity to the magisterium on the part of the ecclesiastical faculty.

"Have you heard the position asserted that the requirement of a canonical mission had fallen into disuse in the late sixties and was therefore inapplicable as a requirement of canon law?" Baine asked.

"I have heard that assertion but I did not accept it," Hickey said. He said that an application of a canon law, such as the canonical mission, does not expire until after thirty years of disuse, and then a formal closure must follow. In the intervening years the mission was given "implicitly," Hickey said canon lawyers has assured him.

Talk of canon law brought Saunders to his feet, disputing the propriety of the court's receiving as evidence a particular person's interpretation of canon law. It was not the last time they would argue this point, and later in the trial it would become a focus of the battle. For the time being, Weisberg wanted no statements by canon law experts as evidence.

WHEN HICKEY HAD BECOME archbishop of Washington in 1980, church officials informed him of the one year of correspondence between Curran and the Vatican regarding the moral theologian's writings. The next period of testimony covered the events leading up to the board of trustees' final decision of 1988 to bar Curran from teaching Catholic theology anywhere in the university. Hickey said he had given Curran fair warning of what the initial Vatican statement implied and thereafter had scrupulously granted him the due process promised by faculty bylaws. Upon receiving the Vatican judgment, Hickey said he was told that the pope "approved both its content and [the] procedures followed," and that he was to take "appropriate action." He had followed proper procedures at the university when he made the administrative decision to suspend Curran, Hickey testified.

Saunders rose to say that on one point of the testimony so far they agreed. "We have no dispute that the proper procedures were followed," he said. "We do dispute the scope of the power of the chancellor." In Curran's view, the chancellor had no power to prohibit him from teaching *outside* the ecclesiastical faculties.

Hickey discussed his decision to prohibit Curran from teaching in the department of theology. Although that department had an ecclesiastical program and a civil program, he said, "it is one department, one ecclesiastical faculty." Hickey said that the question was one of canon law and that he, as chancellor, had authority to interpret the canonical statutes in their description of the department.

The statutes, in fact, stated that they did not apply to all parts of the department. But under the power of canon law Hickey nevertheless had interpreted them as making the department unitary. His interpretation had been sustained by the board of trustees and later supported by Cardinal William Baum, the prefect of the Congregation for Catholic Education in Rome. After the board of trustees assigned a three-man committee to negotiate a new teaching post for

Curran at the university, Hickey explained, he supported the condition that Curran publicly accept and abide by the Vatican ruling. Curran's teachings and dissent had done "a good deal of harm to the church and I felt it was very important that it be clear that he was acceptive of this even though he did not like it," Hickey said.

Why did the board accept the Vatican decree as binding on it? Baine asked, raising a central question to be contested by Saunders.

"It was inconceivable to the board of trustees of the university that we could simply join in what was really the defiance on the part of Father Curran with respect to the decision—the binding judgment of the Holy See."

This ended Baine's questions in his two-hour direct examination of Hickey. Cross-examination by Saunders began.

SAUNDERS WANTED TO highlight the difference between pontifical departments and ordinary civil programs at universities, something he thought Hickey had muddled in describing the school of religious studies. The difference between the departments also raised questions about the sweep of Cardinal Joseph Ratzinger's disciplinary letter to Curran. Saunders asked if Georgetown University was a pontifical university. Hickey said yes. "Does the Ratzinger declaration bind Georgetown University in your view?" he asked Hickey, raising objections again from Baine.

Weisberg suggested a better way to get at the issue, as he would often do. "Is the Ratzinger letter binding on [Hickey] because Catholic University is a pontifical university or because of the ecclesiastical faculties within it or for some other reason?" the judge asked. Saunders put the question.

"It's binding because we would consider anyone so adjudged by the Holy See would be—We could not grant permission for him to teach at Catholic University," Hickey answered. Saunders asked if that would apply even to nonecclesiastical faculties, and Hickey said yes. Why? "It's because of its special relationship with the Holy See, as a pontifical university."

Saunders asked if the Vatican declaration made it clear to him from the outset whether it also barred Curran from the nonecclesiastical faculties.

"I would say that was an initial impression. I did not pursue that because at the time I felt that we should let the canonical procedure take its course to see what would happen," Hickey said.

Saunders now put on pressure, taking a mild impeachment approach, contending that the cardinal had said something different in his deposition. Hickey's deposition, Saunders showed, said that at the outset he had taken the letter to mean Curran could not teach theology even in a nonecclesiastical department. "It was clear as could be," Hickey had said in the deposition. Baine thought the question was splitting hairs, and the judge—who would later raise the issue—apparently thought that Hickey's credibility made him a poor target for such impeachment questions.

Hickey took the challenge anyway. "It just shows an old mind forgets a bit at times," he explained when the deposition was read.

Saunders focused on how the board of trustees finally came to the conclusion that Curran could not teach on the nonecclesiastical faculty. His line of questioning next attempted to show that originally there had been no opposition to allowing Curran to teach in nonecclesiastical departments, a view Baine challenged. Nearly every board member opposed such leeway for Curran, Baine insisted. But Saunders, based on his own assumption, asked why the board changed its policy. Hickey tried to evade the question, finally stating that the board did not "treat [the question] at the time." The board's decision to place a broad ban on Curran's theology teaching only became explicit in its June 2 resolution, Hickey said. To show what Hickey was thinking at the April board meeting, Saunders quoted the minutes: "The ecclesiastical faculty is the department of theology," Hickey had said at the time. "So, withdrawal of the canonical mission doesn't per se bar him from teaching in another department in the school of religious studies."

"Is it correct," Saunders persisted, "that Professor Curran was not ineligible to teach theology at CU outside the ecclesiastical faculty any time prior to June 2, 1988?"

"We didn't formalize it at that [April] meeting, but we certainly had it in mind that he would not be teaching theology," Hickey said.

Saunders, trying to reveal inconsistency in board actions, asked why, if Curran was disqualified from teaching in the nonecclesiastical faculties from the start, did the board find it necessary to pass a resolution almost two years later prohibiting Curran from doing so?

Hickey said that if the board had not barred Curran from teaching the subject in the nonecclesiastical faculties in its June resolution, he as chancellor would have had to do so, but the board's concurrence made that unnecessary.

Saunders then moved to the suspension of Curran in January 1987. Curran had planned to teach only nonecclesiastical degree students in his January classes in the department of theology. But Hickey, arguing that the department was unitary because the same faculty taught in both parts, would not approve such a division. Saunders referred to the language of the 1981 canonical statutes of the school, which said, "These faculties, however, are not exclusively ecclesiastical. They also have other academic programs which do not have canonical effects and to which these statutes do not apply."

Baine objected to the long process of going into the chancellor's interpretation of the statutes. He said Saunders's line of questioning was meant to undermine Hickey's interpretation of the canonical statutes even after it was endorsed by the board. Baine said his own questioning of Hickey had established that interpretation, and that should end it.

Saunders responded: Hickey's "interpretation that the statutes apply to the entire faculty of the department of theology is based upon his understanding of the fact that there has always been a unitary faculty. That's a question of fact and I'm entitled to inquire into it."

On that the court agreed. "I permit you to go a little ways," Weisberg said.

"How do you know it was one faculty?" Saunders asked Hickey.

The cardinal cited a footnote to the statutes which implied that the department of theology was unitary. To counter, Saunders showed the footnote was not in the version adopted by the board but that it had been added later when Hickey went to Rome and the Vatican showed concern over dividing the faculty between ecclesiastical and nonecclesiastical portions. The footnote, Saunders suggested, was not part of the statutes.

"The use of the word faculty has always been a bit confusing in the sense that it's used not quite the same in Europe," Hickey explained.

Saunders asked then if Hickey had relied on his own interpretation to decide that the faculty was unitary.

"Not at all," Hickey said. He drew his interpretation from the statutes and his understanding from the drafting process.

As Saunders proceeded, Weisberg mentioned that they were close to ending and suggested that some of Saunders's details on types of faculties were not relevant to the case. He also showed some impatience at Saunders's long and methodical effort to impeach Hickey's statements.

To Saunders's next question, Hickey said he implicitly granted canonical missions to visiting professors but had decided years earlier not to go through a formal process, which required an amount of paperwork and review that he felt was unnecessary. On this, testimony ended at 4:30 P.M. Hickey would return the next morning. Saunders asked that Baine and Hickey be prohibited from discussing the cardinal's testimony since they were midway in cross-examination.

"Can you talk about the Orioles or something, or more appropriately the Redskins?" Weisberg asked.

"Sure," Baine said.

NEXT MORNING, Hickey's cross-examination continued. He was asked if he or the board took into account Curran's contractual arrangements when they considered action on the Vatican letter.

"We were not attacking his tenure," Hickey said. "We were simply taking . . . action, first of all, to withdraw his canonical mission, then subsequently to try and find a position for him as a tenured professor in the university." That tenure, he said, continued.

Saunders then fired off a series of questions in an attempt to discover why the university, being autonomous, was required to take any action after Hickey received the 1986 letter from Ratzinger. "Was the Ratzinger letter self-executing?" Saunders asked.

While theoretically he could have done nothing, Hickey said that was impossible. "We did not sit in review upon a decision of the highest doctrinal body of the church specifically approved by the pope himself," he said. Canon law, according to his testimony, did not allow the university board of trustees to reject the Vatican judgment.

Hickey could see where Saunders's questions were going—to the disparity between free choice and coercion. The cardinal argued that the university was indeed autonomous in accepting the demands of the Vatican declaration. "We freely accepted that as compatible with our stated aim of fidelity to the Christian message as it comes through the church," he said. Hickey also said that canon law made the letter binding on the university.

Weisberg commented on the apparent contradiction between freely choosing and being bound by canon law to choose. "I would have assumed your position to be, 'we really didn't have any choice, given our relationship to the church and our obligation under canon law,'" Weisberg said.

That is true, Hickey said. But at the same time board members were "free human beings" who could have broken the law; they could have defied everything. "But we were not physically compelled," he said. "If we were to be faithful to our duties, which we were obliged to do as trustees at the university, we had to accept it, of course." But, he added, "Nobody opened our mouth and made us say yes."

Saunders asked, "If the Ratzinger letter was binding on Catholic University in and of itself, the day that it was received as a matter of canon law, why was it necessary to submit any of these matters to the board of trustees?"

"It said take appropriate action," Hickey said. "The letter didn't say fire him today."

Hickey testified that the 1969 Marlowe report—which had found the 1968 public dissent of Catholic University theologians to be appropriate—did not, in his view, constitute official university policy. It was never entirely accepted by the board of trustees, he said, adding that the dissent of 1968 and the Vatican ruling of 1986 were entirely different in nature. Saunders tried to refute that statement in his questioning.

At this point, Weisberg was dubious about whether the historical survey conducted by Saunders's cross-examination was pertinent to the specific contract dispute. Moreover, he told Saunders to avoid going back to the deposition and let Hickey state his position as he saw it in the present.

Saunders wanted to hold the university to its promise to protect dissenters. "Before the receipt of the Ratzinger letter, did Curran have a right to dissent from church teachings consistent with his contract?" he asked.

"There certainly is permitted a type of criticism, a kind of questioning of the argumentation that is used in a particular church teaching," Hickey said. "There is a question of the foundation from which it is drawn and so on and so forth. That is, however, not a rejection."

Weisberg pointed out that he had to decide on the contract, and so asked Hickey what kind of dissent Curran was involved in.

Did he have "any right at all to dissent under that contract, whether there's any part of plaintiff's theory of academic freedom written into this contract?"

Hickey said, "When a professor, through his positions, rejects [church teaching], as Father Curran has in respect to contraception and through certain other points of sexual morality, that in my view is inconsistent with the aim of the university."

"And therefore it exceeds whatever right he had under his contract to take a different view on these subjects?" the judge asked.

"I believe so," Hickey said.

Saunders returned to a question asked by Weisberg that Hickey had said he could not answer: What would happen if, for example, the Vatican said that only clergy could teach theology? Would the university be required to fire laymen? Before, Hickey had responded that the question was "too hypothetical" to answer. But Saunders pointed out that the 1931 apostolic constitution *Sapientia Christiana,* in fact, required all ecclesiastical faculty to be clergy. Indeed, Catholic University, Saunders claimed, had needed an exemption to hire moral theology professor William May, a layman. Saunders's inference was pregnant: If no exemption had been received, Hickey's interpretation of canon law would oblige him to fire May regardless of any contract rights he might have, just as he had fired Curran.

A series of exchanges between Weisberg and Saunders followed, focusing on whether Hickey as chancellor claimed the power to interpret canon law across the board at the university so that, say, a canonical mission was required in psychology or other disciplines. Weisberg said that was beyond the scope of what he had to decide.

"We're only on day two, Mr. Saunders, and you and I are going to have a very hard time. Whether or not he can say, as a matter of canon law, that philosophy is the same as psychology is something I do not have to decide in this trial." The exchange highlighted the challenge Saunders faced in building his case.

After a break, Saunders reviewed with Hickey the dispute on whether the canonical mission had fallen into disuse, which Hickey said he did not believe, and whether he had disagreed with the suggestion of Cardinal Joseph Bernardin, chairman of the trustees, that Curran be allowed to teach some kind of theology courses in the nonecclesiastical faculty. Hickey said he did disagree, but Bernardin's testimony later in trial suggested that originally he had been open to the idea. Saunders ended his cross-examination.

Maureen Ward, a lawyer for the graduate students, now questioned Hickey. Ward tried to explore what chilling effect the action against Curran might have on other moral theologians. But Weisberg said it was only relevant what chilling effect it had on the university. "We intend to show or think we will be able to show that there is a course of conduct at Catholic University . . . that we think has diminished the quality of education available to the interveners," she said. She asked Hickey if he believed the students had a right to certain expectations at the school.

Hickey said that when he was a student professors at times disappointed his expectations, but that did not give him an absolute right to compensation. "We would have our courts absolutely flooded with suits," he said. "If I went into a classroom of students and felt at least one of those people out there was going to sue me if they didn't have full rights, I would be very inhibited." Hickey said he would grant the word "expectation," but not the word "rights."

Ward tried to point out inconsistencies. The school said it wanted to give students a wide exposure and so required them to take courses in the Washington Theological Consortium from different denominational perspectives, she said, and yet it wouldn't allow them to be taught by dissident Catholic teachers.

Weisberg said he did not think the line of questioning was relevant.

Ward asked if the action against Curran would hurt the school's reputation.

"Not in the long run," Hickey said. "I don't think we will help the situation any by becoming less faithful ourselves."

When he was a student, he said, all the conflicting positions on Christian issues were presented, but the teacher clearly upheld the view of the magisterium. "If the professor himself does not make clear that he is not rejecting the teaching of the church then our whole purpose falls apart," he said.

Ward asked whether the action toward Curran would affect the marketability of the degrees given, and Hickey said no. Did the department of theology have difficulty attracting highly qualified faculty members? she asked. "Not in my opinion," Hickey said. The lawyer then produced two letters by two professors, one of them department of theology chairman David Power, to show that the university indeed had experienced difficulty replacing Curran. Hickey said there had been three candidates but that Power and the other professor had not recommended them, a view he attributed to their "mind-set" rather than the candidates' qualifications.

Weisberg mentioned a decade-long battle at Howard University Law School about hiring based on ideological leanings and said that if such hiring policies guided the department of theology at Catholic University it was not part of their concern in the litigation. Weisberg suggested the questions Ward wanted to raise be put to another witness later during the plaintiff's case.

Baine was given a chance to examine the witness further. He read the first paragraphs of a resolution by Cardinal Krol's special committee, which the board of trustees set up to evaluate the Marlowe report. That report, which affirmed the right to academic freedom, had been only partially accepted by the board, Baine showed. The Krol committee had said the report's recommendations were beyond the scope of the Marlowe committee's inquiry, touching on matters of policy under purview of the board alone. Hence, the Krol committee resolution said, the Marlowe report was accepted under a "rule of review" but that "in no way indicates any agreement or concurrence with the findings of the board of inquiry."

Saunders came last, reading further from the Krol report and noting that the board had accepted the conclusion of a June 5, 1969, academic senate resolution on the Marlowe report. Saunders implied that this meant the board of trustees had concurred with the report's notion of academic freedom, though it had stayed neutral on policy or theological positions expressed by the dissenting theologians.

Hickey said that in his view the board's acceptance of the academic senate's recommendation did not mean it accepted the proposition that dissent was appropriate.

With a few minutes before the lunch break, Weisberg asked whether the board was in effect saying it disagreed with the dissenting theologians but would defend their right to dissent. Hickey said that may have been the distinction made by the senate, but that it was not the one made by the board of trustees when it accepted the Marlowe report. After six hours of testimony over two days, Hickey was excused.

NINE

Two Sides to the Story

Like a master storyteller, Paul Saunders had prepared his witnesses to narrate the tale of Catholic University's tumultuous years in the late 1960s. The mood, characters, conflicts, and finally the changes in the institution itself would build Charles Curran's legal case: He had a contract, and it guaranteed academic freedom. Of the trial's fifteen witnesses, Saunders would call eight for the plaintiff, most of them eyewitnesses to the events in question. Stacked around the witness chair were several binders containing four hundred and sixty exhibits, used to look up the facts during testimony. The chronicling began Thursday afternoon, December 15, 1988. It would have been an unbroken sequence for Saunders except that two defense witnesses from out of town, a theologian and a cardinal, also had to be heard before Friday.

Saunders began by calling Nivard Scheel, who had been the acting rector of The Catholic University of America during the period of its bylaw changes. A member of the Xaverian religious order, Scheel had been assistant to the rector who took over after Bishop William McDonald was ousted. Scheel held the university's top post from September 1968 to July 1969 and was the last to be called rector; the bylaws changed the title to president. When the first lay president came in, Scheel served as vice-president for student affairs for the next decade. Prompted by fear of losing accreditation, Scheel said, the university set out to revamp its bylaws and governance in 1967. An American cardinal oversaw the process and the Vatican approved it, but the final outcome was, in effect, to free Catholic University from church control.

The bylaws were revised to put the university in "accordance with American law and to remove control of the Holy See," Scheel said. The trustees had been advised by lawyers that since the university charter did not provide for any church control, the bylaws requiring that were, at worst, unlawful. The process to change that, Scheel added, was given its own word at the time: "depontificalization." It made Catholic University an ordinary university but with pontifical schools. Scheel confirmed an exhibit presented by Saunders, a letter from a Middle States Association of Colleges and Schools official congratulating Catholic University on its "new freedom" since "the authorities in Rome have released their hold on the university."

Overlapping the history of the bylaw change was the 1968 dissent by Curran and others over *Humanae Vitae* and the university investigation that followed. An investigating faculty committee headed by Donald E. Marlowe, dean of the school of engineering and architecture, upheld the right of theology professors to dissent from church teaching without penalty. As acting rector, Scheel said, he understood the course of events to be conclusive evidence that academic freedom for theology professors "was the same as the academic freedom rights of any other professor at Catholic University." Those rights included, he said, "the freedom to teach and to write and to speak in their area of expertise as long as they spoke responsibly and wrote responsibly."

"Was it your understanding that there were any constraints, any ecclesiastical constraints on that academic freedom?" Saunders asked. "I knew of none, no, sir," Scheel said. The point implied was that both Curran and Scheel, as parties to Curran's contract, had agreed that the pact included academic freedom.

In related testimony later, Scheel defined tenure as a review process including a professor's department and school, the academic senate, and finally the trustees. "To me it is apparent because of the university-wide process that takes place that the person is tenured to the university and not to the department," he testified. Saunders hoped to prove that even were Curran legitimately disqualified from teaching in the department of theology, he still had the contractual rights to teach in some other department within his area of competence.

In an effort to show what the understanding of the parties was at the time the contract was entered into—something Saunders would do repeatedly—the lawyer asked Scheel what he would have done if the Ratzinger decree on Curran had landed on his desk back in 1969.

"Probably I would have felt I could not ignore it," he said. "At the same time, I would not feel that this directly could force me to implement something within the university itself." He said peer review would be his only course. "I would deal with someone in theology in exactly the same way I would deal with someone in history or chemistry or wherever." Curran would later testify that he had held the same view; a "meeting of minds," he called it.

Efforts by Cardinal Patrick O'Boyle of Washington and others to give the 1969 bylaws a means to uphold orthodoxy was discussed. In an effort to show that Curran's contract did not include such a control, Saunders offered a 1969 letter sent to O'Boyle by Cardinal Gabriel Garrone, prefect for Catholic education: To "protect the university from the danger of unorthodox teaching," the letter recommended that ecclesiastical faculty contracts make failure to uphold authentic Catholic doctrine "grounds for dismissal." Since that recommendation had not been followed, Saunders argued, it could not later be said that such a requirement was a part of the contract.

As an aside, Saunders and Kevin Baine told Judge Weisberg that to offer Garrone's letter into evidence Baine "broke into Cardinal O'Boyle's safe over the weekend" to obtain it. "No one has looked at those documents for probably twenty years," Baine said.

"Maybe we should call up Geraldo Rivera," the judge said, evoking laughter at the talk show host's dramatic, live foray two years ealier into a barren cellar of Al Capone's Chicago headquarters.

Saunders was quick: "He always comes up empty-handed."

IF SAUNDERS WANTED to tell the Catholic University story from a view favorable to Curran, then Baine, lawyer for the university, wanted to show the witness's vested interests. Scheel, for example, would not meet with the university's lawyers. Moreover, his affidavit submitted in opposition to the university's summary judgment motion had been written for him by Curran's lawyers.

Baine also set out to refute certain impressions Scheel had made in recounting university history. Contrary to Scheel's earlier statements, Baine pointed out, the board of trustees had been examining changes in the goals and structures of the university before the Curran strike of April 1967. Scheel acknowledged his error.

A pattern emerged in how Saunders and Baine would dispute the outcome of the historical events in question. Saunders, through his witnesses, would show that new bylaws, statutes, and understandings established university autonomy and academic freedom. Using the same events, Baine would show that with each victory for the autonomy lobby, the hierarchy or the Vatican had inserted a subtle condition that left an opening for later reestablishment of church authority.

So, for example, Baine produced another 1969 letter from Garrone showing that a Vatican concern over orthodoxy had led to a specific change in the special statutes for ecclesiastical schools. The new phrase said: "The rights and duties of the chancellor shall be in accordance with the norms and regulations of the Holy See." Baine recalled the events surrounding that change. "And Cardinal [Lawrence] Shehan [of Baltimore] explains at the [board] meeting that the reason those words were put in was to respond to Cardinal O'Boyle's concerns about safeguarding orthodoxy," Baine said. Scheel agreed, but when Saunders had the chance to question him again, he testified that the board had rejected O'Boyle's effort to insert a provision in the statutes that would have required orthodoxy in teaching. What remained in the canonical statutes, however, was the provision for the "right and duties" of the chancellor.

During Baine's second cross-examination he had tried to show that even Shehan, one of the more liberal bishops on the board, believed that there was a mechanism to enforce orthodoxy. At the crucial board meeting of 1969, Shehan had said, "The chancellor has the authority and the duty to judge orthodoxy and if he finds a professor lacking in orthodoxy he had the authority to withdraw from him the faculties of the archdiocese, including that of teaching." Saunders interjected, making the point that the "faculties of the archdiocese" had never been withdrawn for any professor, including Curran.

OUT OF ORDER, the defense called its second witness, James Burtchaell, a priest and theology professor at the University of Notre

Dame. Burtchaell had been chairman of his department of theology from 1968 to 1970 and provost of the university from 1970 to 1977. He was expected originally to testify on the question of academic freedom, but instead was led by the university's lawyers to focus on tenure rights. The direct examination was conducted by Baine's partner, Stephen Urbanczyk.

During the financial crisis among colleges in the early 1970s, Burtchaell had served on an American Association of Colleges committee that sought to find an equitable model to terminate professors, even those with tenure. That experience had formed his views. Tenure, he said, was continuous appointment until retirement or resignation. Academic appointment usually involves a contract, he said, but professors' contract terms can change even after tenure, such as when they are dissatisfied with the salary, have a leave of absence, or medical leave. Changes in bylaws or other academic guidelines, he said, can affect the rights of currently employed faculty members, according to the prevailing practice and custom. Changes or small adjustments in bylaws and academic guidelines were regular at most colleges, Burtchaell said. At Notre Dame, where he'd taught since 1966, there had been several modifications.

At the heart of Burtchaell's testimony was his view that the right of tenure did not include the right teach. This was an important point for the university to make. For it held that Curran's tenure rights had not been violated when the university prohibited him from teaching theology.

Urbanczyk, who would later cite the section on "general obligation" in the faculty handbook, continued: "Is teaching a right or obligation?"

"I suppose that many faculty haven't had the occasion to ask themselves that question, although almost all administrations have," Burtchaell said. "And those who do consider it for much length I would think would emerge regarding it as a duty to which one could be assigned."

In the Curran case, he observed, "I do not see anything that would have converted the obligation to accept assignments to teach into a right to demand assignments to teach." Department chairmen, after consultation with faculty and division heads, make teaching assignments that can then be up for review by higher authorities.

Faculty members can be assigned, Burtchaell said, by aptitude, by strengths in research, by the needs of a department, and even by loss of ability from age, poor health, or negligence. Catholic University's decision barring Curran from teaching certain courses "would be an unusual decision," he said. "But I don't understand that it would violate the rights conferred by academic appointment." Loss of teaching rights was not a severe sanction, Burtchaell said later, because professors have many other outlets.

Weisberg asked if a tenure appointment included academic freedom, and the priest said that was in the general understanding. Weisberg had thus put the question Urbanczyk was reluctant to ask, and the answer showed why: Academic freedom strongly implied the freedom to teach. Burtchaell, trying to save the situation, quickly added that tenure might include the right to academic freedom but it did not include the right to teach.

Hence, the basic guarantees of the contract were salary, benefits—and the right to parking, he said facetiously.

So, Weisberg posited, if Notre Dame told Burtchaell he could not teach anymore on campus but could keep those three guarantees, would that be a violation of his contract?

"My ego but not my contract," Burtchaell said.

IN CROSS-EXAMINATION Saunders probed that testimony almost immediately. He asked Burtchaell if his contract would be violated if his teaching were terminated because the Vatican disagreed with his views on, say, birth control.

Burtchaell said he was guaranteed academic freedom not by his contract but the academic articles of the school. Whether academic freedom was violated depended on what punitive action was taken, he said.

Saunders read from Catholic University's 1968 articles: "The university does not place any restraint upon the freedom of a member of the faculty in the conduct of his research or in the classroom or elsewhere."

Burtchaell agreed that the statement was a guarantee of academic freedom but said it was conditioned by what classes a professor was assigned to teach. Yet he agreed, "Once the faculty member is assigned to the class the faculty member is understood to have the freedom to state within his or her competence what seems best on the subject of the course."

Saunders again put the hypothetical question of the effect a Ratzinger-like declaration would have against a tenured faculty member like himself at Notre Dame. "I don't think that I would be protected against that decision by academic freedom," Burtchaell said.

"Let's assume," Saunders said, "that instead of completely removing you from the classroom the president imposed a slightly lesser sanction. He said, 'You can teach but you can't teach about birth control.' Does that affect your academic freedom rights?"

Burtchaell quibbled. He said the university had the right not to assign him to courses on a certain subject but added, "Once I were, however, assigned to a course the university would lose its freedom to control my operation within the course."

Weisberg wanted to know who controlled that right to decide what subject matter is properly part of a particular course.

"The chairman, by designating what the course name is generally," Burtchaell said. If, however, there would be a specific forbidden subject under the general course name, enforcing the taboo was a hard question, and Burtchaell said he had no obvious answer.

The day closed with a brief cross-examination by the students' lawyer.

IT WAS FRIDAY MORNING and everyone—lawyers, judge, plaintiffs, and witnesses—could feel the weekend coming. Two full days in court had been tiring. Some big-name witnesses were up that day, and the next eight hours promised absorbing testimony. They began with canon law professor, Monsignor Frederick McManus, whom Saunders called to the witness stand.

The opening subject was the nature and effect of the Marlowe report. As dean of the school of canon law in 1968, McManus had been one of five faculty members on the Marlowe committee. He kept a close eye on the statutory and canonical changes at Catholic University for the next two decades, as chairman of the 1979 self-study done for Middle States and as vice provost of graduate studies from 1974 to 1983. McManus said professors widely believed the process and outcome of the Marlowe report had confirmed their academic freedom and other rights.

Citing the American bishops' pastoral letter *Human Life in Our Day,* which contained norms of licit dissent and appeared to permit the kind of expression in which Curran engaged, McManus said that in his view professors at Catholic University were entitled to rely on those norms of conduct. Significantly, McManus said, the Marlowe committee's inquiry into the university's practices had led them to conclude that the canonical mission requirement of 1931 was dead. He referred in part to the Marlowe report's finding that certain parts of Catholic University's statutes "are patently incompatible with modern American university practice." There was no canonical mission requirement in *Normae Quaedam,* he added, and the reference to "mission" in the document simply meant to be in "full communion with the church." That meant "not excommunicated, not to have rejected those truths which we would hold to be of divine [origin] in the Catholic faith," McManus said. In his opinion, mission did not refer to a canonical mission.

Weisberg again got to the heart of the matter. He asked whether the faculty's opposition to the 1981 canonical statutes—with their requirement of a canonical mission—stemmed from their knowing that it gave Rome power to give and withdraw their license to teach? McManus said yes.

McManus said he was in a way responsible for the idea of an "implicit canonical mission," a view Cardinal Hickey had argued in his testimony. McManus said he had told Hickey that, having fallen into disuse, the canonical mission at most must have been given "implicitly" since he could find no evidence that it had ever been given outright.

Weisberg asked what would have happened if the Vatican declaration of 1986 had been sent to the chancellor in 1970. McManus said about the same thing would have happened. But he added that even a Ratzinger-type letter in 1970 would not have been sufficient to block Curran from teaching in nonecclesiastical faculties. His point was obvious: If at the time Curran received tenure—1970—a Ratzinger-type letter could not keep him from teaching, how could it do so in 1986?

Moreover, after the bylaw changes in 1969 the chancellor no longer had a juridical role in the ecclesiastical faculties of the university, McManus said. "To my knowledge there was no role left to the chancellor, with regard to the teaching in the nonecclesiastical faculty, such as the department of religion." This begged another obvious question: If the chancellor had no such role, how could he keep Curran from teaching in the nonecclesiastical faculties?

Returning from a brief recess—court transcribers had to be switched every hour and a half—McManus traced the history of what he called excessive church control over the university in the 1960s, leading to a "crisis of credibility" and Middle States's bad review in 1967.

"Some excesses on both sides in the sixties?" Weisberg asked, couching his remark in the form of a question.

Saunders moved on to questions about the 1981 canonical statutes, which imposed the canonical mission requirement. McManus had chaired the council of the ecclesiastical faculties which had drafted the statutes for the university based on *Sapientia Christiana*. That papal document's call for a canonical mission was perceived as reintroducing the requirement, and the theology faculty especially disputed its inclusion. Though McManus had taught at Catholic University since the 1950s, he said, "I never had anything like a canonical mission that was ever communicated to me."

Unlike Burtchaell, McManus believed tenure was meaningless without the right to teach. "It should be the principal thing, I suppose," he said. Even under the 1981 canonical statutes, he said, a professor who lost a canonical mission could still teach in a nonecclesiastical faculty. McManus said he believed that professors at the university did enjoy the right to academic freedom. "In fact, the university had gone through years of turmoil in order to get this recognized as strongly as they could," he said. Saunders had finished with his witness.

BAINE TOOK ON McManus's view of the canonical mission in his cross-examination. "You have maintained over the years, have you not, that the canonical mission was granted implicitly?" Baine asked.

"I would not say that I have maintained that," McManus said. "It was a notion that occurred to me or was presented to me in my early days at the university." The notion came up again when the canonical statutes were being drafted. "I don't want to say, however, that I was at all consistent over that whole period of time because it was not an issue for the most part." But when he used the "implicit" argument, McManus said, it was as a defensive position—"an explanation of why we did not have a formal canonical mission." And that is what he had told Hickey in 1980.

According to Baine, McManus had so far proffered several differing views on the canonical mission, but the point for trial was to show that McManus had at one time asserted that the mission was given "implicitly." When Baine asked about how canon law lapses, McManus was compelled to say, "I think I have probably given different explanations of it. Maybe some of them contradict me." Baine then established that a requirement for a canonical mission could not lose its force unless a contrary custom had developed over a period of thirty years—forty years under the new 1983 Code of Canon Law. He asked whether "from 1931 to 1968, at the very least it could be argued that as a matter of canon law the requirement was continuously in effect at Catholic University?"

McManus said it could be argued that way but added that it could also be argued that the requirement had lapsed in a particular case.

At that point the courtroom lights shut off.

"Do you take this as a sign?" the judge asked.

"I'm waiting for the next sign," Baine said.

"Should I withdraw my offer of proof?" Saunders joked, suggesting that God had intervened on behalf of the defense.

Weisberg said electrical work was being done in the building. "As far as I'm concerned we can continue in the darkness. Maybe it will bring us into light."

Baine cited *Normae Quaedam,* the temporary Vatican norms, which included a paragraph stating that religion professors do not teach "in their own names" but "in virtue of the mission which they have received from the magisterium." Was this not, he suggested, a reference to a canonical mission requirement?

McManus disagreed, saying, "The absence of the word canonical there has significance."

Moving to the Marlowe report, Baine asked McManus if it was not common knowledge that the board of trustees had not fully supported the findings of the Marlowe committee. "We realized there were many things in there by way of recommendations that the board of trustees would be unlikely to embrace," McManus said.

Then Baine set out to establish that McManus himself had disagreed with the Ratzinger declaration. He pointed out that during the 1987 faculty hearings, McManus had said the committee should inquire into the merits and correctness of the conclusions Ratzinger had reached, a sort of challenge to the Holy See that the committee judged was inappropriate. Asked if he thought Ratzinger's finding was erroneous, McManus responded: "The statement of Cardinal Ratzinger was inadequate at the least."

Weisberg tried to pin down McManus on what the faculty committee and board would have done if they had decided, in contradiction to Ratzinger, that Curran was eligible and suitable to teach theology. McManus's answer meandered, but basically suggested the university would not have sent a defiant response back to the Vatican. But on the other hand, he said, "They would not have taken the action of withdrawing the canonical mission." He said his response could be taken only as speculation.

On the question of tenure to the department as opposed to the university, Baine established that in fact there was no precedent for moving a faculty member to another department when he was ruled ineligible in his former post. All previous cases had stemmed from financial exigencies and department closings.

They turned next to questions of academic freedom in the discipline of theology, and McManus agreed that academic freedom was not an absolute, conceding that fidelity to the magisterium was "an element that enters into competence."

"The Holy See in this case has determined that Father Curran is lacking in the requisite fidelity to the magisterium, right?" Baine asked.

"I don't think that is the precise language that was quoted but I think that is a fair statement," McManus said.

Baine ended his cross-examination, and Saunders began his second examination on the last point. He emphasized that peers at a university determine competence, not the magisterium. In conclusion, Saunders elicited testimony that the canonical statutes were also civil in nature; Baine countered by getting McManus to agree that the canonical statutes had to be approved by the Holy See's Congregation for Catholic Education. Once again, two different ways of looking at the same thing.

CARDINAL JOSEPH BERNARDIN had expected to testify and catch a 4 o'clock plane back to Chicago, but he rescheduled for 5 P.M. As he took the stand, both lawyers promised to finish in twenty minutes. Bernardin had become ensnared in the Curran affair because he was the chairman of the university's board of trustees. The Vatican's ruling had come down one year into his three-year term. Twenty-two years a bishop, he had seen his share of controversy but had never before been cross-examined in court.

Bernardin began by saying the trustees had the ultimate governing authority at the university, not the academic senate. Baine asked him about the board's treatment of a June 26, 1969, academic senate resolution upholding the right to academic freedom. Bernardin responded that the statement had never been approved by the board, which alone had the authority to make binding statements on the subject of academic freedom. In fact, he said, while the bylaws of the university made general reference to academic freedom, the board had never accepted a statement defining just what academic freedom was. This was grist for the news media, and that testimony was featured in the next day's *Washington Post* headlines: "Cardinal Denies Academic Freedom at CU."

The great metaphysical question with which Hickey had grappled at length was put to Bernardin: In terms of academic freedom and autonomy, how is the Vatican not external to the university? Citing the Vatican's theological concerns, Bernardin said the actions toward Curran were neither arbitrary nor extrinsic—two conditions the academic senate warned against. "I would not see this as being an extrinsic relationship but rather an intrinsic relationship," he said. The actions were not arbitrary, he explained, because they were built on several years of investigation.

Bernardin reviewed the history of his involvement: meetings with Curran since 1985, the final efforts to find a compromise teaching post in early 1988, the board's resolution revoking Curran's canonical mission, and finally its June 2 resolution barring him from teaching theology in any of the nonecclesiastical faculties. That last action, Bernardin said, was the result of Curran's intransigence. Baine then sought to establish that as a priest, Curran had a special obligation to obey the Ratzinger declaration. Professors are bound by the faculty handbook, Bernardin said. But another binding aspect is the priesthood. "We make a priestly commitment," he said. "It's part of the . . . contractual relationship affecting the cleric—the cleric on the faculty of the university."

Baine put emphasis on that. "Although Catholics have such a responsibility, priests have a special relationship of reverence and obedience to the pope?" he asked.

"Yes. I think that is clear," Bernardin said.

After Bernardin explained how the university's papal charter made it impossible to ignore the Vatican ruling, Baine asked what would have happened if the board of trustees had rejected the Vatican declaration. "I would find it difficult to imagine a board like this, especially since it consists of a number of cardinals, archbishops, and bishops," Bernardin answered. To reject the declaration would have disturbed many people. "There might have been some who would have applauded it but I think a greater number of the people would have been scandalized by this," he said. Admitting his speculation, Bernardin said that such an action would have put the school's relationship with the Holy See in jeopardy.

"If you want to look at the worst possible scenario, since it's a school that has been chartered by the Holy See, if we were to directly defy the Holy See there was always the possibility that that charter would be removed, withdrawn," Bernardin said.

Saunders began cross-examination by exploiting a problem with logic in Bernardin's testimony. If the board had not defined the right of academic freedom, he asked, how would a faculty member find out what his right consisted of? Where would he go? Bernardin sat mute for a long time. But then he referred to the authority of the board on the matter of academic freedom, a topic mentioned in university documents but not officially defined. For Saunders, this exchange showed that the right was illusory; only the board could say what it meant but it had never done so. Bernardin added, "I don't think that it's totally unlimited. I think a great deal depends on the particular field that you're concerned about and in this instance we are dealing with the field of theology, which has its own canons, its own norms." He said Catholic theology cannot be totally divorced from the church's teaching and its teaching authority, a connection that "would have to be taken into account, even though it may not be spelled out in a particular document."

"Sounds to me, the way you've described those, Cardinal Bernardin, as if they impose more of an obligation than define a right," Saunders said.

"Well, with every right I guess comes an obligation," Bernardin said. "I think that the very nature of the theological enterprise is that you have to have a certain amount of freedom to explore, to develop, to refine. But at the same time we're talking about . . . revealed truth" preserved by the magisterium. "Maybe it can be looked on as an obligation but I see it as something that I freely subscribe to as a member of the church."

Weisberg had a question. If the board was required to withdraw the canonical mission under canon law, what required the board to bar Curran from teaching Catholic theology on a nonecclesiastical faculty? Was it the special relationship and religious conviction? The question foreshadowed Weisberg's final opinion.

Bernardin said there was a canonical aspect to the issue because the university was a juridical person chartered by the Vatican, but that the religious loyalty also played a part.

Saunders asked whether the Ratzinger declaration was self-executing or not, implying that if it was not, the board was not required to enforce it. Bernardin said the board had to act on it; theoretically, however, it could have defied the Vatican. "A negative decision on our part would have had severe consequences in terms of the Catholic community, also in terms of the status of the university," he said.

"Then in what sense did you have the freedom not to implement it?" Saunders asked.

"Well, you can just say no but then you have to take the consequences," Bernardin said.

"Civil disobedience," Weisberg remarked.

"Canonical disobedience," Baine said.

"In other words," Bernardin said, "I feel I have an obligation to obey civil laws. If I decide that I'm not going to, then I put myself in jeopardy. I may end up here [in court] again."

To illustrate the authority church officials were trying to exert over Curran, Saunders began a line of questioning. He reminded Bernardin that Curran had been asked to sign a statement accepting the Vatican ruling as a condition for him to teach. The cardinal said it was only a draft statement, and that it was not required finally in the negotiations—a point contrary to Baine's letter to Curran's lawyers. Saunders then asked if any claim had been made that Curran had disobeyed his direct superior, Bishop Matthew Clark of Rochester. Bernardin said he was not aware of any.

"I will say, your honor, we have made no claim that Father Curran has disobeyed Bishop Clark," Baine said.

"Isn't it correct that you and Cardinal Hickey tried to persuade Bishop Clark to recall professor Curran to the Rochester diocese because of the Ratzinger letter and that Bishop Clark refused?" Saunders asked.

Baine objected, disputing the relevance of the question. Weisberg sustained the objection, noting that because Bernardin agreed that Curran had several authorities he was accountable to besides the bishop, the question was moot. Any priest hired by a university must have his bishop's approval, and in turn, the bishop can recall him, Bernardin explained. "But once a cleric becomes a member of the faculty of this [Catholic] university, then there are other superiors that have to be taken into account as well."

Saunders believed that Bernardin and Hickey disagreed about the nature of an alternative teaching post for Curran, and he produced a letter exchanged between the two cardinals to make his point. Pundits, the news media, and church-watchers had always labeled Bernardin the liberal and Hickey the conservative. Now Saunders suggested that on the teaching matter Hickey was strict and Bernardin lenient, even to the point that Curran could have accepted Bernardin's offer. The letter showed, Saunders said, that Bernardin had told Hickey that in his view Curran could teach ethics—with the flavor of theology—and still abide by the Vatican declaration.

"Isn't that exactly what Professor Curran told Father Byron [Catholic University's president] he was willing to do?" Saunders asked.

"No," Bernardin said. Contrary to his testimony a few minutes earlier—that Curran was not required to take a loyalty oath—Bernardin said that Curran asserted "that he could not or would not accept that declaration, that he was a professor of Catholic moral theology and what he would teach would be moral theology. When it's put that way it gives you no room to negotiate." While Bernardin viewed the so-called loyalty oath as an informality, for Curran it had been a line drawn in the dirt; a line he would not cross.

SAUNDERS CALLED THE final witness for that Friday, a leading American theologian. Richard McBrien, a specialist in theology and ecclesiology, was chairman of the University of Notre Dame's department of theology and widely known among American Catholics through his popular two-volume textbook, *Catholicism*. Like the erudite Protestant scholar Martin Marty, who commented on American religion from the University of Chicago, McBrien was the plain-spoken Catholic scholar most called upon by the secular media and liberal Catholic press to make statements on disputes of the day.

Do you agree, Saunders asked, with the proposition that an intrinsic relationship exists between the discipline of theology and the church's teachings?

"Yes, but it depends on how you understand the key word there—church," McBrien said. "Church means the whole community." The hierarchy, which is not the only source of teaching authority, makes "judgments about theology insofar as they see it having an effect on the pastoral life of the church. But it's my judgment that that doesn't enter into the academic sector."

Consequently, he said he did not see respect for the magisterium as a limit on academic freedom. "It's one of the considerations you have to take into account but there's much more to the discipline of theology than that," he said. "In academic freedom the real judgment is always ultimately a peer judgment."

In an effort to respond to the university's argument that Ratzinger's judgment on Curran's competence amounted to a "peer judgment" and thus did not violate academic freedom, Saunders asked if the magisterium, or Ratzinger's office, could not be considered "super-peers" in this case? No, McBrien said, "It is essentially a nonacademic, external act."

Saunders asked whether a letter to him from Ratzinger would have a negative impact his teaching ability. "None whatsoever," McBrien said. The president of Notre Dame "would be bound by the laws of the state of Indiana, the laws of incorporation, and by all the statutes of the university. It wouldn't permit that sort of intervention." Research, teaching, and communication are "the three fruits of academic freedom," McBrien said. "If I were told I could publish whatever I wanted, that I could do all the research I wanted but I can't teach in this classroom, that's a violation of academic freedom because my profession is to teach."

Recalling that Burtchaell, his colleague at Notre Dame, had said loss of teaching rights would not violate academic freedom, Saunders asked McBrien whether academic freedom be would violated if, say, Burtchaell was prohibited from teaching because of the substance of his speech. McBrien said yes.

"You'll be pleased to learn that all he cares about is his parking space," Weisberg interjected humorously.

"As far as I know he doesn't own a car," McBrien responded.

As Saunders closed his questioning, Philip Malet, lawyer for the five graduate students who had intervened in the lawsuit, asked about the reputation of Catholic University and its theology department. McBrien said both used to be held in very high opinion in the academic community.

"What's the reputation today of that department?" Malet asked.

"I think sadly it's much lower than it was. I mean, frankly, it's a bad reputation . . . obviously the whole episode surrounding Father Curran's case is the principal cause. It's not the only cause." He cited other disputes at Catholic University in recent years, saying the common element was that academics appeared in hearings before nonacademic church officials. "Those things are known generally, so it isn't just the Curran case."

Baine knew that McBrien had conceded things in his writings that he had not in his testimony, and he set out to show that in cross-examination. But first he asked: "You're a friend of Father Curran's?" He cited McBrien's support for Curran in statements and letters. Then he produced articles by McBrien that appeared to support the Vatican's right to make judgments on theologians.

Item: An article in *America,* the Jesuit weekly. "One might have to concede that the terms of Father Curran's contract at CUA left him exposed to removal of his canonical commission to teach within the ecclesiastical, Vatican-chartered faculty of theology," McBrien had written. Yes, McBrien said, the Vatican "has a right to intervene but not as the sole intervener."

Item: A June 1986 article by McBrien in *The Tablet* of London. "Whatever the outcome of this case, Father Curran will continue to enjoy the full protection of American law to teach, to write and to lecture, that is except in a theology department of a Catholic seminary, college or university."

Item: Another *America* article. "It is true in principle that the academic freedom of the Catholic theologian is limited by revelation and the teaching authority of the church," McBrien had written.

Now Baine went on the offensive. McBrien had testified that only a peer judgment of incompetence could be the basis for restricting a professor's right to teach. Baine attacked that proposition by posing a hypothetical question. Is it true, he asked, that a Catholic theologian who denies that Christ is present in the Eucharist forfeits his right to be called a Catholic theologian? Yes, McBrien said. That's not because he's incompetent, Baine continued, "It's because what he's proclaiming is heresy, isn't it?"

"Not necessarily," McBrien said. "Heresy is a technical term," he said, that might not apply here.

Baine persisted: "If a professor at Notre Dame denied the real presence of Christ in the Eucharist, would you permit him to teach a course in Catholic theology that covered the subject?"

"I can't answer that question yes or no because I'd have to find out what in fact his position is and how he or she arrived at it," McBrien said. There may come a time, he conceded, when a person in the academy is ruled ineligible to teach Catholic theology based on the substance of his views.

"One can teach Catholic theology competently and deny the presence of Christ in the Eucharist, deny the Sacraments, deny the Ten Commandments and deny the divinity of Christ?" Baine asked.

"I wouldn't call that Catholic theology, no," McBrien said.

"Couldn't one quite competently and in a scholarly fashion arrive at some of those conclusions?" Baine asked. McBrien said yes. Baine thought he had made his point: Although a professor who took those positions might well be competent, he would nevertheless be regarded as ineligible to teach Catholic theology.

Believing that McBrien's testimony helped the university more than Curran, Baine concluded his cross-examination, and the day, with one more shot. Item: Another McBrien article in *America*. "Most, if not all, would acknowledge that there are reasonable limitations on academic freedom in church-related institutions but acknowledging that is the easy part. The hard part is applying those limitations."

TEN

Four Witnesses

The system of canon law, set in place by the church in 1300, expanded over the centuries into every aspect of Catholic life. Its domain included The Catholic University of America, making the trial more than a simple contract dispute, according to Kevin Baine. That is what he had told Judge Weisberg as the trial opened, and Monday morning it became a contested issue again.

From the outset, Weisberg tried to steer clear of any interpretation of church law, though it invariably cropped up in testimony. Paul Saunders and Baine had sparred on the subject a few times already. Baine argued that Cardinal James A. Hickey and the board of trustees had the sole authority to interpret the 1981 canonical statutes. These, he said, were part of the canon law of the church. In fact, he argued that the question of whether Hickey and the board were the proper interpreters of the statutes under canon law was strictly a matter of canon law into which the court could not inquire. Accordingly, when Hickey said he was the proper interpreter, stating his interpretation, that was the end of the matter, Baine suggested. For the court to question that interpretation would be improper.

Saunders argued that whether the 1981 statutes were or were not canon law was irrelevant; they were also the civil bylaws of a civil corporation—the university—and as such the court must interpret them. Even if that were not so, he added, the court could not accept without question Hickey's statement that under canon law he was the proper interpreter simply because he "got to the microphone first." Through the testimony of canon law professor Frederick McManus, Saunders established that Hickey was not the "authentic legislator" of canon law, and so, in McManus's words, "He's certainly not the authentic interpreter." At first, Weisberg was reluctant to allow this testimony. He discouraged having witnesses testify on what canon law was. He painted a verbal picture of what would happen if he allowed such testimony, putting the words in Saunders's mouth: "The defendants can call their canon law expert on that issue and we will call our canon law expert on that issue and you, Judge Weisberg, decide who is right about that." And that, Weisberg said, the court could not do, "by the dictates of the First Amendment and about one hundred twenty years of Supreme Court jurisprudence."

Saunders's claim that canon law was irrelevant prodded Weisberg to make his most vivid analogy of the trial. He asked Saunders, by illustration, why he could not accept that the university felt compelled to act under the weight of canon law. If persons A and B have a contract with each other, Weisberg said, but B has to breach it because C has a gun to B's head, how would it be argued in court? Saunders was arguing that "all we're saying is that you had an obligation to us and you didn't perform it," Weisberg said. "Don't you think B is entitled to rely on the fact that . . . B could show that the gun was at B's head and that you can't claim otherwise? And if my analogy is worth anything at all you are now saying, well, it was a toy gun."

But Weisberg was clearly troubled about this debate. He ultimately agreed to allow testimony on the question of whether Hickey was the proper interpreter. As court opened on the fourth day, Weisberg wanted additional clarification about the canon law issue, something brought to mind by the testimony of Cardinal Joseph Bernardin, past chairman of the trustees. "I have a less clear understanding of what it is in canon law that required the decision that Professor Curran could not teach Catholic theology on a nonecclesiastical faculty without a canonical mission," he said.

"I believe that to be an important question in this case," he said. It was important for the defendants and thus they didn't want it examined in court, Weisberg added. But if the special relationship to the Holy See is the only determining factor, he said, then the university would say that was sufficient to justify its action toward Curran—but then it would also be liable for any contract it breaks.

The judge noted that usually when a question of canon law arose the defense drew a line. "You take the position that those words are like a shibboleth, and once they're said that's the end of my right to inquire into it," he said. That was okay, the judge said, but he still did not understand what in canon law obligated Hickey and the board of trustees to follow the Vatican declaration.

"Canon law is a whole structure," Baine said. Its objects were juridic persons, such as Catholic University, which had obligations according to their nature. Those obligations were binding because the church is hierarchical. The result, he concluded, was, "When the higher authorities of the church make a judgment . . . lesser authority is bound to the judgment and cannot say we reject it."

That made the university, then, like a "baptized Catholic," Weisberg offered, and Baine agreed, elaborating on the obligation of a faithful church member.

Saunders rejected that, offering to produce evidence that by canon law the Ratzinger letter was not binding on the university or its board. "It was not addressed to the board of trustees, it was not addressed to the university," he said. He also doubted whether the board of trustees at Catholic University, a civilly incorporated entity, was a juridic person. "We say that is not correct as a matter of canon law," Saunders said. Saunders said religious conviction and civil law were not always coextensive, as court rulings against polygamy—a religious conviction of the early Mormons—prove. Appeal to religious conviction and canon law did not earn immunity from all judicial scrutiny, he said. There is a civil dimension to every aspect of the university and its contracts, Saunders said. And cries of "canon law" should not "insulate an action that has civil, legal significance."

Indeed, it was a hard issue, Saunders noted. But Baine disagreed, holding firm that pretrial rulings had excluded the topic, which Saunders denied. Saunders said that his position throughout had been that whatever the board felt it was compelled to do as it perceived canon law, the issue at trial was the contract and the obligations to Curran under it. Canon law, he said, was irrelevant. But, he added, Baine had raised the canon law defense through Hickey's testimony. "I'm still entitled to deal with that defense as it is presented on the merits," Saunders said. Baine, in a final word on the matter, said the defense had been consistent in arguments, not "shifting and evolving" as Saunders had suggested.

Weisberg finally decided that it did not matter what the parties had or had not agreed to because he was not going to let Saunders try to prove that Hickey's interpretation of canon law was wrong. "So I think we're back to first base," Weisberg said. Next witness, he said.

A PRIEST AND LONGTIME theology professor, Carl Peter of Catholic University was the first of four witnesses to be called in the next two days. Baine called him for the defense. A former chairman of the theology department, Peter also had been dean of the school of religious studies for eight years, a period covering the Vatican's investigation of Curran's writings. What was more, he was one of two American theologians on the thirty-member International Theological Commission; Curran's successor in teaching sexual ethics at the university, William May, was the other.

Peter had defended Curran in 1967 when the trustees attempted to fire the moral theologian, joining the campus strike to reverse their decision. "First of all I thought he had been treated unfairly in terms of not being given due notice," he said. "And secondly, I thought what he had said up to that point didn't warrant any such action." The next year, he had defended the right to dissent from noninfallible teachings but had not joined the public protest of *Humanae Vitae*. In his testimony, Peter said he understood that he had a canonical mission and believed that statutes adopted after his tenure applied to him. "The university is an institution that is alive, and to stay alive it has got to change," he said. The alternative would be for every professor to be treated differently, an impossible situation that would "atomize the institution," he said.

Peter had helped draft the canonical statutes of 1981 that required teachers in the department of theology to have a canonical mission. And since both civil and ecclesiastical degree students sat in the same courses, the faculty was unitary, he said. He went on to give a traditional definition of academic freedom but said there were limits. "Freedom exists in a context and freedom exists with regard to a discipline." The canonical statutes implied, he said, "mutual restraints, restraint on the part of trustees and on the part of faculty."

Baine quoted from a document of the church's International Theological Commission that said some theologians had "an exaggerated esteem" for academic freedom. "Modern sentiments in favor of democracy sometimes give rise to a tendency to close ranks against the magisterium when it intervenes to prevent some harm to faith or morals," the document said. Peter agreed. Respect for the magisterium "means fair and objective exposition of the teaching," the professor said. "It is quite compatible with critical analysis of that teaching. And I think in certain circumstances it is compatible with dissent from the teaching." The range of respect, he said, extended from absolute assent to key beliefs and a general "religious submission of intellect and will" to others. Baine then implied that in this area Curran had been ruled wanting and thus ineligible to teach Catholic theology.

Theologians disciplined in the past had mixed records, Peter said. Some had obeyed, some had not, some had been treated unfairly and others had left the church. In the Curran case, he had argued that the Vatican declaration constituted a "most serious reason" to withdraw the canonical mission. Curran's academic freedom was not violated, Peter had reasoned, if he could continue to teach in an area of his competence.

"Does academic freedom require that the board of trustees follow the judgment of peers?" Baine asked. No, Peter said, "They are not rubber stamps." The board can certainly disagree, he said, "because I think at times peers are very reluctant to criticize peers."

JUANITA CROWLEY, a lawyer from Wilmer Cutler & Pickering, the Washington law firm assisting Saunders, rose to cross-examine Peter and, in a typical tactic, tried to impeach his testimony. She established that when he was chairman, Peter had not advised members of the theology department that they needed a canonical mission, nor had he thought he himself had one until 1980. The theology department was not unitary because it drafted its own statutes separating ecclesiastical and civil faculties, she argued, citing the minutes of a particular department meeting. On academic freedom, she asked if its limits were the same at Catholic University and at Notre Dame. Peter said yes. "Is the nature of that limit a subject of debate among theologians?" she asked. Peter did not disagree with her implication that it was. From Baine's point of view that did not hurt the university's case; one of its key arguments was that, indeed, there were several views and therefore Catholic University had the right to chose its own.

Using the secular context of a Harvard or the University of Chicago, a common motif of the plaintiff's lawyers, Crowley asked if Curran would have lost a job teaching at either of those schools just because he been ruled unfaithful to the magisterium. Peter said he did not know what would happen but supposed the nature of Catholic University had led to the outcome at hand. "We as professors of Catholic theology have to exercise a restraint that might not be called for elsewhere because of the nature of the institution," he said. Under Crowley's aggressive questioning, Peter, who was trying to qualify his answers, nevertheless agreed with certain of her statements: Peer review was important in the Curran case; denial of teaching in the area of one's competence wrecks academic freedom; not all church laws are retroactive. "Are you going to dispute whether there is a core understanding of academic freedom?" she asked. "No, I don't think we are going to dispute that, but we are going to dispute its implications. The core understanding can lead to different conclusions," Peter said.

Philip Malet, lawyer for the five intervening students, queried Peter on whether both civil and ecclesiastical degree students, who shared the same teachers, were bound by the same requirements and policies. Peter made a distinction between faculty members, who he said were bound by the canonical statutes, and students, who had only academic requirements. He said there were limits on student rights, however, and that the burden of proof was on them in a complaint. Malet asked whether Peter knew that Curran had been offered a teaching post, but only if certain students did not take the course. Peter said he had heard something about that, but his thoughts turned to the theology department, and he made a comment. "If they have taken away the canonical mission for ecclesiastical students and he's not going to be able to teach civil students, then who would he have taught in the department of theology?" Peter asked rhetorically.

"Good question," Malet said. "I will end there."

Baine's redirect was brief, asserting that Curran had received his peer review in the faculty hearing, which then had been subject to board review. "The operative norm is the decision by the board of trustees," Peter agreed. "They decided that they would accept the letter. There were other courses of action open to them. I maintain they decided freely." On that basis, he said, the board had decided ethics was a subject in Curran's competence, although Curran did not agree it was different from Catholic theology. Crowley returned to point out that Curran had not accepted the offer to teach ethics as it was defined.

SINCE 1952, WHEN he began teaching physics at Catholic University, James Brennan had been one of the most active lay professors in the cause of academic freedom. He had supported Curran to the hilt, and Saunders called him to explain why. His view came from considerable inside experience: Chairman of the physics department from 1962 to 1975; associate dean of arts and sciences for the next three years; member of the academic senate and once its chairman. He and Peter had been the first two faculty members elected to the board of trustees after the bylaw changes in 1968.

For telling the dramatic story of Catholic University in the late 1960s, Brennan was the witness par excellence. He had been on the faculty team that had collected the complaints against Bishop William McDonald, the university's last clerical "rector." He had heard the urgings of Cardinal Patrick O'Boyle in closed meetings on how to handle dissenting professors. He had sat in on the vote to promote Curran and had seen the faculty reaction when the board rejected it. "This was clearly another violation of academic freedom, and a gross one at that," Brennan said. All this he told in blow-by-blow detail.

Brennan said the issue of academic freedom underlay all the discussions between the faculty and the board's survey committee, which finally had led to the statement of aims adopted in July 1968. The statement's assertion, "The only constraint upon truth is truth itself," had been hotly debated between faculty and hierarchy, but its adoption, in his view, had established the university's commitment to academic freedom and peer review. The statement had passed even though some faculty and board members had thought it ignored the role of the magisterium.

Perhaps for the first time in a public forum, Brennan recounted the 1968 board of trustees meeting, held at the plush Madison Hotel in downtown Washington, at which Cardinal O'Boyle had held forth against the professors who dissented against *Humanae Vitae.* A letter, written in Italian, had arrived from the Vatican's secretary of state, Cardinal Amleto Cicognani, commending O'Boyle's disciplining of his own rebellious diocesan priests and implying the compliment had papal origins. As Brennan recalled, the letter had implied that O'Boyle should do the same with the twenty dissenting theologians at Catholic University. But the letter, which Baine produced for the court, in fact had counseled restraint.

Cardinal James McIntyre of Los Angeles had made a motion at the Madison Hotel meeting to fire the Catholic University twenty, and O'Boyle had shown his concurrence dramatically, Brennan said. "In fact, I remember Cardinal O'Boyle throwing the letter down, saying, 'It's been two weeks, I move we fire them all.'" Saunders had asked the university to produce the letter. Baine said he had looked for it but would look again.

As interesting as the narrative was, Judge Weisberg, the ultimate timekeeper, asked Saunders to move on quickly. The history showed, Saunders said, that in 1968 a letter very much like the Ratzinger letter to Curran in 1986 had been received. The judge was not convinced the two letters were alike, as he would say later when he saw them, but Saunders argued that their implication was great: Despite Cicognani's letter to O'Boyle, neither the cardinal nor the board of trustees felt compelled, or bound by canon law, to dismiss the professors or withdraw their canonical missions.

On the contrary, Saunders said, the university's Marlowe committee had produced a report defending the professors' right to dissent. "The faculty considered this to be a great victory for academic freedom," Brennan said. By limning this testimony, Saunders wished to show that the university's claim that canon law had compelled its actions against Curran was inconsistent with its view toward the dissenting professors in 1968. Curran had been given tenure shortly after the 1968 protest.

When the apostolic constitution *Sapientia Christiana* came out in 1979, a new debate arose in the academic senate on whether this would lead to a rollback of academic freedom, Brennan said. He said he believed that whatever Rome may have thought, the document could not alter the essence of peer review and the university's commitment to academic freedom.

Saunders asked if tenure was to the university, the department, or both. The university, Brennan answered, using his physics teaching position as an example. By implication Curran was tenured to the university, not just the department from which Hickey had barred him. Curran's annual appointment letter, in fact, showed that in his last year, during the dispute, he had been appointed to the school of religious studies, not the department of theology from which he was finally suspended.

For Baine, Brennan was probably one of the least neutral professors on campus. More than a year before, he had successfully protested Brennan's being on the faculty committee that heard the Curran case. In cross-examination he produced a letter Brennan had written saying the faculty "deplore the action taken against our colleague."

Baine explored the norms that govern physics and theology, illustrating the difference. "You certainly don't profess to be an expert on what the norms of the discipline of theology are, do you?" he asked. Brennan said no.

Baine proceeded to argue, by showing documents and the minutes of board meetings, that Brennan's recollection of the events of the late 1960s, like Nivard Scheel's, was somewhat selective and one-sided. The laudable victories won for academic freedom in the statement of aims, bylaws, and statutes, he said, were always amended or nuanced with some condition of church authority through the chancellor before Vatican approval was given.

On the Marlowe report, Baine said the board of trustees had not accepted it entirely and in a resolution receiving it had also upheld church authority. Although the board had adopted the Marlowe report insofar as it dealt with academic propriety of the conduct of dissenting professors, the adopting resolution said: "In accord with the usual academic practices and the statutes of the university, the faculty in its teaching of doctrine continues to be subject to the teaching authority of the church with specific recognition of the supreme teaching authority of the Holy See." Brennan said there indeed had been a tension, when he was a faculty representative to the board, regarding the obligations of professors teaching sacred sciences.

In a brief return, Saunders reaffirmed Brennan's testimony that the board's acceptance of the Marlowe report indicated its support of academic freedom, the essential element at issue for Curran.

A SLIGHT CONFLICT over the order of witnesses arose, as Saunders wanted to call his next subject to keep the testimony on a roll. Baine, however, thought he had been promised the next slot for a witness who had delayed going out of town and was sitting outside the courtroom. Saunders gracefully relented, backed by Weisberg's assurances that he would not lose the sequence if the plaintiff's witness took the stand the next day.

Baine called Benedict Ashley, a professor of theology in the John Paul Institute for Studies in Marriage and the Family, a Washington D.C. branch of the Lateran University in Rome. He previously had been with the St. Louis University-related Klienman Institute of Theology and was professor of philosophy at the Aquinas Institute, where he had been president from 1962 to 1969. What was more, as a full professor in theology he believed he had been given a canonical mission, even though he had received no documents. "That was a common understanding," he testified later.

But Saunders requested a voir dire—a verbal examination—to challenge Ashley's expertise. He showed that Ashley's current and past positions had been with Catholic institutes, which were different from accredited colleges or universities, institutions with which he had never been affiliated. "I don't think this witness is relevant to give any testimony on relevant issues in this case," Saunders said.

Naturally, Baine argued that Ashley was a man with degrees comparable to those given at ecclesiastical departments, that his schools underwent civil accreditation, and that Ashley was familiar with the principles of academic freedom as it pertained to Catholic moral theology. Weisberg, who said he could use more substance on the differing views of academic freedom in the dispute, allowed Baine to proceed.

Ashley said he was familiar with the university accreditation process in general because North Central Association of Colleges and Schools, like Middle States one of the nation's six regional accrediting agencies, had reviewed and accredited the Aquinas Institute. He also had been involved in investigations for the Association of Theological Schools. Ashley said there was no difference between the accrediting standards required at theological schools and at universities. Theological schools, he asserted, enjoyed academic freedom. "I even remember a case when I was president of Aquinas in which we had an actual dispute with the local bishop," he said. "I was in the position of defending the rights of the faculty against a lack of due process. So I am acquainted with some of these problems."

Academic freedom, Ashley said, "is not simply freedom of speech." A professor is bound by the norms of his field. "The limits, if you want to call them that, are simply that he must exercise his teaching responsibilities and his publications according to the standard of the discipline." Theology operates within the teaching of the church, making it different from science or the humanities, he said. "It is a truth which is a truth of faith rather than a truth of science," he said, and its study, especially in ecclesiastical schools, is to train persons to serve the church.

Dissent can have several meanings: If it means the right to criticize and analyze and even to propose changes, "That's in no way out of the competency of the theologian," Ashley said. "If 'dissent' on the other hand means that theology attempts to take the role of the bishops of the church and assumes the authority of the bishops, then there is definitely a conflict between the theologian and the church."

Referring to the university's decision to implement the Holy See's declaration, Baine asked if, in his opinion, it violated academic freedom.

"It does not," Ashley said.

He explained: "It is necessary that the scientist respect the data that is proper in his field which happens to be the empirical facts that he deals with. In theology it is necessary that the theologian respect the data of his field and the data in this case are the teachings of the Catholic Church." Because schools for this discipline are created to serve a specific need in the church, "The church has a real interest and concern about this," he added. "This should be understood by the theological faculty itself if it is to call itself Catholic."

Ideally, peers would deal with a theologian who has strayed, Ashley said. But if they do not act or their action is not sufficient, he said, "Then I think the interests of the church come into play and I think that's what happened in this case."

Saunders, in cross-examination, referred to Ashley's testimony that there was academic freedom at the John Paul II Institute. What would he do if a superior challenged his writings? Saunders asked.

What if, for example, Cardinal Hickey wrote a letter telling him to stop writing about a certain subject?

"There would have to be due process," Ashley said. But that would have to include the local ordinary, he added. "My peers would have to make a judgment on that matter, but the final say on that question would belong to the church," he said.

Saunders asked who inside the academy decided when a professor had crossed the line in his dissent from the magisterium, and he used the teaching of Catholic theology at Harvard as an example. Individual professors drew the line, Ashley said. Saunders asked about professor Frances S. Fiorenza, a lay theologian who had left Catholic University to teach Catholic theology at Harvard. Would the Vatican declaration have any effect on Fiorenza's rights to teach at Harvard? Saunders asked.

Whether at a Catholic or a secular institution, Ashley said, the Vatican letter would simply strip a professor of the title Catholic theologian and inform the public of his standing in the eyes of the church. The juridical effect, Ashley said, would depend on the institution. "If he's teaching at a school which claims to have Catholic sponsorship, then I think it would make a difference," he said. "If it's simply a secular institute which is in no way representative of the church, I think it would be a different matter." Again, by implication, Saunders was trying to show that there was a difference between the ecclesiastical and nonecclesiastical faculties and that disqualifying Curran from teaching in one did not necessarily bar him from the other.

Saunders asked about the legitimacy of dissent. Some disagreement exists on every question, Ashley said. "But there is such a thing as a traditional meaning and standard tradition which is upheld by prominent theologians and which is concurred in by the church, and that's the one that I try to present." Ashley had critiqued some Catholic teachings, which he called "quite permissible," but he explained that the criticism had not been full-blown dissent.

"Who makes that judgment in the academy?" Saunders asked.

Ashley said that the professor, in the context of his peers, the church, and his discipline freely determined the limit of acceptable dissent. But if the dissent extended so far as to seem un-Catholic, the church finally would have to make that judgment, he said.

Continuing interrogation for the student plaintiffs, their lawyer Elliot Feldman asked Ashley about the beliefs of "mainstream" Catholic theologians. He noted that Ashley, in fact, had given the principal address at the 1986 annual meeting of the Catholic Theological Society of America, the very one at which a statement supporting Curran had been approved. Explaining the implications of the speech, Ashley said, "You can only find a new truth on the basis of something you already know." In other words, he said, "We have to stand up for the truth that we have already achieved in order to explore further."

Though not an expert on the subject of students' academic freedom rights, he said they probably were the same as for teachers. Ashley distinguished between two types of dissent, one that criticizes and suggests change and one that lacks respect for the proper teaching authority of the church. The first arises when a theologian finds one teaching inconsistent with others in the church, he said.

Feldman cited Ashley's textbook *Health Care Ethics: A Theological Analysis,* in which he said an individual Catholic is "always morally obligated to follow a prudently informed conscience," even in deciding whether to have an abortion. Ashley said he stood by that, but noted it was a statement about moral action, not about moral teachings.

The testimony brought the fourth day to a close, and, it turned out, the midpoint in the trial.

THE FIFTH DAY, Tuesday, Saunders called James Coriden, a priest, former chairman of the department of theology at Catholic University, and a specialist in canon law. Coriden was then dean at the Washington Theological Union, a theological school generally considered to be liberal. At that point, ten witnesses into the trial, a clear motif had been established, a visual symbol of where the witnesses stood in their views of the church. Coriden, like all the priests Saunders had called to defend Curran, wore a casual suit or sport coat; in contrast, most of the priests Baine had called wore the clerical collar.

Saunders and Baine quickly got into an argument over Coriden's right to say whether Catholic University was a pontifical school. That was a question of canon law, Baine said. But Weisberg allowed the question, and Coriden said it was not, but rather was a university that contained three pontifical faculties. Coriden said that while he was chairman of the theology department from 1973 to 1975, no one had been told he had a canonical mission. After the events of 1968, he said, "that sense of academic freedom pervaded the university, it was accepted from top to bottom." The judge and lawyers looked at the handbook circulated during his time and agreed it incorporated academic freedom. On the Marlowe report he said, "Everyone's perception was that it was a high mark, a high-water mark for academic freedom at the university."

Coriden, who had read the Vatican declaration on Curran, said that if such a missive had been sent in the period 1968 to 1975, "It certainly would not have any effect on the right to teach in the department of theology," an ecclesiastical faculty. "We looked upon ourselves as a very proud, old-line institution, compared ourselves to places like Vanderbilt [University] and [Johns] Hopkins [University], as a research-oriented graduate school [and] autonomous university," he said. "Any outside interference from any source was seen to be foreign to that concept."

Weisberg said he understood how that might be so for the nonecclesiastical faculties, but did not comprehend how it was the case for ecclesiastical faculties.

The canon law and theology faculties were seen as integral parts of the university as an academic institution, Coriden said. Weisberg pressed again. The Vatican had say on requirements in course work, Coriden said, but not on hiring and firing faculty members. If the requirement of the content of the course work is that it be genuine Catholic theology, Weisberg asked, could the Vatican judge some teaching not genuine? Coriden said that had never happened when he was there. Weisberg continued, asking how the Vatican declaration would have been applied if it had been received in 1968.

Coriden said another professor might have been asked to teach the courses in question—sexual ethics—but that no one would have been dismissed. "So there is something different about the ecclesiastical faculties as it pertains to the question of academic freedom?" Weisberg asked. To this, Coriden gave an analogy. "If the bar association protested the kind of courses that were being offered in the school of law, I think the school would take it seriously, but they would not dismiss the faculty members." But Weisberg said there were other implications to the bar ruling; the bar might block graduates from taking the bar exam. Perhaps, Coriden said, but "the judgment about [the faculty member's ability] to teach would be made by the law school faculty."

In the ecclesiastical faculties, the Vatican dictated the degrees to be offered and the general course work required, Coriden said. But during his time of teaching, he added, fewer than ten percent of students in the department of theology had sought ecclesiastical degrees; the rest had pursued civil degrees. Coriden said the Holy See had no control "whatsoever" over the civil degree programs. To illustrate the flexibility for even ecclesiastical degree students, he noted that they sometimes took courses in the Washington Theological Consortium, an alliance of six theological schools that included United Methodist, Lutheran, and Episcopalian seminaries.

Coriden repeated that he had never been given a canonical mission, nor had he told professors they needed one. "None was ever mentioned to me, none was ever given to me. Implicitly, explicitly, visibly or invisibly," he said. Based on the faculty manual, Coriden said he thought the academic freedom rights of all on the faculty were the same—all were free of ecclesiastical control. Coriden said that while he was at the university any church interference "was unimaginable," although the Vatican's concerns would have been taken seriously.

In cross-examination, Baine established that Coriden had long been a close supporter of Curran's, had signed statements in his support, and had been his canonical counsel in the faculty hearing after the Vatican ruling. He had left Catholic University in 1975 because he did not receive tenure.

What was more, Coriden would not talk to the defense lawyers, Baine said. "Did you tell Mr. [Charles] Wilson that you didn't want to talk to us because you were easily intimidated by lawyers?" Baine asked.

"I may have said that," Coriden responded.

"Just certain ones," Weisberg added.

"Tall ones, your honor," Coriden said. Wilson, who was second counsel on Baine's team but did not participate in questioning because of a neck injury, was more than six feet tall.

Over objections by Saunders, Baine put the question of whether it would violate Curran's academic freedom rights if the chairman of his department assigned someone else to teach sexual ethics after the Vatican declaration, even if Curran disagreed. "That's a close call. I think it could be construed as an infringement of his rights," Coriden said.

"Are peers more competent than the highest authorities of the church to judge a theologian's fidelity and respect for the magisterium? Baine asked.

"They may or may not be competent," he said. "But they are the ones who make judgments in our university system."

"Do they have greater authority than the church to determine respect for the magisterium?" Baine asked.

"Within the university they do," Coriden said.

Coriden said he disagreed with the Vatican ruling on Curran but said the university could have allowed Curran to teach Catholic theology without rejecting the Vatican's directive.

"How can it do that?" Baine asked. By letting him teach what he was hired to teach, Coriden said. He said the board must follow the view of the professor's peers. But Baine clarified the point that peer review is only a recommendation, according to university statutes. "And so the peer judgment is not binding on the board of trustees under the university procedures, is it?" Baine asked.

"Not absolutely," Coriden said.

After Coriden agreed with Baine that the chancellor had some authority over the ecclesiastical faculties, Baine focused his last question on his primary theme regarding the canonical mission requirement: that the chancellor's stated obligation in the "special statutes" to follow the "norms and regulations of the Holy See" must have been a reference to *Normae Quaedam,* the temporary norms issued by the Vatican, which in turn referred to "a mission."

Saunders, on his second examination, challenged Baine's interpretation and sought to show that the norms affecting the chancellor were binding on him alone. The judge then asked if, as the chancellor was obligated under the special statutes to give the canonical mission, there likewise was an obligation for professors to have one? Coriden said no. "I don't think there is a reciprocal obligation."

"Why do you think the rights and obligations aren't reciprocal where they intersect, that is, the duty of the chancellor and the obligation of the faculty member?" Weisberg asked. Coriden said the statutes could not impose such an obligation because that would have meant a one-sided alteration of the contract. "It would be an additional jeopardy. It would be an additional burden not bargained for, and rather thrust, unilaterally, upon the faculty members." Yes, Coriden said in answer to the question, a professor could always resign, but in some cases, as with an elderly faculty member, it would be an exceptional burden.

"So your answer, I guess, in short is that if that happened you'd be in superior court arguing breach of contract," Weisberg said.

"Exactly," Coriden said.

THE TRIAL TESTIMONY revealed the contradiction, or at least the balancing act, both sides wrestled with in presenting key arguments. The university's conundrum, shown in testimony by Hickey and soon by university president William Byron, was its claim to be free and autonomous and yet bound by a Vatican ruling. The argument went like this: The university could have rejected the wishes of the Holy See, but it was bound by canon law and compelled morally not to—and so the university made the "free choice" to obey. For Saunders, this was impossible to reconcile, and he generously pointed that out to the judge.

Curran's side had its own conundrum, also a major one. Does peer review always supersede rulings of the magisterium on the status of a Catholic theologian in a Catholic university that chooses, for whatever reason, to have a "special relationship with" or to be subservient to the church? And given the church's historical battle with heterodoxy, what could maintain orthodoxy if a majority of peers were heterodox? Baine brought out that contradiction in his final questioning of Coriden.

"What if the board said we seem to have a conflict here between peers who judge this professor competent and church authorities who judge him lacking in respect for the church's teaching and, therefore, ineligible to teach Catholic theology?" Baine posited. "And we, the board, don't think we're bound by either, but this is a difficult case, and in this case we are going to prevent the professor from teaching Catholic theology. Would that also violate the professor's academic freedom?"

"Yes, indeed," Coriden said.

"Why?" Baine asked.

"Because they have violated his academic freedom, not in rejecting what the recommendation of the committee was, but in their own action."

"How?" Baine asked.

"By changing the terms of his contract, by breaching his contract," Coriden said.

"What's the breach?"

"The breach is not permitting him to do what he was hired to do."

"But there surely are circumstances under which he can be prevented from doing that, indeed, under which more extreme action can be taken. He can be fired," Baine said.

"Yes, there are conditions. But the condition is not simply a letter from the Holy See."

"But I thought we established that [the letter] was entitled to great weight in the proceedings."

"It is entitled to great weight," Coriden said.

"What if the board says it's entitled to great weight, and in this particular case the board took the judgment of the Holy See to outweigh the peer judgment of competence and that leads us to conclude that we're going to assign him to teach something else other than Catholic theology, would that violate his academic freedom?" Baine asked.

"Yes, indeed," Coriden said.

Baine asked if Coriden objected to such action because it ignored peer review or because it came from the Holy See. The professor said that any outside interference, whether from the Holy See, the mayor of the District of Columbia, or the president of the United States, was improper in the university setting.

"Are you saying then, Professor Coriden, that the Holy See's declaration is not entitled to consideration after all?" Baine asked.

"No, indeed, I said it should be considered, it would always be considered seriously. But it is not determinative."

"Well, it weighs heavily?" Baine asked.

"Weighs heavily," Coriden agreed.

"Can it ever tip the scales?"

"I trust that it could tip the scales," Coriden said. With that concession, Baine had no further questions.

ELEVEN

The Ecclesial Limit

William J. Byron, the Jesuit president of The Catholic University of America, had been described as a man having forty-one bosses. They constituted the board of trustees, the owners of the university. He was their agent. Byron thus was the principal representative at the trial for the defense, and he sat next to Kevin Baine throughout. The university president was the only witness Paul Saunders called who was not friendly to the plaintiff's case. Like Cardinal James Hickey, Byron would be on the stand for almost an entire day, from Tuesday afternoon to the lunch break on Wednesday, the sixth day.

Baine was ready to defend Byron, and the chance came as soon as Saunders began his examination. Byron was asked whether there was a right to academic freedom at Catholic University, and Baine objected, bringing him and Saunders into a discussion with the judge. Baine's objection was that the question asked Byron to state legal conclusions.

Byron took the question as best he could. "It's my judgment that provision for academic freedom is made and that anyone teaching there could expect it," he said. "And indeed most people teaching there would say they have enjoyed it."

"Is academic freedom at Catholic University a right of a faculty member?" Saunders asked.

"I am not a lawyer," Byron said. "Can't answer that question. I presume you're putting it to me in terms of a legally enforceable right."

Saunders persisted and Byron responded. "There are a lot of definitions of academic freedom. There are probably as many understandings of academic freedom as there are institutions of higher education."

Saunders asked if there was any "authorized definition" of academic freedom at the university, and Byron said the lawyer was obviously referring to an erroneous report in the press three days earlier. The *Washington Post* had reported Saturday that Cardinal Joseph Bernardin, former chairman of the trustees, had said there was "no assurance of academic freedom" at the university. Saunders moved to strike that reference to the press, but Byron continued, saying that Bernardin had been misunderstood and that the report had "provoked dismay among people on the faculty." The judge said he made a point of not reading any press reports related to the trial. "I would rather not hear about it," he said. "I have to find facts from the evidence in the courtroom, not from the media."

Saunders altered his question to whether there was an authorized "description" of academic freedom. Byron said the faculty handbook contained such a description but that it was not an authorized "definition." He added that the faculty handbook mentioned academic freedom in two places. He noted that in one place the phrase, "There are no constraints on truth except truth itself," implied a limit. "There are a number of limits on academic freedom," he said, "limits of the discipline, the canons of the discipline, and the expected competencies of those working within the discipline, limits of prudence, I would argue, and an ecclesial limit." Handbook references guaranteeing academic freedom did not provide mechanisms to back the guarantee up, but due process was followed in disputes. Likewise, he said, there was no "specific definition" of ecclesial limits but rather a common understanding of the phrase.

The next day, Byron made another allusion to how the Washington newspapers reported his idea of "limits." In reporting on Byron's view at the trial, editors had not found the term "ecclesial" in their dictionaries and so had changed his terminology to read "ecclesiastical limit." Byron said his use of ecclesial rather than ecclesiastical was intentional. Ecclesial, from the Greek *ecclesia,* a community or assembly, implied that limits were imposed by the church community and a continuity of tradition rather than the hierarchy. "Ecclesiastical," he implied, smacked of hierarchial heavy-handedness, a connotation he wanted to avoid. Some Catholic educators had already told Byron that, in their opinion, that was a distinction without a difference.

Saunders continued, asking Byron how long he had been of the view that there were "ecclesial limits" in the teaching of theology.

"I never thought much about the question until the past year or two," he said. He spoke of a meeting in January 1987 with ten bishops, ten theologians, and ten university administrators at the University of Notre Dame to discuss the question. It was then that the notion of ecclesial limit had come into focus for him.

Suggesting that Byron's explanation was simply a justification he had invented to rationalize the university's actions against Charles Curran, Saunders showed that in 1967 the assistant to the president of Catholic University had signed the Land O'Lakes Statement, which declared that Catholic universities were independent from Vatican control. The statement contained a view of academic freedom in theology that differed from Byron's current view. Saunders wanted to know if Catholic University had incorporated into its governing statutes any of the positions taken in the Wisconsin statement. Apparently not, Byron said.

Saunders next moved to the question of institutional autonomy, which Byron said Catholic University enjoyed. Paraphrasing the Land O'Lakes Statement, Saunders asked, "Do you mean to say that . . . Catholic University has that institutional autonomy in the face of authority of whatever kind, lay or clerical, external to the academic community itself?"

Byron said yes. "It makes its own decisions."

Saunders had set him up. "Do you consider the Holy See to be internal or external to Catholic University?" he asked.

It is external as an entity, Byron said, but "as standing for values which are freely internalized by the university through action of the board of trustees. Much of, if not all of, what the Holy See stands for has been freely internalized." For Saunders, the answer did not make sense. He believed that after Hickey had said the university was autonomous, that was the only explanation the university president could give.

Saunders moved closer to Curran's case. He asked if peer judgment was central when judging competence; Byron said that depended on circumstances. Where, for example, would it not apply? Saunders asked. In the case of mental illness of a professor, "and I would suspect there could be a whole variety of examples like it," Byron answered.

Saunders asked directly about Curran. "It's not my impression that the judgment is made about his competence," Byron said. "It's about his eligibility." Nothing from the Congregation for the Doctrine of the Faith in Rome had said he was not competent. This was a point important to Curran, who believed that no disciplinary action could be taken against him without the peer review. Saunders reminded Byron that, according to university statutes, peers were to decide whether there was "sufficient reason" for the chancellor to take action against any professor. Byron said he assumed the chancellor's position was that "the academic senate or one of its committees is not to sit in judgment on final, definitive, binding sentences of the highest doctrinal authorities of the Roman Catholic Church."

Judge Frederick Weisberg, to clarify, summarized the university's position. Since the Vatican had already ruled on the substance of Curran's teachings, the faculty committee was only required to decide if that merited withdrawal of the canonical mission. The committee said it did—so long as Curran was allowed to teach elsewhere in his area of competence. That led directly to the question of teaching in a nonecclesiastical department.

Saunders picked up on that and pursued what he found contradictory in the university's view of the Vatican declaration. What was it that made the board decide, he asked, that the Ratzinger letter penalizing Curran was binding on the university? Saunders's question was how, if the declaration was not "self-executing," it could disqualify Curran. How could it be "binding" on the board if it required no board action?

"The declaratory judgment of the Holy See was not self-executing," Byron said. "It simply applied to [Curran] personally. And the words of the declaration were that he's neither eligible nor suitable."

Saunders asked if the board of trustees had ever received a letter from Ratzinger making the declaratory judgment binding on them.

"The board of trustees to my knowledge never precisely considered itself bound by the letter," but it did "consider itself bound by canon law and religious conviction to take what it considered to be appropriate action," Byron said. In a later legal brief for the judge, Saunders cited what for him was the key contradiction in the testimony: Byron first had testified that the board was "bound by canon law" to act in the Curran case. But later he had said the Vatican declaration was directly "binding on both the chancellor and Father Curran," implying that there was no need for the board to play a role.

Saunders cited Byron's press conference with Hickey in August 1986 in which Byron seemed to say that Ratzinger's letter was self-executing. Because of the letter, Byron had said, Curran could no longer teach in the department of theology.

"My understanding has always been that a canonical mission is required in the department of theology," Byron said.

But at the time Byron announced that Curran could no longer teach theology, the professor still had his canonical mission. It was not removed until almost two years later. In testimony, Byron also said that at the time in question the Vatican declaration had not yet led him to conclude that Curran could not teach on the nonecclesiastical faculty. "I didn't even consider the question," he said.

Saunders was still trying to get at something. What exactly was it, he asked, that disqualified Curran from teaching theology on a nonecclesiastical faculty—the declaration or the action by the board of trustees? In the former case, he would argue, the university was not truly autonomous. In the latter, he would contend, the board was not really bound by canon law.

Byron tried to evade the conundrum. The action boiled down to an administrative decision to disqualify Curran until the board of trustees officially did so in its June resolution, he said. He had taken that administrative action, Byron added, after considering a recommendation by the dean of the school of religion that Curran teach in religious education, which Byron would not allow. Barring Curran administratively, Byron said, had been his "prudential judgment about what was best for the university at that time while these procedures were moving forward." Permitting Curran to teach theology anywhere "would be perceived to be an act in defiance of the declaratory judgment rendered by the Holy See."

After a break, Saunders returned to the question of autonomy. He asked Byron who owned Catholic University. Byron said the board of trustees.

Weisberg was now somewhat confused, and he asked Byron if he was saying that canon law only bound the board to consider the

Holy See's declaration but not necessarily to follow it, though it had chosen to do so in concert with the chancellor? Byron said yes. "My understanding would be that the board was free and the board could conceivably have acted contrary to a law under which it is bound. It could have broken the law," Byron said.

Saunders elaborated from Byron's answer. Why, if the board's action was bound by canon law, Saunders asked, did the process for removal of the canonical mission even take place? Due process required it, Byron said. But again Saunders recalled that Byron had taken the view that the university had been bound by the Vatican's judgment about Curran as soon as it had been issued. The two positions, Saunders held, could not be reconciled. Byron tried manfully to do so, obviously recognizing that on the one hand he would be forced to say that the university did not enjoy autonomy and, on the other, that the university was free to disobey the Vatican. As a prince of the church, Hickey could answer that question easily; as a university president Byron could not.

Weisberg again asked for a clarification. What in canon law would have been violated if the board had not removed Curran from teaching theology? he asked. Byron, noting that he was not a canon lawyer, said respect for the magisterium and the definitive nature of the Vatican's judgment required the board to obey.

Byron said the letter itself was not the trigger, but the board had to comply with it. "It was a major problem," Byron said. "And boards deal with problems. My job as administrator is to bring the problem to the board."

That brought the testimony back to questions about Curran's competence. Saunders wanted to establish that the university's actions had not been based on competence.

Byron said he had never sat in on one of Curran's classes and had read few chapters from his books. He had sat with Curran on panels several times. He said he did not disagree with a litany of commendations Saunders produced about Curran's competence to teach theology. Baine cut short the line of questioning by stipulating that the university had not judged Curran's incompetent to teach theology; it has said he was ineligible to do so.

Saunders compared Bernardin's testimony that Curran could teach social ethics from his perspective as a Catholic theologian, and

Byron's letter to Curran saying that he could not. "If Bernardin was correct, then we say it is part of our case that Professor Curran should have been permitted to do that and he wasn't," Saunders said. Baine's position was that neither Bernardin, Hickey, nor Byron disagreed among themselves and that Saunders was exploiting the semantic subtlety of the terms theology and ethics to portray a dispute.

Questioned about tenure, Byron echoed James Burtchaell, the Notre Dame theologian who had testified earlier: It provides employment security and benefits but not the right to teach. The university, Byron said, was free to bar a tenured professor from teaching. "There are tenured professors who do not teach and don't claim violation of rights. Some of them are full research professors."

Next Saunders contrasted Byron's current views on academic freedom in theology with an article he had written in *America,* a Jesuit weekly, in late 1986. Byron explained that he had started working on the article as an interpretive framework. He had sent it to Hickey as a discussion paper on April 7, 1986. "I didn't even think then about publishing it as an article. So in an abbreviated form, and I might add with a lot of incorrect assumptions on my part in the earlier draft, I used it as a discussion paper with Cardinal Hickey." Later he enlarged on it for publication, but it had been written before he saw the Holy See's judgment, Byron said.

The key statement in the article, according to Saunders, was Byron's assertion that even if Curran's canonical mission were withdrawn, "That decision would not of itself exclude Father Curran from a position on a nonecclesiastical faculty . . . This freedom to teach theology in a nonecclesiastical faculty at CUA or elsewhere is a separate question." Obviously, according to Saunders, Byron believed along with Curran that Curran could still teach theology in nonecclesiastical faculties.

Saunders asked if the passage was still correct. Byron said that in essence it was. Saunders showed that Byron had written in the discussion paper, "The university can provide an alternative faculty position to a professor whose competence and integrity has been reaffirmed by due process." Hickey, he showed, had written in the margin, "NO!" Nevertheless, the sentence, in a slightly altered form, appeared in the *America* article.

Saunders produced a letter in which Byron had told Curran that there was "no direct relationship" between tenure and canonical mission. "The canonical mission, as I understand it, affects only your status as a member of the faculty to the department of theology. There are wide and narrow constructions applied to the understanding of tenure, whether it is to the department or to the university. In your case I would want to adopt the wider construction and would be prepared to do so when and if the occasion arises," Byron had written.

Saunders asked whether that "occasion had arisen," and Byron explained that his letter was not definitive and that his final judgment was that tenure related to the department, not the university. Saunders then produced another letter in which Byron had told a fellow Catholic priest that although case law supported the narrow construction, he supported the broad one—tenure to the university—for Curran.

Gingerly, Saunders approached the question of Canon 812. Added to the Code of Canon Law in 1983, it required all Catholic theology professors in any establishments of higher learning—not just Catholic universities—to have a "mandate" to teach from the local bishop. Virtually all American Catholic college presidents, and many bishops, had lobbied unsuccessfully against its adoption. Byron's letter referred to "invoking a canon."

"Can you tell me what that is?" Saunders asked.

"So bad you can't even say it. 812," Byron said.

"812," Weisberg said.

"812 of the Revised Code of Canon Law. Does canon 812 bar Curran from teaching theology on a nonecclesiastical faculty?" Saunders asked. The canon had never been used to dismiss a theologian anywhere, Byron said.

To suggest that Byron was among the Catholic educators who still opposed the canon, Saunders produced a 1986 document by university presidents that critiqued the Vatican's 1985 "Proposed Schema for a Pontifical Document on Catholic Universities." Byron had signed it. The document criticized the idea of a bishop's having control over the orthodoxy of faculty members or departments.

"Yours is the first name, is it not?" Saunders asked.

"Alphabetical order," Byron said.

Saunders pointed to a paragraph that criticized the schema's solution to the conflict between orthodox teaching authority and theological inquiry.

"It wasn't written to apply to Catholic University," Byron said. "We would have to take it piece by piece." Saunders finished his examination with a few more questions, some about academic freedom for theologians based on Catholic University's autonomy. The day had ended, and Weisberg suggested they would be pushing it to finish the trial by Friday.

DAY SIX, A WEDNESDAY, began with Baine's friendly cross-examination of Byron. Under questioning Byron explained that he approved of the instruction to cancel Father Curran's courses, that he believed there were a variety of types of academic freedom, depending on the institution, and that he had written his *America* article before he had seen the Vatican declaration. He had submitted the article to *America* on July 29, 1986. The September 1985 letter from Ratzinger, which had occasioned Byron's article, spoke of Curran's teaching "in the name of the church," whereas the last letter said that Curran was neither "suitable nor eligible" to teach Catholic theology, which Byron testified "is broader."

Byron pointed out that his *America* article did not deal with the question of whether Curran could teach on a nonecclesiastical faculty and that the article called that a "separate issue." He again defined "ecclesial limit" in terms of the community of faith. He said he thought there was support in the university handbook for such a limiting principle. Baine found it in the canonical statutes: "Faculties are intended to assure fidelity to the revealing word of God as it is transmitted by tradition and interpreted and safeguarded by the magisterium of the Church and to safeguard academic freedom," he read.

Byron said the issue at Catholic University was the university's religious freedom, and he went on to define theology and its limits. "Theology is not catechism. A theologian isn't doing his or her job unless he is pushing that tradition forward and there may be new formulations, indeed, new understandings of the data of revelation," he said.

"Now that's where theologians get into a relationship of tension with the church authorities," he continued. "They are there not simply to repeat past formulations. And they are there to help develop new understandings. This is an area that I'm struggling for my own personal understanding and the ability to articulate it."

He recounted that after the faculty committee hearings, Curran had been given due process in his chance to address the board of trustees with counsel at his side.

Byron repeated that the Land O'Lakes Statement defining academic freedom in theology had never been adopted by the university's board of trustees. But he said the board's decision on Curran was "consistent" with that statement. With respect to the university's 1970 report to Middle States Association of Colleges and Schools, which contained an articulation of academic freedom in theology that was different from the university's present position, he explained that the board of trustees did not approve such "self studies" prepared for accrediting groups. He implied that the board was not bound by what was said.

He said the faculty was bound by revisions in the handbook. "There would be administrative chaos if that were not the case," he added. Faculty members, he continued, always participated in handbook revisions. The testimony was important because it countered Curran's claim that his rights had been frozen before the canonical statutes had been adopted. Byron further said that Catholic University was still a pontifical school based on its charter.

Testimony turned to the May 25, 1988, letter to Curran in which Byron offered the social ethics teaching option. Byron said he did not consider the course Catholic theology but did consider Curran competent to teach it. The letter had been read to Curran over the phone, and his lawyers had telecopied a message that he would meet with Byron and Cardinals Hickey and Bernardin about the offer, but the meeting had never taken place. Why?

Byron gave two reasons: It was not convenient and Curran, through his lawyer, had conveyed the impression that it would not be productive.

As to the "loyalty oath" required for the teaching option, Byron said that he was looking for "simply an expression of willingness to comply with [the Vatican declaration] . . . It was not expected that he would say that he agreed with it but that he would comply with it."

The judge pointed out that the question of whether Curran would teach social ethics or theology sounded like a semantic dispute, and wondered what was the difference. "What difference does it make other than a semantic one if he calls that theology and you call it social ethics?" he asked. Byron said that if he had had a meeting with Curran that might have been ironed out.

After Curran refused to accept or comply with the Vatican ruling, Byron said, he had to decide what to do. "At that point," Baine asked, "why didn't you just let Father Curran go ahead and teach the course in social ethics anyway?"

"Because he would in effect be inviting the university to join in his dissent from the declaratory judgment. The university is unwilling to do that," he said.

Saunders now had a chance to question Byron again. He quickly focused on the issue of Curran's teaching theology in a nonecclesiastical faculty. He asked if the ecclesial limit idea applied to teaching Catholic theology in a nonpontifical school or in a non-Catholic school.

Byron said, "My understanding of an ecclesial limit on theology would apply wherever Catholic theology was done."

Saunders asked if that included Harvard. Byron said he did not believe Catholic theology was taught as Catholic theology and "in service to the faith community" at Harvard. What about Notre Dame? Saunders asked.

"You had the opportunity to inquire of the chairman of the department of theology at Notre Dame," Byron said, referring to earlier testimony by Richard McBrien. "So I wouldn't propose to speak for them." When Saunders asked again how an ecclesial limit might work at Notre Dame, Byron would only refer back to his general explanation.

Saunders again brought up the university presidents' response to the draft of the Vatican schema on education that Byron, among others, had signed. Saunders pointed out that the response had contained no reference to anything like an "ecclesial limit" on the teaching of theology. Had the board, Saunders asked, considered whether Curran had breached the ecclesial limits or was it simply an issue of accepting the Vatican's determination? Byron said that the board had not delved into the ecclesial limits. Saunders claimed that the board simply had accepted the Vatican decree without question. Byron said that was not so.

Saunders challenged the university president's contention that only after seeing the 1986 Vatican declaration did he believe it called for a Draconian limit on what Curran could be permitted to do. Saunders argued that it was clear from the 1985 letter from Ratzinger—which Byron had read before he wrote the *America* article—what the Vatican's final judgment would be.

DURING THE CURRAN affair, Byron had made one visit to consult with church officials in Rome and had corresponded frequently with other inquiring hierarchs and clergy. Saunders wanted to put some of these conversations on the record. Baine objected that it was improper to delve into communications between church officials. There is no legal precedent, Saunders responded, to exempt communication between church leaders from disclosure in a court. "I contend that if the court were to find that such a privilege existed for the Catholic Church, that would be a violation of the First Amendment because it would be in effect an official establishment of the Catholic Church," he said.

The judge said he doubted Saunders's assertion but was not ready to rule on it. For Baine, this was another measure of Weisberg's sensitivity to the issue of religious freedom. In the end, correspondence with the Vatican stayed out of the record, though exhibits on other correspondence was allowed.

When reading aloud portions of letters that Byron had written to clergymen about the case, Saunders asked Baine whether he wished to have one particular sentence read out loud. Baine said no, but Saunders read it anyway, to laughter: "We had the best legal counsel available in the U.S.," Byron had written. The reference was to Baine, who stoically took it in.

"I would certainly repeat that if I were writing the letter today," Byron said.

"You're under oath," Saunders said, evoking another round of laughter. Such humor and banter often eased the courtroom tension, which even the lawyers felt as they knew they must pin their unfriendly witnesses into a corner of contradiction. After that release, however, Saunders again pursued Byron. The subject was the university's definition of academic freedom. Byron said that Catholic University did not adopt specific definitions created by other associations, such as the American Association of University Professors.

Saunders asked why Catholic University never had come up with an official definition of academic freedom on its own. "I have no idea," Byron said.

The judge asked if it would be consistent with the Vatican declaration if Curran taught a course called "anti-Catholic theology." "He would say at the opening of the course, 'I consider myself a Catholic theologian. The church does not. This course is about what I think Catholic theology is, even though the church disagrees.'"

"That would be inconsistent with the declaration," Byron said.

Aiming at the heart of the university's defense—that its deference to Vatican directives was acceptable because of the university's "special relationship"—Saunders wanted to know if the special relationship applied to the whole university or just to the ecclesiastical faculties. "The entire university," Byron said.

Saunders returned to the loyalty oath requirement, asking, "What is it in the governing documents that, in your judgment, requires Professor Curran to agree to be bound by the Ratzinger letter?"

Nothing he could cite specifically, Byron said, but he opined that the requirement generally was based on "the whole spirit, the tradition, the founding purpose, the declared mission, the statement of aims, all of those things include a special relationship with the Holy See which is one of respect and fidelity."

When asked if professors at the university were expected to comply with canon law, Byron said all Catholics were. Saunders asked what would happen if a Catholic who was teaching at the university violated canon law. The judge sustained Baine's objection.

Saunders instead asked whether Curran had breached any obligation of canon law under his contract with the university. Byron said nothing in the contract had been breached, but he implied that Curran had failed to live up to obligations placed on him by Article 23 in the faculty handbook. That article, added five years after Curran received tenure, provided that clerics on the faculty had "primary obligations to ecclesiastical superiors."

Before Byron finished his testimony, Weisberg asked him again to clarify the distinction between teaching Catholic theology and teaching social ethics. If a professor wanted to teach a course on "Why the Holy See Does Not Consider Charles Curran a Professor of Catholic Theology," Weisberg asked, "is that a course you would approve if the dean recommended it" and would it be consistent with the Vatican declaration? Byron said yes.

Would academic freedom include the right of students to be exposed to that kind of discussion, the judge asked. Byron said yes. "What if Professor Curran wanted to teach it in a school other than the department of theology?" the judge asked. Byron said that if he taught it as a Catholic theologian he would be defying the Ratzinger declaration. Weisberg summarized the answer by saying that it would not be much different from teaching a course in social ethics as a Catholic theologian. Byron agreed.

Saunders had a follow-up question on that subject. He asked whether Curran could teach the course on social ethics, which included two papal encyclicals, from his perspective as a Catholic theologian. Byron said he wished Curran had taken the offer to teach the ethics courses, but that if he had the courses could not have been taught as theology courses.

To Baine, the line of questioning raised the same issues the disputing parties had negotiated over when they had tried to secure Curran a teaching post, and he said it was inappropriate to raise them in trail testimony. "If Mr. Saunders wants to negotiate, let's negotiate," Baine said in objecting. The judge agreed that the discussion should take place somewhere other than the courtroom. Baine also objected that the questions about the teaching offer ignored the fact that Curran had said he would not accept the Vatican ruling as a condition.

"This has nothing to do with facts," Saunders said, drawing laughter. "It has to do with a purely hypothetical situation."

DAVID POWER WAS the chairman of Catholic University's department of theology, a post he had accepted in September 1986 with the explicit purpose of helping defend Curran. He had done it in letters and hearings and privately—and now he was doing it on the witness stand. Power, the twelfth witness, was called by Saunders. Juanita Crowley conducted the examination.

The professor reiterated what other witnesses for the plaintiff had said: There was no canonical mission given before 1981; the faculty "took for granted" that it had academic freedom; and tenure included the right to teach. He said students seeking ecclesiastical degrees got credit for courses in the nonecclesiastical departments. The magisterium, Power said, should receive its due respect. "All of its statements must be taken into due account, according to the particular weight which is attached to the particular statements." But, he added, there was disagreement on how much respect was due to the magisterium.

And who resolves that dispute? the judge asked.

"It goes on for centuries sometimes," Power said, provoking laughter.

Power said he disagreed with the Vatican action and said Curran's status was protected no matter what faculty he was on. He said peer review would determine if Curran had shown proper respect for the magisterium. Asked about the Vatican letter that had declared Curran not "eligible" to teach theology, Power said, "The notion of eligibility is something new to me. I would always have judged the matter on the basis of competency."

The contradiction of loyalty to church and to the principles of a university are resolved "through open discussion," Power said. "If there were no contradiction, there would be no room for theology." Power said that when he had joined Catholic University in 1977 he had not thought it was a pontifical institution, and since being on faculty he had never heard of the university's special obligations under canon law. He said there was "no relationship" between the nonecclesiastical faculties and canon law. Power portrayed Curran's reputation among his peers as "exceedingly high" and confirmed that in June 1987 the Catholic Theological Society had approved a resolution supporting Curran.

The Ratzinger declaration, he said, could not validly bar Curran from teaching theology. Such an action would contradict the purpose of the university. The "authority has to be internal" in judging the professor, he said.

Baine began his cross-examination. Power acknowledged that not all theologians would have the same view of academic freedom he had. Baine showed that Power had asserted at the faculty committee hearing on Curran's canonical mission that the Holy See's procedures were deficient.

"It was within the authority of the Congregation for the Doctrine of the Faith to review Father Curran's writings and to come to conclusions about those writings, was it not?" Baine asked.

"It was, but there are times, of course, when people may legitimately protest the particular exercise of authority in question," Power said.

Baine asked if the judgment of the Vatican as to whether one shows sufficient respect for the magisterium takes precedence over the judgment of peers. Power said no. "It must include some investigation into the judgment of peers. It is a statement about respect which of itself also deserves respect," he said. On a reference by Baine to Power's earlier use of the term "magisterial authority," Power said that although it might be a priority, the authority can be dissented from—a debate going back a thousand years.

"Is it your view that the judgment of peers in this case is entitled to greater weight?" Baine asked.

"I go back to my concept of the church as organic body," Power said, "and I think a variety of parties have to be called upon to consider this question before a responsible decision can be arrived at." He said the board of trustees was but one of the parties. Many theologians, he said, "believe that [Curran] has not transcended the permissible bound of dissent, and according to a reckoning of numbers, I would say the majority of Catholic theologians on the continent [agree]."

Baine asked if he meant to say that a majority vote should resolve the question. Power said no, an inquiry would determine that. He said he had no evidence that an adequate inquiry had been made into Curran's competence. In closing, Baine elicited from Power his overall view—that even though the congregation in Rome had ruled that Curran had crossed permissible bounds, the university should have rejected that in order to protect Curran's right to teach.

It seemed to Curran that more than six days had passed. He had sat quietly behind Saunders since the trial's beginning, occasionally leaning forward to point out, in a whispered but animated voice, facts or discrepancies in the testimony. The afternoon remained and Curran was to be called next. As expected, his testimony would be the longest.

TWELVE

"I Can't Deny Who I Am"

For a university professor, Charles Curran was in an unusual position. He had not been fired. He still had tenure. His financial benefits were still in place and would be for the foreseeable future. By most accounts, he had taught his subject with distinction for twenty years. And yet because of an uncompromising face-off between him and the administration, he could not, or would not, teach. He was in a state of limbo. The American Association of University Professors would describe the situation thus: He "went on a leave of absence rather than teach under conditions he considers unacceptable."

A few months earlier Curran had begun to teach at the University of Southern California, and the change of clime had left its print. His complexion was rosy from sunburn, part of it accumulated around the campus of the bustling downtown university. Before that, in 1987 he had taught a year at Cornell University, occupying a visiting chair of Catholic studies. In both cases, Catholic University had offered to make up any differences in salary, but it was not necessary. Both schools paid him more than the $26,000 salary and $9,000 in free room and board he had been getting from The Catholic University of America.

Called to testify, Curran began by explaining what he believed to be his contractual rights. "I have a right and an obligation to do research, to communicate the fruits of my teaching and research, in the area of my competency, of moral theology, for which I have a right to salary and what is connected with it," Curran said. "And I have this within the context of the rights of academic freedom, tenure, and due process."

The first part of his testimony, which scanned the history of his ideas in moral theology, was designed to show that Curran's dissenting positions had been well known by those who had hired him at Catholic University. He hoped to show that by prohibiting him from teaching because of those views, the university, not he, had changed positions. In legal terms, he believed that meant the university's understanding of its side of the contract—a contract being a mutual agreement—recognized his freedom to dissent. To prevail, Curran had to prove that both he and the university had held the same understanding at the time the contract was entered into, or that the contract had been changed after mutual agreement.

Curran said that in about 1963 he had been called before the auxiliary bishop in Rochester and told "that my theology was too progressive, to avant garde." That view was known to those at Catholic University and was repeated after he moved there in 1965, he testified.

Curran said that when he joined the staff at Catholic University he understood the department of theology to be an ecclesiastical, or pontifical, faculty. But he said he also knew "there was academic freedom, that I could dissent from church teachings." So from the outset, he contended, both he and the university had believed he was permitted to dissent.

He described the 1967 strike as confirming his right to academic freedom. "After having both confrontations and meetings, et cetera, by that time I was certain I had the right," he said.

His right to academic freedom, he said, had been further confirmed by the events surrounding his 1968 dissent over *Humanae Vitae,* the encyclical upholding the ban on artificial contraception. Curran said that Cardinal Patrick O'Boyle, then archbishop of Washington, had called him and other dissenting professors together. "There was no doubt that the whole tone and demeanor of the meeting was that he was very unhappy with what we had done," Curran said. But the significant outcome, he testified, was that the board of trustees had neither fired the professors nor sought to withdraw their canonical missions. Rather, it had convened a faculty committee, the Marlowe committee, that ultimately concluded that the professors' dissent was "within the bounds of academic propriety."

"It was obvious to all of us at the time that [the Marlowe report] was a landmark recognition that academic freedom fully existed at Catholic University," Curran said. "Note, I do not say it [the report] granted it. It was proof that it already existed." He continued: "There was great discussion on campus. I mean it was looked upon, as I say, as a vindication of the living proof of who we are . . . truly an American institution of higher learning."

As evidence of the Marlowe report's importance, Curran cited articles written about it in 1970, including in *Academe,* the bulletin of the American Association of University Professors. In fact, he said, the AAUP's academic freedom committee had been so impressed that it no longer recommended the so-called limitations clause in its 1940 statement on academic freedom and tenure. That clause, which singled out church-related schools as suspect, provided that if such schools wished to limit full academic freedom—and keep the AAUP's blessing—they were required to give written notice to prospective faculty members before hiring them.

Curran was very enthusiastic during the recollections and gave some of the longest answers of any of the witnesses. He said that throughout his time at Catholic University he had opposed efforts to curtail academic freedom for theologians. After the events of 1967 and 1968, he said, he had been vigilant. Through voracious reading, Curran said, he had become "the resident expert on academic freedom." Activist faculty battling the administration of St. John's University in New York sought his support, a request he demurred because the dispute involved unionizing more than academic freedom. In 1975 Curran had fought unsuccessfully in the academic senate against the proposed Article 23, an addition to the faculty handbook to prevent priests who left the priesthood without being laicized from continuing on the faculty. And in his testimony he rejected Byron's implication that Article 23 called for unflinching obedience to the Vatican and strict orthodoxy in the teaching of theology. He had written letters and sent out press releases in support of other professors whose academic freedom was challenged, such as in 1979 when the trustees blocked religious studies professor John Dadek from tenure. He also had fought the canonical mission requirement of the 1981 canonical statutes.

Curran said he had never heard the idea that the university was governed by canon law until it was raised in his case, and he was firm in his belief that a judgment by the Holy See would have no effect "whatsoever" on his contract rights. Probably for the first time in trial, the judge was presented with a clear difference of opinion as to what were the contract rights of professors at Catholic University.

In his opening statements of the trial, Saunders had emphasized that there was a distinction between theologians as academicians and theologians in the church. Curran returned to that theme. There was the "Catholic theologian, qua church theologian," Curran said. There was the "Catholic theologian, qua academician." One was part of the church; the other part of the academy. And the only limit on teaching in the academy was peer judgment. "What is new about the American scene is precisely the fact that we say now that a theologian in the academy should have now the same rights as any other scholar in the academy," he said.

Curran said he had never heard of the idea "ecclesial limit" before William Byron, Catholic University's president, articulated it. He said it didn't make sense, unless the limit was understood to mean competency. "I have always said that Catholic theology must give due weight to authoritative teaching. However, the ultimate judgment about that is not made by authority external to the academy," he said.

Judge Weisberg asked what would happen in Curran's contract if the trustees gave heavier weight to the external judgment than to the peers. Curran rambled a bit, then gained his focus. He said that there were limits on what even the board could properly do, referring to a 1915 AAUP document that said the board had a public function and was not solely concerned about employing professors. Curran said it was like a separation of powers. The board had a defined role, but so did peer judgment.

Yes, Weisberg said, but what if the trustees, even in that public role, still gave more weight to the authoritative teaching of the magisterium?

Curran said if the board decided to go that way, "That would be an invalid use of the power of the board of trustees." He made a distinction between American universities, always run by boards of trustees, and German universities, which were run by the various faculties of colleges. He said peers could indeed make mistakes or be prejudiced, so the checks and balances were necessary. But he insisted the trustees had to go by what was "on the record," the inquiry by peers. In Curran's situation, of course, the peers had "assumed" his competence. In fact, Curran said, neither the faculty nor the trustees had made a substantive inquiry into his writings and teachings. Speaking of the board's acceptance of a part of the Marlowe report in 1968—the part dealing with the academic propriety of dissent—Curran said, "I thought the trustees should have gone further than they did, but still I accepted the fact that we have proved to the world that we could hold our head high as an American institution of higher learning. This is the principle I fought for for the last 20 years; you can be both Catholic and university at one and the same time."

The Ratzinger letter on his ineligibility to teach Catholic theology, he said, had violated that academic freedom and hence had breached his contract because it represented an external judgment on his fitness to teach not made by his peers. He said he believed that his tenure guaranteed academic freedom, and between 1970 and 1980 no one at the university had ever told him that his writings were inconsistent with his right to academic freedom. Some scurrilous mimeographed sheets had been left around campus a half dozen times, Curran said, but John Whalen, acting rector, had apologized to him for that.

The time and the testimony had flown by. It was 5 o'clock, and the twilight had come, bringing with it the chill of a winter evening. Spectators parted, and the lawyers stuffed their papers into briefcases. The players in the Curran case fled under gray skies to warmer, more personal enclaves. The day had tired everyone; a rest was due, for there was more to come.

THURSDAY WAS CURRAN'S day. His testimony consumed the six hours allotted in the 9-to-5 court sessions.

Paul Saunders began by asking Curran about a particular passage in his book, *Faithful Dissent*. Kevin Baine had read it at the beginning of the trial to show that Curran believed he was teaching his theology for the good of the church. "Academic freedom for the Catholic theologian is ultimately for the good of the church," Curran had written. The church was free to protect itself from error by pointing out the erroneous nature of a theologian's work. "And in a certain sense, yes, theologians in the academy will make error, and the church will have voluntarily given up juridical control over them. But in the last analysis, I think that that ultimately is for the good of the church."

Saunders pointed out that the church had not disciplined Curran in the way that it had others. He had not been excommunicated, silenced, or censured, and he continued to have the support of his bishop and permission to teach outside his home diocese. No restrictions were upon him. The point, obviously, was that the Vatican declaration imposed only academic sanctions against Curran. There were no grounds for church discipline. Yet Curran believed academic sanctions were solely the business of the university, not the church.

Curran said he saw the Vatican ruling as "very definitely affecting my roles as a Catholic theologian qua theologian." And yet, he added, "In and of itself, it could have no direct juridical effect within the academic world." He said the Ratzinger letter had tried to go around that. "They want to say eligibility is sort of the first hurdle you have to go through. You don't get competency until you overcome the hurdle of eligibility." But Curran said that "eligibility" was a new concept and that he had never heard the term "suitable or eligible" until Ratzinger had used it.

A canon lawyer had told Curran there was no such thing as a "declaratory judgment," which is what the university said the Ratzinger letter was. Tribunals make judgments and take actions, Curran said, "but the Congregation for the Doctrine of the Faith is not a tribunal." Since the congregation was an administrative arm of the church, all the letter had done "was make a declaration," he said. "That letter contains no action to be taken against me." If so, then how could the board of trustees be "bound" to do anything because of it? he asked.

Moreover, Curran said that Cardinals James A. Hickey and Joseph Bernardin knew about the investigation but had taken no action against him. Hickey was chancellor and Bernardin chairman of the trustees. "They knew everything I knew, and, I presume probably more," he said. And yet neither of them had said the investigation would lead to termination of his teaching at the university. Nor had they said he should curtail his public dissents.

Curran spoke of his compromise offers to Hickey—that he

would not teach sexual ethics, would move to the department of religion and religious education, and would even be a professor at large. All had been to no avail. All these offers, he said, "might be looked upon, then, as a way of avoiding any kind of confrontation." Curran said he had objected "strenuously" to Hickey's decision to suspend him before the faculty committee even started work. He had capitulated only because Hickey had threatened to invoke Canon 812 if he did not. "I did not want to [be] the occasion for the invocation of Canon 812 in the United States," he said.

With respect to Byron's offer to teach social ethics, Curran said, "If I am going to teach a course in social ethics, I am going to teach it as a Catholic theologian." He had rejected Byron's condition that he acquiesce in the ruling that he was not "suitable or eligible" to teach Catholic theology. "I mean, I can't deny who I am," Curran said. "I just thought that put me personally in an untenable position, to say nothing about how it was ever going to be policed or carried out."

In response to Baine's contention that Curran was calling on the university to "defy Rome," Curran said that defiance was not necessary for the university to defend his academic freedom; it had not been necessary in 1968. Catholic University was not a pontifical school, he asserted. It was owned by a board of trustees with bylaws barring outside interference and guaranteeing autonomy. "Sponsorship" was a better word to describe church ties to the university, he contended. The relationship of the church to the ecclesiastical faculties, he continued, was like that of an accrediting association that set down norms for degrees and competence. And yet, he said, the church did not—or at least should not—control the university.

WHEN THE ECONOMIC crunch of the early 1970s began to displace faculty members at Catholic University and elsewhere, Curran contended in his testimony, the idea of tenure shifted from tenure in the department to tenure in the university as an institution. "The theory, obviously, is that tenure itself is granted by the university. It's not granted by the department," he said. Curran spoke of a letter from Byron saying that the university viewed tenure in the same broad sense. He used to believe his tenure was to the department of theology, he said, but his view had evolved along with university practice.

"Do you believe the 1981 canonical statutes apply to you?" Saunders asked.

"No," Curran said. In earlier testimony he had put it this way: "I think that any future event which derogates essential rights is not obliging on me." As a result, he told Saunders, his contractual relationship had been broken both when the chancellor relied on the 1981 statutes to suspend him and when the board barred him from teaching theology anywhere because of the Vatican declaration.

Saunders asked him what damages had resulted from those breaches. Curran had made no claims, but it was a necessary part of his proof to establish that damage had occurred because of the breach of contract. Curran said he had lost access to the scholarly environment, the graduate students, and the library. At Cornell and the University of Southern California he had had to make trips to other libraries for his research.

Those university jobs had come to him without pursuit, so he accepted, he said. "What else was I supposed to do? Teaching has always been a very important part of who I am." He could not endure as a research professor, he testified. "My life has obviously been ruptured a bit, just in terms of the time it takes to learn a new library." Curran said he had not tried to quantify the damages, because to him it was a matter of principle more than financial loss.

He conceded that many American universities had started as church-related and become secular. "I am not asking for that," he said. His commitment, he said, was to both concepts, "Catholic" and "university."

Regarding his students, Curran said there was a good market for specialists with the right degrees in social ethics and moral theology. He spoke specifically of the five students who had intervened in his case and whose situation was the subject of cross-examination by Paul Andrews, one of the students' lawyers.

Judge Weisberg probed the professor's concept of academic freedom. Imagine, he said, a case in which the ad hoc faculty committee and the board of trustees took no action based on the Vatican ruling—neither revoking the professor's canonical mission nor barring him from teaching or wrote back and said they did not understand what the Vatican meant by "no longer suitable or eligible."

In the judge's hypothetical instance, the Vatican's response to the inaction or request for clarification was: "What we meant was no Catholic theology at Catholic University of America. Period. If you do not reconsider your position, and if you continue to allow Professor Curran to teach theology either on an ecclesiastical faculty or on a nonecclesiastical faculty, we will (a) decertify the ecclesiastical faculty and not recognize those degrees, and (b) withdraw what we have always viewed as the charter of the Catholic University of America for its formation by Pope Leo in 1887, and you can be whatever you want to be after that, but you will not be in that relationship with the church."

Weisberg continued. "Would you say that that's the price the university would have to pay for academic freedom?"

"I would have to say, yes, your honor," Curran said.

"Okay," Weisberg said.

"But, interestingly enough, they didn't say that," Curran added.

"I know," Weisberg said.

BAINE WOULD BEHAVE toward Curran as Saunders acted toward Hickey and Byron: as a gentlemanly antagonist. In his normal style, Baine got quickly to the point about the rights of the church and the obligations of its priests. He established that Curran did not deny the congregation's right to investigate his writings and protect church doctrine. They agreed the Vatican ruling was on discipline, not doctrine.

"And this disciplinary document was issued by your ecclesiastical superior, was it not?" Baine asked.

"Yes. I mean, insofar as it came from the dicasteries of the Roman Curia," Curran said.

"All Roman Catholics have obligations to respect the judgments of the Holy See, do they not?"

Curran acknowledged that they did.

"And as a Catholic priest you have a special obligation to show reverence and obedience to the pope?" Baine asked.

"Yes. We could debate what that might add to the other, but I will accept it as special."

"And both as a Roman Catholic and a Roman Catholic priest you are required by church law to observe all directions of the Holy See that pertain to you?"

"That is correct," Curran said.

To Baine, who tried carefully to read Weisberg's reactions, Curran's admissions had just closed the case. So far as his contract went, if both Curran and the university believed the Vatican declaration was binding on them, there was no way to reject the disciplinary action taken, Baine reasoned. Past concepts about the contract paled under that current understanding. In case Curran had not made these admissions, Baine had the priest's deposition ready with references to his being bound by the ruling.

"The disciplinary document in this case was addressed to you and pertained to you, does it not?" he asked the theologian.

"It does," Curran said.

"For that reason, Father Curran, you said to the faculty committee in this case that the declaration was binding on you and you alone?" Baine asked.

"That is correct."

"And it is binding on you as a matter of church law?"

"Yes."

"You also said before the faculty committee that because the declaration was forwarded to the chancellor of the university for appropriate action he is also bound in some way by the declaration?" Baine asked.

Curran again agreed.

"Now, although this declaration is binding on you as a matter of church law, you believe you are free to disregard it. Is that true?"

"Disregard is a broad term," Curran said. "I have to regard it, but I can disagree with it."

Baine had laid his groundwork meticulously. He was ready to challenge Curran. "What gives you the right under canon law to dissent from a disciplinary decision about you? " he asked.

"The only one who can take action against me for violating church law is an ecclesiastical superior," Curran said. "No ecclesiastical superior of mine has taken any punitive action against me for my actions with regard to this. I don't think you have any right to bring this up in this court, and I think you are impugning my reputation."

Baine said the university had taken the position that as a priest Curran was to observe directives of the Holy See.

"What is that based upon?" Curran asked.

"Are you aware that is the university's position?" Baine asked in a voice that had abandoned some of its earlier gentlemanliness.

"What is that based upon?" Curran snapped.

Baine explained to Curran that he had to answer the questions.

"Let him ask," Weisberg interjected, "and if you can't answer the question, just say I have no answer or some other answer, but this is not a forum [in which] you are permitted to ask back." The exchanges continued testily.

They turned then to Curran's deposition, in which he had said he was only obligated to give the Vatican's declaration the "respect of intellect and will." For the church to extract more, he claimed, his ecclesiastical superior had to say he had violated church law. Curran acknowledged, however, that the board had accepted the limitation the Vatican had put on his teaching.

So Baine asked, "Despite that fact, you would still continue to go on teaching Catholic theology at the university unless the university stops you from doing so?"

"That is correct," Curran said.

Baine referred to Curran's June 9, 1988, letter to Byron after the faculty hearing. In that letter he said he could disregard the Vatican declaration. Curran, in his response to Baine's question at his deposition, had said that the university should in effect join him in dissenting from the Vatican declaration.

Curran said he would have added a nuance to that answer as he looked back on it. "I do believe there are other places where I answered that question the other way," he said.

Baine focused on Curran's explanation: "But it [the university] would have to agree with you that the congregation was wrong when it said you were ineligible to teach Catholic theology?" Baine asked.

"No, it would not," Curran said. "It would only have to say that it was not applicable to Catholic theologians qua academics." The university, however, had relied on the Vatican declaration's words that Curran was a "professor" who taught, a point Baine would bring out in later testimony.

But for now he cited an analogy Curran had made earlier, that the declaration was like an unjust law that does not need to be obeyed. Curran agreed with Baine that the chancellor was bound by the declaration to do something, but he continued to reject the extent to which Hickey and the board had acted against him.

Weisberg asked Curran what would happen if Hickey wrote back to Ratzinger saying he did not know what to do with the declaration because Curran was competent. In that negotiation, the judge continued, Ratzinger would write back and say, "Begin proceedings to withdraw the canonical mission and consider barring him from teaching." What happens then? Weisberg asked.

Curran said the chancellor could ask the university president to begin an Article 24 dismissal proceeding based on a challenge to his competency. That, he said, would have to go to a hearing. And there peer judgment on his competency would have to be the deciding factor. At one point, Weisberg asked whether the distinction being made between "ineligible" and "incompetent" was not just a word game because whatever word was used, the Vatican claimed final authority on the decision of whether Curran was ineligible. But Curran insisted there was a difference.

Curran admitted that professors could be dismissed for reasons other than incompetence, such as demonstrable "dishonesty in teaching or research, for manifest neglect of duty or for other adequate cause."

"Adequate cause must be something different from incompetency, would you agree?" Baine said.

Curran said it came down to "fitness to teach."

"Is it your judgment that your peers have greater competency than the Congregation for the Doctrine of the Faith to judge your writings?" Baine asked.

"I have never said that," Curran said. But he agreed that the process in the academy was "much more adequate" than the congregation's process.

"Is there any way in which the congregation speaks with greater authority than your peers do?" Baine asked. That was a question Curran did not say "no" to, but neither was he able to explain the congregation's role when it and the peers disagreed.

Baine wanted to show that even if Curran said he was an academic theologian, that was exactly what the Vatican declaration targeted. He asked if the Vatican ruling did not "include your role as theologian qua academician?"

Curran said that according to his understanding of an American university the ruling had no authority, and hence no effect.

"On the face of the document it says you are ineligible and unsuitable to exercise the function of a professor of Catholic theology. Isn't that what it says?" Baine asked.

"That is correct," Curran said. "In one place it says professor. The other place it says teach." Curran said he did not know the congregation's view of the difference between an academic theologian and church theologian, only that he himself relied on academic freedom in the university context. To conclude the line of questioning, Baine pointed out that no church disciplines or restrictions on writing or research had been imposed on Curran, implying that the Vatican's focus was his teaching status as an academician.

In further questioning Curran agreed with Baine that the Vatican letter was universal, affecting his teaching of Catholic theology anywhere at the university. This roused Weisberg's interest. If everyone assumed that the letter was binding on the university, then would it, in Curran's opinion, bar him from teaching anywhere? Weisberg asked. Curran said it would if two "ifs" occurred: if the letter were binding on the university and if the board had an obligation under canon law—both points that he contested.

Baine then turned to a more subtle topic: Respect for the magisterium and who decides when enough respect is being given. To illustrate, Baine cited the International Theological Commission's report, which said respect for the magisterium is part of the science of theology.

"Respect tends to be, or can be, interpreted as a more subjective personal aspect of it," Curran said, adding that he preferred to use the words "due weight."

Using Curran's words, Baine asked if the congregation had not decided "that you failed to give due weight to the teaching of the magisterium?" Curran acknowledged that it had.

Curran said that based on Canon 752 such a claim would be incorrect. That canon, depending on the translation from Latin, means "religious respect of intellect and will" or "religious submission of intellect and will" to noninfallible teaching. Curran said giving such respect depended on the level of the teaching and other interpretations. In his case, he said, "I think I have given due weight."

To clarify, Baine asked if Curran meant that he could give respect to something and still dissent from it. Curran said yes.

Baine pointed out that Curran dissented on church limits on remarriage for divorced Catholics, a doctrine that had been established at the Council of Trent and was, according to Baine, a core doctrine. Curran said his idea of divorce was compatible with Trent because, similar to his argument, that council had allowed divorce concessions to members of the Greek, or Byzantine Rite, church who came under Roman jurisdiction.

Referring to Cardinal Ratzinger's letter, Baine noted its reminder that the Second Vatican Council had called abortion an "unspeakable crime," while Curran dissented on that subject. Curran said that a student who answered the complex abortion question that simply on an exam in his courses would fail. According to history, Curran said, the church only opposed direct abortion at all times, not indirect abortion. "Indirect abortion can be permitted for appropriate, for proportionate reasons," he said, using the subtle parlance of the "new" moral theology.

"Father Curran, I can't debate you on theology," Baine said. His real question, he said, was whether the congregation in fact claimed that Curran did not give sufficient respect to church teachings. Curran agreed. He also conceded to the obvious: That some theologians, not just the Vatican, thought his dissent was out of bounds.

Baine then pointed out that in Curran's original complaint, dated February 28, 1987, he had alleged that social ethics was a subset of moral theology. But when the complaint was amended on June 10, Curran had claimed that his only area of competence was moral theology. "Is it impossible for the university to reach an understanding with you that you could teach courses in the area of social ethics without teaching Catholic moral theology?" Baine asked.

"Yes, it is," Curran said.

"If the university is searching for alternatives for you to teach other than Catholic moral theology, I take it there are none?" Baine asked.

"That is correct," Curran said. "I was willing to teach social ethics"—but only, he said, if he did not have to sign an oath or agree to be bound by the Vatican's declaration, which he understood the university was requiring him to do formally.

When Baine mentioned his past course in Protestant social ethics, Curran said the course had drawn comparisons from Catholic theology. "In any event, Father Curran, is it fair to say that this lawsuit is not over whether Catholic University will let you teach Protestant social thought?" Baine asked.

"I think really to be more exact," Curran said, "it is over whether or not I have to admit the Vatican declaration applies within Catholic University. That is the ultimate reality."

The judge asked whether every document that carried papal approval was as strongly binding as, say, an encyclical. Curran said the pope approves scores of letters, dispensations, and other decrees. Weisberg asked about the weight of the term "definitive" in the Vatican ruling on him.

Curran said it carried "no more weight than it ordinarily would have by being approved by the pope."

They turned next to the Marlowe committee report. Baine tried to establish the difference between the Marlowe hearings and the hearings in the Curran case. In Marlowe, Baine asserted, there had been no evidence, witnesses, adversary proceeding, or Vatican ruling. By comparison, all these elements had been part of the ad hoc faculty hearing for Curran in 1987. Although Saunders disagreed with this comparison, Baine got it before the judge and on the record.

Baine went on to establish that Curran's tenure had been given to him through no formal process and that it had taken twenty pages of transcript in the deposition to establish when Curran had gotten his tenure, and still the time could only be pinned down to 1970 or 1971. Curran said his view of Catholic University had evolved. On arrival, he said, he had believed it was a pontifical university. Over time, however, his understanding had become more sophisticated. By analogy, he said, the Vatican's relationship with the ecclesiastical faculties was like that of an accrediting agency.

Weisberg jumped in again. Why was the Vatican ruling then not a removal of the department's accreditation, he asked. Curran said it would have been. Then the judge asked what happened to peer review in that case. Curran's answer wandered.

"Then what is unreasonable about the university's response to that without getting into competence at all?" Weisberg asked. "To just say by the board, well, we don't want to lose our accreditation. We interpret this letter to mean either Curran goes or we lose our accreditation?"

Curran went on a circular discussion about Rome's approving all sorts of aspects of the new bylaws, not just the canonical statutes.

"For some reason I am not making my question clear at all," Weisberg said diplomatically—as he often did when he sensed the evasion he had often seen on the witness stand during his career.

If Curran believed the Vatican was like an accrediting agency for the ecclesiastical faculties, the judge asked, why couldn't it disaccredit them? Because Rome also promised academic freedom, Curran said. "That is why they can't do it."

Baine returned to his questions. He asked about the 1931 apostolic constitution *Deus scientiarum Dominus*. Curran said it was never clear to him that it applied to Catholic University since he was aware that many parts of it were not enforced at the university, such as the rule that all courses be taught in Latin.

Curran added that although the canonical statutes of 1981 required that professors on the ecclesiastical faculty receive a canonical mission, he was not bound by the canonical statutes since they were enacted—over his objections—after he had received tenure. Weisberg, understanding that Curran believed the new statutes could not curtail his earlier rights, probed the issue by asking about the corollary: "Would you take the position that [any provision in the 1981 statutes expanding your rights] would apply to you because it would expand your rights?" Curran said he already had the most expansive rights.

"Knowing that statutes and bylaws change from time to time, when they change in your favor it is applied retroactively but when they change against you, it is not," Weisberg said, summarizing Curran's point of view. Curran agreed that was his position.

Baine noted that although Curran had objected to many provisions in the 1981 statutes, they had in fact been adopted. Indeed, the faculty committee finally had said that Curran was bound by the statutes' canonical mission requirement, though it also said it wanted to protect his rights to teach. Didn't that mean he had a canonical mission? Baine asked.

"Frankly, again it was the hoop that I had to go through in order to get some kind of hearing," Curran said. Later, on the redirect examination, Saunders pointed out that Curran had conceded, for the purpose of the proceedings only, that he had a canonical mission.

As further evidence that Curran had the mission, Baine cited the analysis of canon law professor Frederick McManus that it was very likely the mission had been given "implicitly" since the 1940s, a conclusion the faculty committee and board also had made.

Baine now tackled one of Saunders's key arguments: that the board's June 2 resolution barring Curran from teaching in the nonecclesiastical faculties had violated his tenured contract. Baine framed the board's action in a different light. Cardinal Hickey, as chancellor, had not asked the faculty committee to address anything more than whether the canonical mission should be withdrawn, he said. When, in addition, the faculty committee made recommendations on Curran's teaching rights, Hickey had objected. But he still passed on all its findings to the board of trustees. And so, Baine said, the board also was required to address the teaching status question. It finally decided in the June 2 resolution to bar Curran from teaching theology anywhere at Catholic University.

Baine then pointed out that the 1969 statement on academic freedom, which Curran used as an articulation of his rights, had been adopted by the academic senate but never approved by the board. Other documents showed that that statement still had not been approved by the board of trustees as late as March 1973. Baine noted that under the bylaws no statement related to academic freedom or tenure was binding on the university unless it got that highest approval.

When asked earlier, Curran had said that while he no longer considered Catholic University a pontifical school, he accepted its special relationship to the Holy See. Baine wanted to emphasize that further for the judge. He showed that Curran had written that his case affected only ecclesiastical schools and, when meeting with Hickey and Bernardin in January 1986, he had not challenged their characterization of Catholic University as pontifical. In fact, a transcript of

Curran's press conference of March 11, 1986, showed that Curran had said that Catholic University had been founded by the bishops. Curran was asked at the press conference why he had been singled out. "The college is a pontifical university, a pontifical faculty. Obviously this is very much an official Catholic institution," he had said, according to Baine's transcript.

Curran responded that the transcript was unreliable, not verbatim, pointing out that there were several errors.

Baine then cited the commentary of James Coriden, canon law expert and dean at Washington Theological Union, on what the new Code of Canon Law said about the Vatican's relationship with universities. The commentary said, "Except in the case of a very few dioceses and colleges and at The Catholic University of America, ties with the institutional church generally have been informal and implicit at most."

Curran said that had been Coriden's view, "but it changed."

Baine produced another transcript, from an August 1986 press conference in which Curran had said Catholic University had a different statute than Georgetown or Notre Dame. "A limitation on academic freedom," Baine read from the transcript.

Curran denied that he had said that.

Baine then produced a press release by Curran's lawyers that said the Vatican and hierarchy applied Roman Catholic governing norms in regard to "Catholic University itself and the teaching of philosophy, theology, and certain subject matter at Catholic University." This implied that the university "itself" had canonical obligations. Again Curran said that was not his statement.

Finally, Baine turned to Curran's statement in his book *Faithful Dissent* in which he said that he chose to teach at Catholic University because of its special status and because he wanted to, in Baine's words, "do his theology within and for the church." In the book, Curran also distinguished himself from an academic theologian. "Some theologians will be properly classified as doing their theology for the academy but that is not my role," Curran wrote. "I stayed at Catholic University despite numerous offers to go elsewhere because I wanted to do theology for the Catholic Church. There would be no better place to exercise that role than at the Catholic University of America."

Baine asked him if because of his relationship to Catholic University "you have this special role in the life of the church?"

Curran said, "It is part of it, that's correct."

That was the last question for the day.

WEISBERG OPENED THE eighth day of the trial, December 23, by saying his calendar would permit holding court January 3 and 4 if more evidence or argument needed to be heard. But the lawyers agreed they would try to finish on schedule. Indeed they did, that very day.

With a final question for Curran, Baine established that extensive testimony on the subject of Curran's competence had been given before the faculty hearing. He cited names of those who had testified, a letter from German moral theologian Bernard Häring, and 141 letters from individuals, faculties, and organizations, all attesting to Curran's character and scholarship. The point was to show that competence had not been overlooked. Yet it was not the final issue before the committee and board of trustees.

Curran acknowledged that evidence. But again he made the point that the faculty committee had not attempted to judge his competence but rather had assumed it. He again pointed out that no judgment of competence had even been made about him.

Saunders asked Curran if he had correctly answered Baine's question of the day before regarding the 1969 special statutes. The question was put again, and Curran answered that the statutes "apply to the chancellor" and did not place any obligation on him.

Weisberg said he did not understand. He asked Curran whether it could not be said that one of the obligations imposed on the chancellor by the 1969 special statutes was to confer the canonical mission. In that case, perhaps it could be said the statutes indirectly placed obligations on Curran to have one, the judge suggested.

Curran cited "an old canonical principle that says those things that are harmful to you are to be interpreted in the most restricted sense" and said that was how the statutes should be viewed.

Weisberg said he was making a different point. If the 1969 statutes, which included a clear obligation for the chancellor to grant the canonical mission, had existed when Curran joined Catholic University in 1965, Weisberg asked, wouldn't there also be an obligation for faculty members to have one? Curran said that if that was intended, "they should be explicitly stated as such, as the rights and duties of the faculty."

Weisberg asked if in 1970, when Curran was up for tenure, the chancellor had said he didn't have the credentials required for tenure, such as a canonical mission, and Curran simply had said he didn't know he needed one, would that have been the end of it? Curran answered, "We might have wound up here fifteen years ago, your honor."

Saunders turned to church law. Curran gave the example of the concordat between the church and Germany, which is both church law and civil law and governs the appointment of bishops, such as a recent controversial one in Cologne. Saunders asked if in such a case the church had an exclusive right to interpret the concordat, or whether the state had an interest. Curran said both had a claim. "I don't think that the state in Germany would accept the Vatican's interpretation without question," Curran added.

Based on that example, Saunders established that the 1931 statutes, the 1969 special statutes, and the 1981 canonical statutes were all civil law as part of the civil bylaws of the university. "I understand my contractual obligations to the university to be governed by civil law," Curran added. "I mean, basically I think this is the whole point of the discussion."

Saunders read back a colloquy between the judge and Curran about whether the university trustees had taken any action based on the Vatican letter, and Saunders asked if Curran would add to that.

Curran said the Ratzinger letter affected only him, not the university, and that it affected him wherever he went.

"All over the world?" Saunders asked.

"I think so. I hope not to heaven, but at least all over the world," Curran said.

"Do you plan to continue your teaching?" Weisberg asked.

Much as he had done in the classroom, Curran quoted a medieval theologian to answer the question. According to Duns Scotus, he said, "heaven will consist of half your time teaching and half your time learning, a marvelous part of the Catholic tradition." Curran continued: "So the Ratzinger letter follows me. It has no effect on anybody else."

The other element, Curran said, was the letter from Ratzinger to

Hickey, telling him to take "appropriate action." What kind? he asked. "With regard to the nonecclesiastical faculty of the university, Archbishop Hickey can take no action by statute," Curran said. He could only talk to the university president and urge him to start an Article 24 hearing, Curran continued. "That is the only thing that could be done in the nonecclesiastical faculty." Even in the ecclesiastical faculty, Curran said, promises of academic freedom protected him from every adverse action without peer judgment of incompetence.

With that Saunders closed.

Baine did not have a question but wanted to read for the record the full text of the discussion between the judge and Curran. That was the text Saunders had used to ask Curran if he had answered the judge's question correctly the previous day. Weisberg joked, "I think that was my most embarrassing moment in the trial, I sort of wish you wouldn't." Baine read it anyway.

Saunders then read, for the record, a piece of Byron's testimony before the faculty committee. He offered some exhibits and rested his case.

THIRTEEN

Past Presidents

After Paul Saunders rested his case, Kevin Baine moved for dismissal of Charles Curran's complaint. The plaintiff's evidence was all on the table. Now, he said, "the court may weigh the evidence, resolve any conflicts, and decide where the preponderance of evidence is."

Curran had not proved breach of contract, Baine argued. The Catholic University of America had never contracted away its right of religious freedom, and there was nothing to show the university had promised to protect Curran from a Vatican declaration of his ineligibility. To prove the contrary, Curran "relies upon a course of conduct, three events," Baine said: the 1967 strike, the 1968 dissent and the Marlowe report about the right of dissenting faculty members, and the university's revision of the bylaws in 1969.

"Nothing in any of those events satisfies his burden, assuming that course of conduct and custom is at all relevant here, and we say it is not," Baine said. He said that legal precedents demands a clear, uniform, and definite custom, which did not exist at Catholic University. "It is crystal clear that the university board of trustees was not of the view twenty years ago, as Father Curran has suggested, that the views of the church were irrelevant," Baine said. In fact, he added, the university had not gone as far as it could—firing Curran—but instead had tried to find him an alternative teaching post. And in the current case, he said, "there was certainly no understanding on the board of trustees that the views of church authorities were to be disregarded or merely weighed in the balance."

Curran "could be teaching at the university right now if he were willing to broaden his own definition of his field of competence," Baine told the court. Adding a few other examples of university generosity, he concluded, "Under the circumstances, we think there is no basis [to claim] that his contract has been violated."

Saunders rose for a brief rebuttal. According to the evidence, he said, "It is clear that the understanding of the parties at the time of the contract was that academic freedom was an integral part of the contract." The faculty had that right and could rely on it, he said, and it could not simply be taken away.

Judge Frederick Weisberg asked how that guarantee became part of the contract if it was not written?

Saunders said that it did not need be written. "It was a part of the contract in the beginning." The events of 1967 and 1968 had not created the right, he said, but were evidence of everyone's expectation and belief that the right existed.

Weisberg said he had to deal with the case as a contract issue. Both sides, he noted, agreed that the contract was not written. He said he understood Baine to be saying that the relationship between the Holy See and the university was so special that the university would not give up its rights without an explicit waiver. He understood Curran to be saying that the mere fact that he had entered a university implied his rights to academic freedom. From the university's point of view, he added, this wasn't "just any old Catholic university"—it expected faculty members to observe the appropriate church-given limits on academic freedom.

"That is where I think the heart of the case is," Weisberg said.

Responding to Baine's argument that there was no explicit waiver of the university's right to religious freedom, Saunders said he would not expect that Harvard University had explicitly waived its right to religious freedom when it had severed its connection to the Congregational Church. "That is, Harvard University is a corporation in the same sense that Catholic University is a corporation," he argued. "They are both American corporate entities. Catholic University has no more or less right to the free exercise of religion than Harvard does."

Weisberg asked if the Catholic University documents that formed Curran's contract didn't speak of a special relationship to the Holy See. Saunders, who believed the contract documents were two civil handbooks for the faculty, attempted to show that they did not speak of such a connection. Baine looked on, knowing that both handbooks contained the explicit phrase "special relationship."

Saunders said there were church institutions in Washington,

some just across the street from Catholic University, that had a "special relationship" with the Vatican. "No one disputes that there is not academic freedom in those institutions in the same sense in which there is in a university," he said. "It is the nature of a university that requires academic freedom and institutional autonomy." He said the university and church could have set up a separate religious institute for the teaching of theology but instead had chosen to teach theology in the university context.

In final response, Baine said the plaintiff's case was not based on a contract but "on the plaintiff's idea of a university." To suggest a comparison between Harvard and Catholic University belittles the case, he said. "Harvard University abandoned its relationship with the Congregationalist Church a number of years ago." Academic freedom, Baine argued, was not an abstract concept floating around a university campus. "It develops meaning through its application in particular cases, and this case is an unusual case," he said.

Weisberg asked Baine if his claim of religious freedom allowed the university to say that it might have had a contract understanding that included academic freedom before but that the situation had evolved and the university was not liable for breach in taking away that freedom? That's right, Baine said. Even if the university had made an explicit contract with Curran that ensured academic freedom, which it had not, and even if the court would say the university's free exercise right was not absolute, there would still be the question of what was the "compelling state interest here that requires us to somehow enforce this contract," he said.

After a short break to consider the motion for dismissal, Weisberg ruled that Curran had made a prima facie case and that Baine had to put on a defense. Because of how the testimonies had proceeded from the first day, a patchwork of prosecution and defense, Baine had already called five of his witnesses. There were two more to go.

BAINE CALLED THE two men who had run the university from 1969 to 1982, the only two lay presidents in the university's history, Clarence Walton and Edmund Daniel Pellegrino.

Walton, a graduate student at Catholic University before the war, had returned to his alma mater from Columbia University, where as dean of general studies from 1964 to 1969 he had been in the center of the student riots. As a professor he had taught economics. Baine's partner, Stephen Urbanczyk, questioned Walton.

Walton, who had become Catholic University president in 1969, had participated in some of the board of trustees' meetings to draft the new bylaws that year. Some on the board, he recalled, had resisted change. That opposition party had included three cardinals—John Krol of Philadelphia, James McIntyre of Los Angeles, and Patrick O'Boyle of Washington. The strength of this group had prompted those advocating the new bylaws to work quickly to head off the opposition, Walton said. He, Cardinal Lawrence Shehan of Baltimore, and two assisting priests had gone to Rome in November 1969 to present their case for the new bylaws to the Congregation for Catholic Education.

He recalled a little Italian priest who had asked whether the changes meant the university was severing its ties with the Holy See. Shehan answered definitely not, "The tie with the Holy See remains." The board had approved the new bylaws in September, hastened by Shehan's trip to Rome.

Walton said that during the debate leading to the bylaw changes, the Vatican had suggested that a statement be added: "The duties of the archbishop of Washington as chancellor of the university are repeatedly reaffirmed regarding the entire university and in particular regarding the ecclesiastical school." But no such statement had been appended.

The relationship between the university and the Holy See continued, Walton said, "but the internal governance of the university was very substantially enlarged." Walton said his selection as president had been a breakthrough for the laity. He could reconcile the university's claim to autonomy, on the one hand, while on the other maintaining a special bond to the Holy See because there was a mixed board of trustees with clergy and laity. Early in his term, he recalled, he spoke out of prudence to the chancellor about appointments of deans to ecclesiastical schools. But he said the conversations were only consultative; he made the final decision.

Finally Urbanczyk asked the question that the judge had asked several witnesses: What would the board have done if the Ratzinger letter declaring Curran ineligible to teach Catholic theology had come in 1970? Walton said that about the same thing would have happened.

Saunders began his cross-examination by asking what Walton thought the board would have done in 1970, having received the hypothetical Ratzinger letter, to consider Curran's teachings and competence. And how, he added, would the board have taken into consideration Curran's academic freedom?

"This is a tricky one," Walton said. "What do you mean by academic freedom?"

"It doesn't seem too hard for me," joked Weisberg, who had heard the word hundreds of times.

"Does it seem clear to you?" Walton asked.

"No. I am just kidding."

"I haven't heard all of the definitions," Walton said.

"Well, we have been here for a week," Weisberg said.

"It's called cabin fever," Saunders added, and he restated the question.

Walton said he believed academic freedom existed at Catholic University but said the prefix Catholic in the institution's name was important. A state university, he pointed out, was beholden to state guidelines and the votes of a state legislature. In Ohio, for example, the state had overridden an admissions policy set by the faculty with the result, in effect, that anyone who graduated from high school was allowed to attend.

"In the case of Catholic University of America, the prefix suggested that the institution was church-related or church-sponsored," he said.

Saunders asked for Walton's definition of academic freedom. Walton said it was the right to teach and publish, but it also contained the responsibilities defined by the nature of an institution. In an effort to establish the point that in a university external authorities did not have the right to determine who could teach, Saunders asked another "what if" question. If the American Society of Physicists wrote to him and said a professor on campus were teaching that the sun revolved around the earth, what would he do?

Walton said he would first invite the organization's leader to meet with the professor and get the information straight. If the charge was serious enough he would call in a faculty committee. Before that outside judgment affected the professor, Saunders asked, would Walton subject it to judgment by faculty peers? "Most probably I would," he said. Seeing where Saunders was going, Walton said, "I want to make an important point. There is a very sharp distinction between physics and Catholic moral theology."

Walton said he had learned the distinction between the "sacred" and "profane" sciences when had come to Catholic University and mused that if he used the term "profane sciences" at Columbia he would "be hooted off" campus. "But there was a distinction made and therefore that distinction in my mind would be important."

Saunders asked whether in 1970 theologians had had the right to dissent from noninfallible church teachings. Walton said they had, as Curran had done in 1968, but that the right must be exercised in the context of an institution's special mission and nature. "Unless you look at that special quality about it, then the definition of the 'rights and freedoms' becomes almost, if you will, so obtuse . . . that they don't have practical meaning. I was a practical guy. I was running a university."

Saunders asked if Georgetown University was a pontifical school, and Walton said it had a pontifical charter but that over time its relationship with the Vatican had changed.

Saunders asked who had severed that relationship.

Walton said Saunders should ask Timothy Healy, then the Jesuit president.

"The D.C. Court of Appeals," Weisberg corrected him jokingly. He was referring to the court's recent ruling that Georgetown was bound by the D.C. Human Rights Act to give equal access and benefits to gay student groups, despite the Catholic Church's teaching against homosexuality.

"Touché," Walton said.

Saunders showed that in fact Catholic University had been established by civil law under an act of Congress two years before the papal charter was given. Concerning the 1969 bylaw revision, Walton said it had been triggered by the visit of the Middle States Association of Colleges and Schools. Some at the university, Walton said, had worried that the university's ties to the church might bring about a lawsuit against the university for receiving federal funds.

Given that the chancellor got his power from the Holy See,

Saunders asked if the university could nevertheless be called autonomous.

"It's a free and autonomous university in light of its particular and specialized history," Walton said. "It is a totally unique kind of institution in the United States." The answers were not totally satisfying to Saunders, so he pressed the point. What would have happened if the board had received the Ratzinger letter in 1970, reviewed it, and decided not to act?

"As Stalin said to the Holy See, count the regiments," Walton said. "There would be no way that it [the Vatican] could force it [the action against Curran] if the trustees said no." Would such a letter be binding on the university, Saunders asked. "Not any more," Walton answered.

"Not after 1970?" asked Saunders.

"That's right," Walton responded. The university might "no longer be The Catholic University of America with a unique relationship to the Holy See," he added, but it would still be a university. A joke had gone around at one time, he said, that if severance from Rome happened the university should be renamed "Brookland University" for the tree-lined old neighborhood in which it stood.

Saunders asked about the January 28, 1970, letter F. Taylor Jones of Middle States had written to congratulate Catholic University on its "new freedom" following the 1969 bylaw revision. "I have just heard," Jones had written, "that the authorities in Rome have released their hold on the university." Evidence was introduced to show that Walton had jotted on the letter a note to his secretary: "Phone Taylor to thank him and impress on him the historic nature of this action for CU." Acknowledging that, Walton said his positive response to Taylor had indicated his concurrence with the new independence of the school. And so, his reply said, "We have now brought the governance of this university into conformity with normal American academic practice."

When Saunders produced a statement on academic freedom—based on the American Association of University Professors' model—that the university submitted to Middle States, Walton said he stood by it but with one qualifier. The university never adopts outside documents, he said. Internal ones had to be adopted by the board. In fact, he said, the AAUP in those days "was turning into a, if you will, a quasi-bargaining board. It was not the same kind of AAUP set up to protect academic freedom that I knew in my early days."

To another question, Walton said that at one time the American Association of Law Schools had recommended that law professors at Catholic University get the same pay as federal judges. "My answer was 'be a federal judge,'" Walton said.

"I would have expected that to be a reduction in pay," Weisberg joked.

"Oh, no, no, you don't know our salary scales," Walton said.

THE FINAL WITNESS was Edmund Daniel Pellegrino, who had followed Walton as president of Catholic University from 1978 to 1982. Pellegrino held a chair in medicine and medical humanities at Georgetown University. His long and varied career, which included university presidencies and department chairmanships, the teaching of medicine, and his current position as director of the Kennedy Institute of Ethics at Georgetown, led to the question of academic freedom. Under Stephen Urbanczyk's questioning, he recalled a case after the war in which, while president of the University of Kentucky, he had defended the right of the dean of the school of economics to hand out tracts calling for withholding taxes because of the bombing of Hiroshima and Nagasaki.

Soon after Pellegrino had become president, Curran had visited him to give him background on the disputes over himself and related issues. He had given the new president two books on the incidents in 1967. He had hoped, Pellegrino recalled, "that I would take the position that his freedom was such that he could take the position he wished to take and that indeed the university should back his right to dissent."

Pellegrino said that he did not agree with Curran's view of academic freedom. As a result of his conversations with Curran he had developed a general response, a sort of deflection, to private Catholic inquiries about the moral theologian. Typically he would say that the orthodoxy of Curran's teaching was to be judged by the ecclesiastical authorities, not the university president, and that until a bishop gave him a directive he would take no action regarding Curran. "To do so would be to usurp an authority which I did not have," he told the court.

"I think the role of peer judgment is limited," Pellegrino said. It can address methodology, rigor of argument, and use of source evidence, he said. "But I do not think in the ultimate determination of whether a matter is of faith or not, that the peer judgment is relevant." That judgment rests with the board of trustees, he said, which had a peculiar role at Catholic University.

Pellegrino said he saw the school as a pontifical university, and this was a significant feature to him. "At the time . . . I accepted the presidency, I had offers from three other institutions to become president. I chose Catholic University of America because I felt that it was a unique institution," he said. "It was the flagship institution of Catholic higher education in America," and he was interested in the intellectual engagement of Catholic and modern thought, he added.

If there were limits on the study of theology, Urbanczyk asked, did that mean theology professors were not free to dissent? "They were free to dissent," Pellegrino said. But if that dissent went so far as to be "no longer considered consistent with the received faith . . . then the freedom was limited."

Responding to Weisberg's question, Pellegrino said the limits on theological academic freedom sprang from several sources, and he emphasized one in particular: "It is also a guideline for the moral and spiritual life of Roman Catholics. And so that what a theologian teaches has implications above and beyond its academic implications."

Weisberg asked if the academic freedom for professors in the ecclesiastical faculties differed from that of professors in nonecclesiastical faculties.

Pellegrino said that in his opinion, "An academic theologian is bound whether he is at a Catholic university like the Catholic University or some other setting." Weisberg wondered what would happen if a theologian dissented elsewhere, and not in an ecclesiastical faculty at Catholic University. Pellegrino said a bishop could declare his teaching wrong, but the university would not make that its business. However, at Catholic University, because of the special relationship with the Holy See, that was different, he said.

Under questioning from Urbanczyk, Pellegrino said it was his view that the board of trustees had been obligated to see to it that Curran didn't teach theology after the Vatican declaration was issued.

Saunders wanted to narrow some of these generalizations down to specifics. In 1980, he asked, would the trustees have been required to act as they had in 1986? He was asking if the Vatican letter was binding merely by its declaration of Curran's ineligibility. "I think the response would be the same in both cases," Pellegrino said, even if Curran were in the nonecclesiastical faculty. Weisberg pursued that topic. "Is there something that [Curran] could have done even in the face of the declaration from the congregation [the Ratzinger letter] at another school that he could not do . . . at Catholic University?" Pellegrino answered that the ecclesiastical faculties were different from the nonecclesiastical faculties.

"What if the [Ratzinger] letter came with respect to a professor of biology?" Saunders asked. Pellegrino said the situation would not be the same. "The Holy See is not qualified to make decisions about biology," he said. "They are, however, qualified to make statements about the theological implications of biological findings." With that, Saunders got an idea.

MUCH OF THE HYPOTHETICAL probing in the trial had lacked concrete examples, but now the lines of Saunders's questioning produced one that was quite specific. He introduced the question of *in vitro* fertilization. The technology, which is condemned by church teaching, allows doctors to fertilize the ovum outside the uterus.

Raising this topic, Saunders implied that the Holy See had indeed spoken on biology. He asked what would result if the Holy See were to intervene regarding a Catholic University professor who taught about *in vitro* fertilization? Pellegrino said a distinction should be made between the biological and theological implications of such teaching. Saunders persisted, but Pellegrino insisted that the Vatican would never "quarrel with the biological facts . . . it's important to keep that distinction in mind."

Weisberg interjected immediately: "But that's the point. I don't mean to steal your question, Mr. Saunders. I think that's the point of the question. I'll use the word interference. I don't mean any pejorative connotation by it.

"The interference from the church would be based on the theological implications of what was being taught, not the biological," Weisberg said. "And the question is what the obligation of the university is in those circumstances, given the special relationship the university has with the Holy See."

In response, Pellegrino said that in his opinion if a professor of biology offered theological observations that were "offensive, dangerous, misled people with the authority of the Catholic University of America behind it, I think it would have the same weight as it would as if he were teaching theology. Because he was making a theological statement." Pellegrino, taking another question from Saunders, said his view would apply even to a biology professor teaching in the nonecclesiastical faculties.

"I don't really think that's fair," Weisberg said. He said the biologist simply would be teaching how something worked mechanically, why it worked, and its scientific implications. "None of this has anything to do with theology," he said.

Pellegrino said that with Weisberg's clarification about what the teacher was doing, "There's no problem."

"But the pope says it does have something to do with theology," Weisberg continued.

"Well, the pope would have to make that point clear. I doubt that he would [intervene]," Pellegrino said. Clearly, he did not like the line of questioning.

"In other words," Weisberg said, "when you answered earlier, to my question and to Mr. Saunders, you were assuming the biologist was standing up there and saying, 'and in fact this is the right thing for a Catholic to believe in?'"

Saunders said that was not the point of the question, however. He continued: "My question is precisely this; let us assume that a professor who is teaching biology at Catholic University received a letter from the pope. And the letter from the pope said, because I don't like what you are saying in the classroom, I hereby declare you no longer suitable or eligible to teach biology and that is a final definitive declaration of the Holy See, nothing more."

Over objections, Saunders said his question needed no distinction between biology and theology. "He is teaching biology and you don't know anything more about what he is teaching."

"Okay," Pellegrino said. "If he is teaching biology and I don't know anything more about what he is teaching . . . I would not feel that that [papal letter] was binding."

Even if it were a definitive ruling by the pope? Saunders asked.

"On biology the church has no authority. On theology the church does," Pellegrino said.

Earlier Pellegrino had listed three natural limits to academic freedom in theology: the discipline itself, its methodologies, and the community its serves—its pastoral dimension. By way of comment, Weisberg recalled that Pellegrino had said the pastoral limitation was stronger on clergy than nonclergy.

Saunders then asked about a hypothetical theologian teaching at Harvard who received a letter from the pope. Would that determine his ability to teach? Pellegrino said no, but that was because teaching in itself was free and the school had no special bonds to Rome. Pellegrino said Curran had every right to teach until a properly constituted authority, such as the Vatican, determined he had crossed the line.

Like an echo in the courtroom, the next question was familiar: How could Catholic University could be autonomous with Vatican control over it?

"One of the most amazing things to me as president of the university . . . was I had less interference in the daily operation in The Catholic University of America than I did as a chief executive officer in the State University of New York, the University of Tennessee, or University of Kentucky," Pellegrino said. By comparison, he added, Stonybrook, a state-founded school, had four levels of control—a local board, an overall state system board, the governor, and the legislature.

Saunders asked what if the governor decided he didn't like what one faculty member was teaching? Would that be proper or would it be interference? Pellegrino said the governor would not have the competence to judge the faculty. He spoke of a time when a governor asked him to admit certain students to medical school. Pellegrino said he refused, threatening to resign if he were forced to. That had ended the inquiry, he said.

Saunders showed him a self-study Catholic University submitted to Middle States in 1979. Saunders asked if there was a section on academic freedom, and Pellegrino said he assumed so. Saunders read the phrase: "The most highly valued right and privilege of the university professor is that of academic freedom." Pellegrino said that

that indeed had been Catholic University's position in 1979. "Certainly, always has been," he said.

"Was Catholic University in 1979 in fact free of arbitrary and extrinsic constraints, be they civil or ecclesiastical?" Saunders asked, reflecting another statement from the self-study.

"I would say that they were free of arbitrary constraints and extrinsic restraints," Pellegrino said.

Saunders, over some objections, asked who determined what an arbitrary constraint was? The exchanges became strained as Saunders sought unqualified answers and Pellegrino attempted to state definitions before he answered. Pellegrino would not agree that the Holy See was extrinsic to Catholic University, at least on the matter of theology.

Saunders read from the university's statement of aims: "The only constraint on truth is truth itself." To say truth is truth is unexceptional, Pellegrino responded. "The question here is who determines truth and what is truth?"

Now Saunders produced a letter in which the former university president had written that the pope "sees the university as a part of the evangelizing mission of the church."

"Does that include Georgetown?" Saunders asked.

"Yes," Pellegrino said, adding that it applied to Catholic universities in general.

Saunders read on: "As a scholar himself, I am sure he [the pope] understands very clearly the intellectual dilemmas in that proposition."

"He does indeed," Pellegrino added.

Saunders asked him to describe the intellectual dilemma.

"There is always a tension . . . between the desire of scholars to examine and question what he wants [and] the responsibility of the church to interpret the tradition faithfully," Pellegrino said.

To conclude, Saunders established that the words not "suitable nor eligible" were never, to Pellegrino's knowledge, used to describe a criteria for professors of theology.

In his second direct examination, Urbanczyk pointed out the crux of Pellegrino's question to Curran in their exchange of letters. "Are the obligations of responsible use of academic freedom different in an institution which has more than a nominal connection with the hierarchy?" That 1979 letter, Pellegrino confirmed, expressed his view of Catholic University. With that, the witness was excused.

Baine had decided he needed to recall Cardinal James A. Hickey, university chancellor, to respond to earlier testimony by David Power, the chairman of the department of theology. Power had testified that Hickey had told him the 1981 canonical statutes would not be applied retroactively to already tenured professors. The cardinal returned to the witness stand briefly. Baine asked Hickey if he had ever told anyone at the university that the 1981 statutes were not retroactive. Hickey said no. He said that all the appropriate faculty members had received canonical missions implicitly and that consequently the norms of the 1981 canonical statutes were fully applicable to them.

Taking the contrary position, Saunders asked Hickey in cross-examination if he had ever told anyone the 1981 statutes were retroactive. Hickey said no.

Weisberg then opened a whole new line of inquiry by asking whether the reference to "mandate" in the Vatican document *Normae Quaedam* was intended to be a reference to "canonical mission." Hickey said it was. Saunders pointed out that the document had no explicit reference to canonical mission. He also asked Hickey if the cardinal knew that the Marlowe committee had been advised by a canon lawyer that the document did not require a canonical mission.

"I am not aware of it, but an individual canon lawyer does not make law," Hickey said.

Saunders stated his concern that the university might argue that the cardinal's interpretation of canon law was binding on the court. Baine argued that the university's interpretation of canon law, a position it had taken prior to trial, was not subject to review by the court. But because Baine believed the court should not have put the question to Hickey, he would argue that Hickey's answer was binding.

Weisberg allowed Saunders to state, for the trial record, that in his view Hickey did not have final authority to interpret canon law.

"Perhaps I should not have asked the question in retrospect," Weisberg said. "I did, and it seems to me we are at the end of the inquiry." Hickey was excused.

Weisberg said that there were only two questions he could

legitimately ask on the issue of canon law. First, could the plaintiff claim that the university's reliance on canon law had been taken in bad faith? Second, in the hierarchical church, who had the authority to interpret canon law?

Baine offered his canon law expert's affidavit to support the view that the board, lay and clergy, could interpret canon law in the issue at hand. However, Saunders said that the affidavit was inadmissible hearsay and, in any event, the issue was not who interpreted canon law but what were the civil law requirements that protected Curran in his contract. "I've said from the beginning canon law has nothing to do with this case. It's a red herring. You're dealing with civil bylaw of a civil corporation in a contract dispute . . . and that question is simply not covered by canon law," he said.

Weisberg accepted the affidavit anyway.

Baine spoke briefly to conclude his case. The trial was over.

Weisberg sat up and leaned forward in his oversized swivel chair. After some fifty hours spent observing the legal jousting, he decided it was time to offer commendation, something rarely heard in routine court cases.

"This is probably one of the most difficult and certainly one of the most interesting cases I've heard in eleven years on this court," Weisberg said. "And I do want to commend all counsel . . . for the thoroughly professional and responsible manner in which you've conducted yourselves in this case. You've made my job much easier, and I do appreciate it very much."

FOURTEEN

Verdict

The trial ended three days before Christmas, and its concerns were overshadowed temporarily by the holidays. Judge Frederick Weisberg took the delicate substance of the dispute into his chambers for final consideration, predicting that a thorough review could take several weeks. Lawyers for both sides were allowed to submit final briefs by January 25.

This legal contest had required a great investment of energy and principles, and perhaps even prayer. The financial investment had been equally heavy—half a million dollars to three quarters of a million dollars in legal man hours for each party. Paul Saunders's firm had done the work free, and Kevin Baine implied that Catholic University had been spared some of the financial burden as well.[1]

When Weisberg issued his ruling on February 28, 1989, Charles Curran and his supporters may have wondered whether the battle had been worth its price. Two years to the day after Curran had filed the original suit, the judge found in favor of The Catholic University of America.

Weisberg's conclusion was direct: "The university did not breach its contract with Professor Curran by requiring him to teach courses other than Catholic theology or, for that matter, by requiring him to agree to be bound by the declaration of the Holy See."[2] To reach this point, however, Weisberg used his thirty-six page decision to dissect the claims of each side.

By way of the trial he had been exposed to Catholicism's quest for both authority and freedom and could see the depth of the tension, especially in how freedom of inquiry and loyalty to church doctrine exist at the same university. "Nowhere is the tension between the two allegiances more acute than in the teaching of Catholic theology at a Catholic university, perhaps especially at The Catholic University of America," he wrote.

But he also said his purview limited him from taking on those larger issues. The questions before him were simply whether the university had breached the contract and, if it had, what was the proper remedy.

To win, the judge said, Curran was required by law to prove with "clear and satisfactory evidence" that the custom and practice forming the understanding of his contract were "definite, uniform and well known." But to decide on that point, the judge said, he was required to consider first many other questions.

His ruling began by asking whether the contract required Curran to have a canonical mission to teach in the department of theology and whether withdrawal of the mission, if it existed, would leave the university with any further obligations to Curran.

What, he asked next, was the merit of Curran's argument that his 1970 tenure did not require a canonical mission and that he was not bound by the university's 1981 statutes, which did require it? "The university may be correct that the existence or nonexistence of the requirement of a canonical mission is a question of canon law, and therefore the court must accept its authoritative interpretation of canon law on that question," Weisberg said. But the court could ignore that issue, Weisberg added, because his concern was whether "the parties to the contract agreed to be bound by it." Here the university's case was weak, as the requirement of the canonical mission was not made explicit in the contract. "If CUA wanted to make it a condition of Curran's contract that he must maintain his canonical mission, it should have told him so," Weisberg said. "Having not made the requirement explicit, the university cannot rely on an interpretation of arcane provisions of canon law to read into the contract terms that could not have been understood by the parties."

And yet, he continued, "Things change and some contracts are no exception." Protection for employees, established in case law under fixed contract rights and obligations, did not totally apply to the Curran situation, Weisberg said. "Both parties to the contract understand that from time to time the university may change its bylaws or other governing documents, which may in turn alter the relationship between the university and its faculty, even those with tenure." If this were not so, he said, universities would be burdened by myriad kinds of contracts with their faculties.

"This doctrine of evolution in the contractual relationship between a tenured faculty member and the university is especially true of the relationship between CUA and its professors in the ecclesiastical faculties," he said. Enough was understood between Curran and the university to determine that such changes may well have come to ecclesiastical departments. When *Sapientia Christiana* made the canonical mission an explicit requirement, "it should have come as no surprise to Professor Curran that he was expected to have one," Weisberg said. Hence, he said, the withdrawal of the canonical mission and the related suspension did not violate the contract.

With those matters dismissed, Weisberg said two questions remained at the core of Curran's charge of breach of contract. Could Curran teach civil degree students in the department of theology and, if not, could he teach Catholic theology in one of the other nonecclesiastical departments? This touched on the question of a unitary faculty and the propriety of the board of trustees' June 2, 1988, resolution, which barred Curran from teaching theology anywhere at the university.

On the first, Weisberg said Curran had "failed to produce any credible evidence that the university has ever divided the department of theology faculty along those lines or made any distinction between professors based on whether their students were in one program or the other." The university had said this too was a question of canon law exempt from court inquiry. However, Weisberg said that claim of exemption did not matter: Curran had failed to prove that he could teach civil degree students without the canonical mission.

WEISBERG HAD COME to the nub of the case. It was, he said, "the issue of Professor Curran's right . . . to teach Catholic theology in a nonecclesiastical faculty within the university." And that issue, he added, was not as easily resolved as the previous questions. First, Weisberg said, the preponderance of evidence showed that faculty at the university were tenured to their departments, not the university as a whole. This undermined Curran's claim to having a tenured right to teach in other departments. That was a guarantee, Weisberg added, that traditionally was given only when faculty members lost jobs because of financial exigencies rather than disciplinary action. But he admitted that the Curran case was different, for the professor's competence had not been questioned under peer review and, for a reason unclear to the judge, his 1986 appointment had been attached to the school of religious studies instead of its department of theology. Nevertheless, the judge said, there was no custom or practice regarding contractual rights to look at in Curran's unusual case. "The simple fact is that it [a dispute like Curran's] has never happened before, at this university or anywhere else," he said.

The judge said he preferred to base his decision on other grounds—the parties' reasonable knowledge of what the contract implied. Though Curran and the university had not agreed in writing what would happen if he was ruled neither "suitable nor eligible," Weisberg said, "certain things were unmistakably known and understood by the parties." He gave a short list: Both knew that the university charter was granted by the pope, that the bylaws allowed the archbishop as chancellor to represent the Holy See, that more than a third of the board must be church hierarchy, and that the faculty handbook spoke of a special relationship to the Holy See. "No one—least of all a Catholic priest and a professor of Catholic theology—could have contracted with CUA without understanding the university's special relationship with the Roman Catholic Church, with all the implications and obligations flowing from the relationship," Weisberg said. For Curran's part, he continued, "As much as he may have wished it otherwise, he could not reasonably have expected that the university would defy a definitive judgment of the Holy See."

The university need not prove its claim that it was bound by canon law because the institution was, at the very least, clearly bound by religious conviction, based on its longstanding and voluntary relationship with the Holy See, the judge said. Only an explicit university waiver giving up those ties would make it possible for Curran to claim a right of protection against the Holy See's ruling, and the university obviously had not agreed to such a waiver. Hence, Weisberg concluded, there was no breach of contract.

In case Curran wanted to appeal the ruling, Weisberg outlined his reasoning in denying the professor's request for "specific performance"—the court's power to order his reinstatement under penalty of contempt. "Even if the court were to find that the university had breached its contract with Professor Curran, it is virtually unthinkable that the court should order specific performance," the judge said. The idea that a court could force a Catholic university to accept a particular professor of Catholic theology was incredible to Weisberg. Usually the courts compel enforcement only when an employee has been discharged in violation of statutory or constitutional rights or the rights of collective bargaining, or where little or no direct supervision of the employee by the employer is required. What was more, Weisberg said, contract enforcement in academia has established legal patterns. He quoted a 1967 ruling of *Greene vs. Howard University*: "A contract to hire a teacher may not be enforced by specific performance . . . It would be intolerable for the courts to interject themselves and to require an educational institution to hire or to maintain on its staff a professor or instructor whom it deemed undesirable and did not wish to comply."

From this, Weisberg drew his conclusion. "If there were ever a case in which a court should decline to force an unwanted teacher on an unwilling educational institution, this must surely be it. Professor Curran is, by all accounts, a popular and highly respected teacher and scholar. But none of the university's decisions in this matter have been based on its judgments of his competence."

Weisberg made several general observations on the case. As he had done in his first question of the trial to Baine, the judge posited what Curran believed to be his ideal, and real, contract. But the judge concluded that Catholic University would never have made such a commitment. Because the bulk of the plaintiff's evidence was historical, that also cut two ways. Though history showed the university had attempted to achieve full academic freedom and institutional autonomy, the general social climate also demanded consideration, the judge suggested. "There is little doubt that the late 1960s was an extraordinary time at Catholic University," he said. "In many respects the events on the campus were a reflection of the turmoil on college campuses all across the country. These were turbulent times, characterized by persistent testing of institutional limits on all forms of expression of individual freedom, including academic freedom. It is hardly surprising that The Catholic University of America, with its close ties to the Roman Catholic Church, found itself in the middle of these struggles."

He said the university had to grapple with its desire to have both unwavering fealty to the Holy See and complete academic freedom. "Perhaps it can fairly be said that the university wanted it both ways; but on most issues it can also be said that the university could have it both ways," Weisberg observed. "The university may choose for itself on which side of that conflict it wants to come down, and nothing in the contract for Professor Curran or any other faculty member promises that it will always come down on the side of academic freedom."

BAINE SAW THE RULING as having limited implications, if any, for other Catholic or secular institutions because of the uniqueness of Catholic University. Weisberg's ruling that tenure relates to the department rather than the entire university, though, may well be used as a precedent by some other university that argues a dispute in court.[3]

Saunders viewed the ruling as an unsettling portent of future disputes. "The Curran case is the shot across the bow," he said. "If we're not careful some day there will be a torpedo to the midships." Weisberg's ruling, Saunders believed, implied that simply by stating that it has a "special relationship" with the Holy See an institution can exempt itself from civil obligations and insulate itself from legal recourse sought by professors. He said Weisberg's decision condoned a "one-way choice" in which the university defined its nature and obligations regardless of contract commitments. What was more, Saunders said, the dilemma of "truth in advertising" continued. Catholic University availed itself of all the opportunities to appear fully committed to academic freedom and the procedures of the modern American university, he said, and then it had reneged.[4]

The tremors hit Catholic University about three weeks after the Weisberg ruling. They began when the academic senate passed a resolution affirming and inviting trustees to support the "essential conditions of university life and growth"—that is, academic freedom and institutional autonomy.[5] They worsened a few weeks later when fourteen professors from the school of arts and sciences issued a statement saying they would teach under protest until the board of trustees gave a guarantee of academic freedom. "The academic freedom which we have enjoyed has been jeopardized, and the reputation of the university in the eyes of the academic community may suffer unwarranted and undeserved diminution" by Curran's dismissal, it said.[6]

As it turned out, Catholic University would work on a more developed statement of academic freedom after its 1990 review by the Middle States Association of Colleges and Schools. Yet the resulting declaration would not be of the kind advocated by the American Association of University Professors. Instead it would proclaim a formulation of academic freedom as it had been argued in the Curran case—that there are limits.

Before the Middle States review, Saunders said that if the university issued an AAUP-type statement on academic freedom, Curran could reopen his legal complaint. That was because the trustees' June 2 resolution had established a sort of precedent on the limits of academic freedom. Any statement that superseded the resolution would give Curran, who still had tenure, a new crack at returning. Of course, Curran's desire to return hardly burned as before.

Reaction and comment in the Catholic community mirrored the two lawyers' divergent views. Fordham University president Joseph A. O'Hare, for example, argued before the trial that the Curran affair highlighted the distinction between pontifical and nonpontifical institutions or departments. Ordinary Catholic institutions need not fear, he said. If anything, what is and is not an ecclesiastical institution or department must be made clear.[7] Columnist Tim Unsworth of the *National Catholic Reporter* lamented the fate of Catholic University, which he eulogized in a column. "Who will apply to CUA now?" he asked. "Who will accept a visiting professorship? How many scholars already active in the field will quietly remove any CUA references from their resumes? How many alumni, now teaching elsewhere, will be denied advancements because their credentials have less market value than a peso?"[8]

Since before the trial, Catholic University president William Byron had been at work presenting his case on what academic freedom meant in the American Catholic community. To the bishops meeting in November 1988 he said that their university was being judged in the court of public opinion. As a result, he advised, Catholic leaders must present their case "that academic freedom is never absolute in any university," whether Catholic or secular.[9] A month before the ruling, Byron presented his case to a more skeptical audience, his peers in higher education, at the annual meeting of the Association of Catholic Colleges and Universities.[10] He expounded the idea of an ecclesial limit in a keynote address: "An American Catholic Perspective on Academic Freedom."

"There can be an ecclesial limit on academic freedom," Byron said, replaying his trial testimony. Ecclesial, he said, means the continuity of tradition and community of the church rather than hierarchical structures. And when there is a dispute between a theologian and bishop on whether certain academic pursuits break from the continuity, the nature of the church gives the bishop the last word. "Theologians and bishops should examine together questions of continuity and break. Then the bishops should decide," he said. Bishops, he added, needed to hone their theological literacy so they could engage in such discussions. Though the Catholic University dispute infused the talk, Byron said his aim was broader. "I don't consider this [speech] about the Curran case," he said.

Byron also addressed the question of how a Catholic university can consider itself autonomous and still be deferential to the church hierarchy. An institution can have both postures when it has a "freely chosen Catholic character expressed in its mission statement and subscribed to by the campus community," he said. In that situation, the church's concerns are relevant to the academic institution. "We should be wide open to influence but resist control," he concluded.

Two respondents to Byron's presentation disagreed with his formulation. A university's "church relatedness" comes not from hierarchical control but from serving a democratic church made up of "the people of God," said St. John's University professor James J. Annarelli, who had supported Curran in statements and articles on newspaper Op-Ed pages during the dispute.

Annarelli, whose paper was read in his absence, said Byron's view of ecclesial limits amounted to an acceptance of direct ecclesiastical intervention that meant a surrender of autonomy. "This is a time when Catholic educators should be jealously guarding the threatened autonomy of their institutions," he said. "Father Byron seems all too willing to surrender that autonomy." A contradiction occurs when the governing board of a Catholic school "invokes its institutional autonomy to abrogate that institutional autonomy," Annarelli said, alluding to Catholic University's argument in the Curran case.

In another response James Heft, a priest and provost of the University of Dayton, said that defining the limits of academic freedom was not the crucial beginning point. First, he said, the Catholic theological community must clarify what is infallible church teaching and what is not, especially in the area of morality. Only then can the limits of theological inquiry be clear.

Curran's departure from Catholic University relieved the American bishops of a no-win situation. While Curran was there he could speak with the authority of that institution, and yet any effort they made to control him smacked of "oppression" in the next day's newspaper headlines. After the dust settled, Catholic University's trustees commissioned an opinion poll of the bishops. The question was simple, but between the lines it read: How was the handling of the Curran dispute perceived, and what were the financial consequences? Their dioceses gave up to $4 million each year to support the university. Of the 213 bishops responding to the 1989 poll, 192 said their impression of Catholic University was "generally positive." Thirteen bishops said their impression was negative; five others had "mixed" reactions.[11]

In their own territory, the American bishops were seeking a way to allay occasional disputes with theologians before they mushroomed into a Curran-type affair. To that end, they considered a set of preventive guidelines, first drafted by canon law scholars and finished off by a bishops' committee. It was not new for the teaching role of the bishop and the theologian to be at odds. But now their disputes could spiral beyond control. Their family quarrels had become fodder for the media and computer-age communication. Positions held by either party often were misconstrued by the time they reached the public.

At their semiannual meeting in spring 1989, the bishops adopted the guideline document "Doctrinal Responsibilities."[12] Nine years in the making, it sought to define the roles of bishop and theologian in a complementary way. With Vatican input, the bishops amended the final version to say clearly that the bishop is final arbiter of church teaching. However, the document advises several ways for the bishop and theologian to talk informally and reach some agreement. It also suggests procedures for submitting evidence, holding hearings, and making appeals when attempts at an informal agreement fail. More than anything, the protocol was to keep local disagreements from becoming issues for the Vatican.

Would the guidelines have led the Curran affair to different consequences? "I would like to think that the Curran affair might have had a different outcome if such a process had been in place early on," said the drafting committee's chairman, Archbishop Oscar Lipscomb of Mobile, Alabama. "But that is only speculation."[13] Looking back on that decade, Curran called the guidelines a "bright spot" in an otherwise dark landscape.[14]

CATHOLIC UNIVERSITY suffered some stress in the aftermath of the trial, most of it the normal discomfort that an institution feels when a controversy is blowing over. There were vocal critics and vocal supporters. Parents thought twice about sending a child to a school portrayed by the evening news as being in turmoil.

Despite the flap, the university hired fifty-two new faculty members for the 1988–89 school year. Enrollment in the 1990–91 school year was down from previous years, but that mirrored a trend at most universities both locally and across the country.[15]

Financial effects of the controversy apparently were, in the balance, negligible. Donors had long been aware of Curran's high profile, according to the court testimony. Curran recalled that at least two presidents and several vice-presidents had joked to him, "Curran, you cost us an awful lot of money over the years."[16]

Yet *The Tower*, the university's student newspaper, reported before the trial that donors lost because of the controversy were being made up by those who backed the university's stand. By the end of 1989, the university reported that alumni and public contributions were at an all-time high. For the fiscal year ending in August 1989, the CUA Fund received its highest annual contribution in its thirty years—more than $2.3 million in contributions from alumni, parents, and friends.[17] By the fall of 1990 the capital funds drive of $100 million had reached $57 million, according to university officials.

Byron reported to the bishops that fall that more than $1 million had been granted to the university to endow a professorship in the school of religious studies. And the bishops gave no mean support: Their dioceses sent $4.8 million during the fiscal year ending in August 1989. In perspective, however, giving in the Catholic Church continued its general two-decades-long decline, and Catholic University was not in the ranks of the heavily endowed Ivy League. As the fall 1990 school year opened, Middle States had completed its every-decade review of Catholic University and renewed the university's accreditation. Yet it offered critiques and suggestions. For one, it said the university sought to do too much with too little; it recommended focusing on priority areas of its own choosing, which might mean cutbacks in others. Moreover, it encouraged the university to formulate a clear statement on academic freedom, a recommendation that clearly rose out of the Curran dispute and some agitation among faculty members.

The heaviest toll the Curran affair exacted on Catholic University was the censure it provoked from the American Association of University Professors. The AAUP began its review in mid-1989, and at its full meeting in June 1990 the assembly voted to approve a censure recommendation.

Though without binding effect, the censure sent a signal across academe, or at least to academics attentive to the AAUP. At most the censure tarnished the university's reputation. That, in turn, might hurt its ability to attract top-notch faculty members. The recommendation to censure began with an AAUP committee on academic freedom, which issued its report in October 1989. That report was published in the AAUP's *Academe*.[18]

Noting the unique situation of Catholic University, the committee report nevertheless highlights what the AAUP considered several injustices to Curran: His suspension came without consultation with the faculty committees; the denial to teach in his area of competence was, in effect, a denial of tenure rights; and his academic freedom was violated when he was penalized for his published views. Finally, the report says, the administration and the board of trustees failed to exercise their right and duty to protect the university's autonomy.

Before the report was published, Catholic university filed with the AAUP a forty-two page critique of the findings. A brief summary of the critique was published in *Academe* alongside the censure report and recommendation. Kevin Baine, author of Catholic University's response, wrote that although Curran acknowledged the authority of the Vatican to rule on his teaching status, he "sought to continue teaching Catholic theology . . . in defiance of the judgment." The AAUP "committee cannot eliminate that conflict by pretending it does not exist," he wrote.

He criticized the AAUP report for ignoring Weisberg's conclusions. He said the association had misconstrued or disregarded everything Catholic that related to the events and instead had substituted "its own standards for the university's." In conclusion, he said an institution must be faithful to its own goals and objectives. "Academic freedom may be limited by the religious aims of the institution," he said. "The university's actions in this case have been vindicated completely by a fair and impartial trial judge."

Many of Catholic University's challenges, whether financial or in retaining good faculty members and drawing more students, were not unusual for most of American higher education. In comparison to some large mainline institutions, Catholic University looked quite stable.

What remained unique, however, was the university's identity, created partly by its "special relationship" to the Holy See and partly by its heritage as an early center of higher education and research. As Byron told the bishops in 1989, the university straddled two realities—that of the church and that of the research university. He stressed to the bishops that a Catholic presence in that secular and scientific world was "for the good of both church and nation."

With the university out of the limelight of the Curran affair, Byron's 1989 message to the bishops was about getting on with their task. "Probably our greatest need in the first decade of our second century is to attract and retain star-quality faculty," Byron said. That takes funding, he implied. But it also hinged on Catholic University's reputation and standing. Since the university opened its doors to the first thirty-six students in 1889, the years had been "good ones," Byron said. "The years ahead look promising."[19]

WHATEVER THEIR QUALITY, however, those years would not include Charles Curran. After the trial, Curran returned to his one-year visiting professorship at the University of Southern California's department of religion. He was there when he heard of Weisberg's February 28 ruling. Saunders read it to him over the phone.

"Within three minutes I decided not to appeal," Curran wrote later.[20] One reason was that the ruling raised no constitutional problems. As Weisberg had said, he refused to enter the First Amendment aspects of the case and so raised no "global constitutional issues." In fact, he said, the university was "forceful" in arguing that its decisions were based on canon law and could not be reviewed by the court "without impermissibly entangling the state in the affairs of the church." Weisberg's flawless handling of the case also made it difficult to appeal.

Even if he could win on appeal, Curran added, the chances were low that the courts would rule he could get his job back. Besides, he said, by now he was tired and saw no promise in returning. "The board of trustees said in 1988 and Judge Weisberg confirmed its right to say that full academic freedom in the American sense of the term does not exist at Catholic University," Curran said. "My appeal would not change that reality."[21]

By the Holy See's formulation, Curran would not accept the rules of his Catholic world. Thus, he was denied its freedoms. In contrast, Curran derived freedom from outside that world of church authority. Perhaps even he saw the outcome as poetic justice. "I am a free man now, and better for it," he said.[22]

As he had done before, Curran presented his case through writing. In the fall of 1990 he published *Catholic Higher Education, Theology, and Academic Freedom,* which had been in the works since 1987. In the closing chapter he argued the rightness of his cause and drew his well-known conclusion about Catholic University: "Full academic freedom does not exist there."[23]

Through the struggle at Catholic University, Curran not only enhanced his notoriety as an academic but also strengthened his own resolve on matters of academic freedom and tenure. He would carry that beyond the walls of Catholic institutions. He did not look for trouble, but it came his way again.

Curran's time at Cornell University and his first year at the University of Southern California placed him in the world of nondenominational undergraduate education. His topics ranged from Catholic social teachings to value systems of the world's ideologies and religions. The endowed chair at the University of Southern California could accommodate him for one more year, through the summer of 1990, but then the funds dried up.

He was looking at an array of offers, but one struck him most—if not for its location at least for its terms. Early in 1989 Curran agreed to take an "eminent scholar" chair at Auburn University in Alabama. The scholar's chair, a type being promoted in Alabama universities by the state government, was endowed with $1 million, and the offer was for a "tenured professorship." In fact, as late as April 16, 1990, university officials urged Curran to accept the long-term position.

Then the university's president James Martin reversed the offer, beginning a rumor mill and finally an open public controversy by the end of the year.

As the first reports of the new Curran dispute leaked out to the secular and Catholic press in early September, Curran's supporters began to float a public challenge. Which Catholic university had the guts to hire this eminent theologian, who was seeking work in secular academe? That message was first editorialized in the *Reporter*: "Why, one asks, have Catholic academics, particularly Curran's colleagues in theology, been so silent?"[24] As if to answer, two of Curran's friends spoke out. Richard McBrien, chairman of the University of Notre Dame's theology department, and his Notre Dame colleague, ethicist Richard McCormick, put forth their case in the widely read Jesuit journal, *America*.[25] Notre Dame and the theology departments of other Catholic universities had inquired about hiring Curran. But the two theologians said that administrations had blocked such efforts. Clearly, no Catholic university was ready to take the political heat.

The Curran legacy was so explosive that the hierarchy was even implicated in the Auburn dispute. The first news reports cited Mobile Archbishop Oscar Lipscomb as the culprit. The archbishop allegedly had gotten the Auburn president's ear through the one Catholic on the university's board of trustees. Lipscomb strongly denied the report. Some observers agreed that he could have no motive—was it not a solution of sorts for the entire American church hierarchy to have Curran established in a largely Protestant domain like Alabama? Still, McBrien thought otherwise: "There isn't any doubt in my mind that Oscar Lipscomb is responsible for the president's flip-flop on the tenure decision." As one Auburn professor put it then: "It's not enough that the Catholic Church had made Charlie a persona non grata. Now they're interfering with state universities."[26]

By November, however, that charge seemed overblown, if not false. A faculty committee investigating the treatment of Curran discovered another possible motive. Auburn had been censured by the AAUP in 1983 for a tenure dispute, and some faculty were disappointed that Martin had not resolved the stigma since he arrived in 1985. What may have lost Curran the Auburn job, faculty leaders said, was Martin's negative reaction to the theologian's inquiries about the AAUP and academic freedom. In this view, Martin and the trustees did not want a firebrand on the faculty. This also explained why the "Curran affair" was a cause for Auburn faculty to rally around.[27]

And then yet another motive was suggested: The trustees of the Bible Belt institution did not want a Catholic added to the two-man religion faculty. One professor was already Catholic and tenured. A Birmingham millionaire revealed this information when he said he was going to cut his endowment to the university for reasons beyond, but perhaps including, Curran's treatment.[28]

Whatever the reason behind Martin's decision, a critical faculty committee report said he had exceeded his authority and violated Auburn's procedures for tenure and promotion. At the least, it added, the president must explain his rationale to the university senate. Martin appeared before the senate and said that he had acted within university procedures and was not required to explain his decision. As threats of a faculty censure of Martin mounted, the university's promotion and tenure committee met with him December 7. To some surprise, it emerged saying that "there was no violation of academic freedom and that the president met the letter of the policy." That left the campus divided. The burden to initiate further action lay with the university senate.

By that time Curran had made another decision, and the hour was ripe for a declaration. On December 13, 1990, he told an Auburn news conference that he had been awarded a tenured "professorship in human values" at the Southern Methodist University in Dallas, where the announcement was also made that day. Curran would teach Christian ethics. When he began in the fall of 1991, he had automatic and guaranteed tenure. The chair in Christian ethics allowed Curran to teach in all departments of the school. The Catholic theologian's arrival, the university said, would "heighten our ecumenical vision of the role of scholarship in the pursuit of a more values-oriented society."

At Auburn that day, as faculty opposition against the administration mounted, Curran spoke out on the cause he was known for. "Auburn's academic freedom, autonomy, and role as a major institution of higher education in the United States is at stake," he said. He recommended changes in the selection, size, and time of service for the university's board of trustees.[29] Whoever was right, in the eyes of the fiercely independent wing of academe Auburn now wore a scarlet letter. The university senate made clear were it stood; on January 15 it censured Martin.

Obviously, Curran had not sought the southern tussle, nor the timing of the serendipitous and dramatic call to Dallas. When it all happened, though, and the media came looking, he knew the ropes. Pursuit of freedom was resurrected as a public cause.

Curran was fifty-six; during his first stand at Catholic University he had been thirty-three. For some he had become a symbol and hero. To others he was the "aging enfant terrible." Whatever else had changed over that time, Curran's statement upon his new—and perhaps final—appointment had a familiar ring. The academic chair, he said, "fits in very well with my own academic agenda in Christian ethics and my attempt to keep the tradition of Catholic moral theology a living tradition."[30]

EPILOGUE

Sparks but not Fire

The claims of authority and freedom, with all their subtlety and variety, clashed in *l'affaire* Curran. The saga made clear that the church ideal of joining the two remains elusive. The Curran case was not a turning point in Catholic history; it neither found a way to unite authority and freedom nor tore the church asunder. The outcome affirmed the formal authority of the pope and his bishops. It also affirmed the nature of Catholicism—an ordered community reluctant to allow deviations.

The Vatican was willing to accept negative side effects to uphold its authority, for the showdown with Curran had nurtured resentment. With one more cause for liberal reformers to avenge, the potential for polarization between the Holy See and advocates of freedom in the Catholic Church had increased.

Curran said during the trial that his academic freedom in the university and in the church was for the good of both. Judge Weisberg later said, "Maybe Professor Curran is right." But he insisted that such value judgments were beyond the court's purview. The Vatican had taken its course. "Whether this is ultimately good for the university or good for the church," the judge concluded, "is something they have a right to decide for themselves."[1]

The 1980s were combustible for the church because its members debated and anguished over the questions of freedom and authority. Some thought the Curran case would be the fatal spark. Yet if it failed to set the Catholic world aflame, it was at least an ember in the kindling. Between 1988 and 1990, his case and other confrontations in the church kept the fire stoked.

THE ISSUES HAD BEEN heating up in Europe, where theologians finally confronted the Vatican. Their incitement began in the fall of 1988 when John Paul II met with moral theologians at Rome's Lateran University. There, the papal adviser Carlo Caffarra, a monsignor, theologian, and ghostwriter of the pope's speeches on matters of morality and sexuality, reasserted the arguments of *Humanae Vitae*—much to the chagrin of many theologians. Then in December 1988, after a period of suspense over the appointment of the archbishop of Cologne, West Germany's most wealthy and powerful archdiocese, John Paul passed over three candidates recommended by local churchmen. He chose his own man, Cardinal Joachim Meisner, former archbishop of Berlin. Similar disputes had arisen over appointments in the see of Chur in Switzerland, and in Vienna and Salzburg.

For many European theologians, the Cologne snub was the last straw. The combined incidents "looked like a full-fledged restoration"—a repudiation of the Second Vatican Council's collegiality—Bernard Häring said.[2]

Impatient that no bishops voiced concern, a group of 163 German-speaking theologians from Germany, Austria, Switzerland, and the Netherlands drafted the so-called Cologne Statement.[3] This January manifesto, signed on Epiphany, decried a "new Roman centralism." It criticized an array of Vatican actions: appointment of bishops without consultation with local churches, interference in free theological research, and arrogation of authority to answer all questions of morals as well as faith. Signers included Hans Küng, Edward A. Schillebeeckx, and Häring. The Cologne Statement triggered supporting statements across Western Europe. Fifty-two members of the Catholic University of Louvain, Belgium, signed a document protesting "a centralism that is limiting local churches and theological freedom as well as pluralism and the ethos of believers."[4] In France, one hundred thirty theologians endorsed the Cologne Statement with their own, asking Cardinal Ratzinger to study the issues "with all the seriousness they deserve."[5] Some sixty Spanish theologians also weighed in behind the Cologne Statement.

Ratzinger would not back down. He denied requests that he hold a special dialogue with the theologians. At the same time, however, he discouraged Vatican supporters in the theological community from firing a countershot. When an alliance of Italian theologians wanted to declare publicly their loyalty to the pope and magisterium, he asked them to refrain for fear of greater polarization. Ratzinger said the protests of the Cologne Statement would be considered by the thirty-member International Theological Commission, an advisory board he hand-picked. The cardinal knew that time was on his side, for a major document on the role of the theologian was already on the drawing board of the Congregation for the Doctrine of the Faith. Moreover, the Vatican was poised to release a new document.

On February 25—three days before Judge Weisberg ruled—the Vatican published a new requirement for the church, the "Oath of Fidelity."[6] As part of the initiative, the congregation had also revised the church's standard profession of faith, but the oath was a new law to be enforced under existing canons. No such loyalty formula had existed since 1967, when the 1910 oath against "modernism" had been dropped. Those required to take the new oath included pastors, deacons, seminary rectors, and professors of theology in seminaries. Alarming to some theologians, however, was that now even they—"teachers in any university whatsoever who teach disciplines which deal with faith and morals," according to Canon 833—apparently were expected to take the oath.[7]

The theological community's response was split. Some expressed dismay, charging that the Inquisition had been resurrected. Theologian Avery Dulles, however, said in his customarily calm manner that the oath should not worry anybody already accustomed to decades of church practice; it was, he said, "an improvement" over the existing profession of faith. Calling the printed reactions hysteria, he counseled: "There is nothing to be alarmed about. The Catholic tradition calls for us to profess our faith at Mass every Sunday."[8]

The words that concerned theologians most, "any university whatsoever," were actually of narrow application, according to canon law expert Ladislas Orsy of Catholic University. "There is solid evidence that the obligation exists for those, and those only, who either are appointed to hold an ecclesiastical office, or are at least mandated to function 'in the name of the church,'" he said. This excluded that vast majority of professors of religion who did not have canonical missions, as Curran once did. The word "whatsoever" was used, Orsy continued, because theology professors in some secular or state universities outside the United States are "appointed by a competent ecclesiastical authority," meaning they hold a canonical mission. Canon law would dictate that only new appointments to such faculties need to take the oath, not current teachers, he added.[9]

Nevertheless, a torrent of opposition to it developed, raising the question of the document's breadth and how it would be implemented or enforced. "We cannot but express our dismay and consternation regarding the additions to the profession of faith, together with extension of the oath of fidelity to theologians and others," said the Catholic Theological Society of America, which had firmly backed Curran. "How, one may ask, can one link obedience with doctrinal declarations? And how can one take an oath to obey whatever may issue from such teachers in the future . . . The very impression of the language leaves the way open to misinterpretation and to the possible abuse of power by individuals in authoritative positions."[10]

The theologians stopped short of passing a resolution supporting the Cologne Statement. But they did form a committee to study the oath's implications. The exemption Orsy had pointed out relieved some of the concern. The burden of the oath was interpreted as resting more on pastors. Strictly speaking, the oath bound them to uphold such precepts as the church's ban on birth control, something increasingly difficult to counsel point blank to parishioners.

Yet the theological society's report, issued in April 1990, was ambivalent, especially about the cultural reaction to taking any oaths in the United States. The report said only those with positions "under church control" must take the oath, which excludes people in "collegial and consusltative bodies" and other teachers. Moreover, it said, "At this time no action should be taken against those who judge themselves in conscience unable to make this Profession of Faith or take the Oath of Fidelity in light of the problems surrounding them." The report asked those in authority who interpret the oath "to repsect the legitimate differences which exist within the church on such matters."[11]

Those matters went mainly to the issue of placing infallible and noninfallible church teachings side by side in an oath of loyalty. The theologians said that even Vatican II was not that explicit. As their report was being completed, the fallible-infallible question became further complicated. In December 1989, the first version of a new "universal catechism" for the church was released for confidential review by the world's bishops. The question raised was salient: How would the catechism distinguish between irreformable and reformable church teachings?

THE AMERICAN BISHOPS steered a middle road of conciliation between the Vatican and the theologians—and between the Vatican and the American church experience. Several of them traveled to Rome in March 1989 for a long-awaited summit on the church in the United States. What caught the headlines during the four-day meeting was the discussion on the impact of feminism in the American church and how dissent from moral teachings reflected the moral climate of the United States.

Conducted like a dialogue, the session had an American bishop present a topic and a Vatican prelate respond. The topic evolved to the role of the bishop, especially his magisterial teaching authority. Archbishop John L. May, then president of the National Conference of Catholic Bishops, took up that issue. He congealed a theme set by all the speakers, that the American church operates in a democratic context that has overwhelming influences on the effectiveness of church teaching and authority. In short, authority and freedom are seen in America through American spectacles. "To assert that there is a church teaching with authority binding and loosing for eternity is truly a sign of contradiction to many Americans who consider the divine right of bishops as outmoded as the divine right of kings," May said. "Accordingly, bishops live and work constantly in this atmosphere."[12]

These concerns, among others, undoubtedly were heard sympathetically by the pope and even Curia officials. Yet in their responses they revealed the traditional prescription: Hold fast. "The criterion for the truth is such that it's worth suffering for it," Cardinal Ratzinger said, not letting the bishops off lightly. "Those who announce the Gospel must also be martyrs in the most profound sense of the word."[13]

Archbishop May returned to the United States and presided at the spring assembly of the bishops' conference, which adopted the new "Doctrinal Responsibilities" guidelines. Armed with this accomplishment, which had taken nine years to forge, May spoke before the June 1989 gathering of the Catholic Theological Society. It was this session that wrestled with the new fidelity oath. Archbishop May gave the theologians his wholehearted support in an effort both to mend a bridge weakened by recent events and to cover unknown incidents of the future. "There are too many sweeping accusations leveled at the theological soundness and credal fidelity of the theologians," May said. "The result of such wanton accusation upon theologians has been a growing fear."[14]

THERE WAS APPARENTLY no fear in Europe as theologians continued their protest. A group of sixty-three Italian theologians, alarmed at the Vatican's decrees and its call for bishops to be more assertive, issued an open letter during the Italian episcopal conference in late March 1989. Though more conciliatory than the Cologne Statement, it suggested that the spirit of Vatican II was being cast out.

The Holy See, according to the open letter, was wrongly asserting that Vatican II had had only pastoral authority and that its proclamations were thus not binding. "We do not believe that the church can renounce *a priori,* through fear of problems which might follow for its unity, the variety of ways of understanding and living the faith which the Spirit inspires in different communities and in the pastoral guidance of the bishops," the theologians' letter said. They asked the Vatican to examine the "delicate problem of extension of the magisterium into the field of ethics," and emphasized Vatican II's respect for a hierarchy of truths. "We do not think that theologians would be doing their job if they simply spread the teaching of the magisterium and gave deeper reasons for the positions which it takes up," the letter said. Theologians must, it added, also address new questions that arise for the church on its journey of faith.[15]

Not one to feel uncomfortable among dissenting Catholics, John Paul addressed the Italian bishops' conference and spoke firmly about a single magisterium. He denounced "overt or surreptitious forms of a parallel or alternative magisterium." The sole and authentic "teachers of faith" were the bishops, he said.[16]

As feisty as ever, the seventy-six-year old Bernard Häring signed the Cologne Statement and wrote an essay calling for the creation of a special commission to reconsider the Vatican's position on birth control, "to prevent the numbers of those leaving the church from reaching catastrophic proportions." Then he made a dramatic proposal: He urged in a public statement that the pope shut down the

Congregation for the Doctrine of the Faith. Likening the congregation to the "nightmare" of the Inquisition, he said its past methods were too deeply ingrained to be changed by procedural reforms. A few days later he released his own book, *Faith, History, Morality,* an unflattering account of the congregation's investigation of his work from 1975–79.[17]

To counter the criticism, Ratzinger shortly after told Italy's private religious television station, *Persona,* that there could not be a relaxation on dissent over official church teachings. "Faith is not a theory of our own," he said. "It is a divine gift."[18]

While the combative exchanges flared in Europe, liberal American Catholics urged their theologians to take a firmer stand. That spirit was expressed in a *National Catholic Reporter* editorial of June 1989: "U.S. Theologians, speak up." "The Curran case has been a symptom of a disease we see within the church today," the *Reporter* said. "Even as the Curran drama has unfolded in recent months, theologians in other parts of the world have been protesting the deeper underlying causes of the illness."[19]

The announcement in early 1989 that Curran lost his case had galvanized a defiant mood, and the mood was quickened at the end of the year by the Vatican's release of the first draft of a universal catechism. This project added a new reference point for debate between authority and freedom. The idea of a new catechism had been around since the 1970s, but it came to a focus when John Paul summoned the world's bishops to an extraordinary synod, the first he had called, in 1985. Coming twenty years after Vatican II, the synod was a forum for three forces in the church, the neo-Augustinian, the communitarian-humanistic, and the liberationist. It was, in effect, freedom against authority, two to one. The synod's closing document melded the three views so that none dominated.[20]

Out of the process emerged a strong call to produce an entirely new catechism for the world church. Several approaches were recommended after Cardinal Bernard Law of Boston first stated the proposal. But the synod's final mandate was simple: to produce a catechism that would be an "important help in guaranteeing the unity of the faith." Thus, it must contain "the whole of Catholic doctrine, both of faith and morals," it said. "The presentation of doctrine must be biblical and liturgical. It must be sound doctrine suited to the present life of Christians."[21] The catechism would be the first issued since the Council of Trent in 1566, though Vatican II had set forth a catechetical directory and national churches drew upon that. This catechism would for the first time address questions of human sexuality, family life, and social ethics.

Under the plan, the catechism would be written for the world's twenty-five hundred bishops. They in turn would use it as a "point of reference" for national or diocesan educational materials. As soon as a draft of the "Catechism for the Universal Church" was issued to the bishops "*Sub Secreto*" (under secrecy) in November 1989, it got around, as the Vatican may have expected, and the debate over how it distinguished between infallible and noninfallible doctrines caught fire.[22] The draft, which a range of commentators on both sides of aisle called dogmatic or top-down in its approach, made no distinction. "There is need for a good clear statement of what we believe—unchangeable truths," said Francis Buckley, a Jesuit professor at the University of San Francisco and an author of catechism books. "But they have equated changeable truths with unchangeable truths. And that confuses the faithful."[23] All matters of faith and matters of morals were equal in the drafters' demand for a "submission of intellect and will."

The catechism's section on moral theology reminded again of the clash between advocates of natural law and proponents of "development." One section, for example, read: "In obeying the natural law man obeys 'the divine law itself—eternal, objective and universal' . . . of which it is the expression." One of the "new" moral theologian's attack on this approach echoed the historic debate in the Curran affair: "Three major developments in moral theology since Pius XII seem to have been ignored in the new Universal Catechism: the shift from law to responsibility, from the particular moral act to the agent and from the pursuit of 'perfection' to loving service of neighbor."[24]

Among the least strident critiques was that of Avery Dulles. "A way should be found to distinguish between matters of faith, noninfallible doctrines and merely theological opinions," he said.[25] Other scholars who scrutinized the catechism worried that the hierarchy could abuse the blurring of such teaching authority. The document was in its early phase and was likely to take several more exchanges over a few years before there was enough consensus for John Paul to give it the imprimatur. The process would provide a generous arena for the continuing debate over authority and freedom.

THE 1990s OPENED with two climactic stands by the Vatican. One was toward the theological profession and the other toward Catholic higher education. The first had the aura of confrontation, a drawing of the line by the Vatican in a juridical document on theologians, who in turn dissented. The second document, on education, ended in conciliation. Both involved the struggle of authority and freedom, but the two came down on opposite sides. For the theologians, authority was maintained. For educators, freedom, in the form of autonomy, was affirmed.

Yet each of these conclusions hinged on documents alone, pieces of paper that were only as permanent as the intentions behind them. How these documents would guarantee the causes of both authority and freedom in the real world rested as much as ever on questions of interpretation, politics, and charitable wills.

The Theologians

Rome's summer air was fresh and cool as Cardinal Ratzinger walked across the Vatican grounds to a small auditorium just outside St. Peter's Square. He made the trek on average once a year to deliver to the world media major teaching documents of the church. The subject that day, June 25, 1990, was the *Instruction on the Ecclesial Vocation of the Theologian*.[26]

Opening comments were made in Italian and then the cardinal took questions in that and other languages. "What made the new document necessary?" someone asked. It was prompted by "a climate of conflict" in the church, Ratzinger answered.[27] For Vatican observers the allusion was clearly to cases such as Curran's and the declarations by European theologians.

The *Instruction,* approved by John Paul, was straightforward: As the magisterium asserts both faith and morals, so the theologian must assent. Analysts said the document was juridical in nature, a guide for both the theologian and bishop to know when sincere questioning of church teaching becomes a form of unacceptable dissent. The church can be expected to use it as the starting point for the possible disciplining of dissent in the future.

Pervasive in the document is the classic formulation of freedom, that it comes by adherence to authoritative truth. One example is the *Instruction's* homage to free theological inquiry, which it called "the hallmark of rational discipline." The magisterium defines limits, however: "The freedom proper to theological research is exercised within the church's faith."

In a second expression of the formulation, the magisterium is given the right to intervene, disclaiming public opinion or dissent to ensure freedom in the truth. "Even when it might seem that they limit the freedom of theologians, these actions, by their fidelity to the faith which has been handed on, establish a deeper freedom which can only come from unity in truth." Indeed, the document disdains the false pretender to true freedom, the ideology of philosophical liberalism, thus: "freedom of judgment understood in this way is more important than the truth itself."[28]

The *Instruction* also builds upon a trend started in the Curran affair. When Curran was disciplined, Vatican officials said it represented the effort to include morals under the rubric of magisterial teaching. The instruction codifies that point: "What concerns morality can also be the object of the authentic magisterium [which] also extends to that which concerns natural law," not only divine revelation. "It is a doctrine of faith that these moral norms can be infallibly taught by the magisterium."[29]

The document begins by speaking of the unity of the truth, yet admits that it "exceeds the capacity of human knowledge." Human reason does not oppose revealed truth, but man's sinful nature complicates the rational search. Hence, theology is prone to "moments of crisis and tension."

The supernatural assurance given to the magisterium so that it "cannot err" comes through the office of the bishops. In unity with the magisterium, these pastors are bestowed with "the charism of infallibility in matters of faith and morals," the *Instruction* says. "It is the bishop's responsibility to guard and interpret the Word of God and to make authoritative judgments as to what is or is not in conformity with it." Indeed, the magisterium is in constant "vigilance."

Theologians who speak for that magisterium need a canonical mission. They are thus "officially charged with the task of presenting and illustrating the doctrine of the faith in its integrity and with full accuracy." A critical mind is welcome, as it is required in rational research, the document says. "The obligation to be critical, however, should not be identified with the critical spirit which is born of feeling or prejudice." As theologians draw on the culture around and use the tools of other philosophies, these must never supercede "revealed doctrine," the *Instruction* says. Theological work is described as slow and careful.

There are three levels at which the magisterium asserts truth, and all of them require the theologian's assent. Theological faith is required when a truth is declared as infallible. But even a truth about faith and morals that is not divinely revealed but which is proposed by the magisterium "'in a definitive way' . . . must be firmly held and accepted." And when the magisterium does not intend to act definitively but teaches a doctrine to aid the understanding of revelation, that too calls for "the religious submission of will and intellect."

When theologians defy truths asserted by the magisterium or propose ideas that threaten clarity, the magisterium may intervene, according to the *Instruction*. "The willingness to submit loyally to the teaching of the magisterium on matters *per se* not irreformable must be the rule," the document says. Because magisterial statements given at certain times may not be complete or made in the best possible terms, there is room for dialogue to reform church teaching. But that must be accompanied by the theologian's cooperation with magisterial officials so as not to disrupt the "unity of truth" or the "unity of charity" between disputing parties.

From this follows prescriptions for the conduct of questioning theologians. They should not state their hypotheses as truth and should "refrain from giving untimely public expression to them." If a disagreement persists, the theologian must continue to talk responsibly with "magisterial authorities" and avoid the "mass media." For a loyal theologian who still cannot agree with a church teaching, "such a situation can certainly prove to be a difficult trial," the document says. "It can be a call to suffer for the truth in silence and prayer, but with the certainty that if the truth really is at stake, it will ultimately prevail."

Dissent from the magisterium has several sources, the document says. First is the ideology of philosophical liberalism, which can lead Catholic thinkers to view independent judgment as superior to any authority. Next is the weight of public opinion on a theologian to say what is more acceptable. Finally, the document says the plurality of cultures and languages can lead to disagreements and dissent. Using the conscience as the basis for rejecting truth declared by the magisterium is sophistry, the document says, for the conscience guides practical action not belief. The document presents the case that a properly formed conscience would not lead to sharp disagreement with church teaching.

For Curran and the large number of international theologians who dissented from many moral teachings of the magisterium, this new definition of the "theologian's vocation" was a dead end. It held out to them freedom by assent to Vatican authority. They would side instead with freedom as they defined it. They would have to take the consequences.

On December 8, 1990, twenty-five years after the close of the Second Vatican Council, the Catholic Theological Society of America issued what amounted to its "Cologne Statement." The document, "Do Not Extinguish the Spirit," went through eight drafts over two years. Its criticism was less specific than the Cologne missive, which cited particular disputes in Europe. The North American document cited Curran's case, for example, in a footnote. But its general tone warned that Rome had reversed Vatican II's progressive stance on collegiality, free theological inquiry, the role of women, and ecumenism. A theologian's work, it said, had been "made more difficult" by the "Oath of Fidelity," canonical mission requirements, and the Vatican's failure to consult with them before issuing documents such as the *Instruction*. The methods used by the Congregation for the Doctrine of the Faith to investigate theologians, it added, "fail to honor fundamental human rights."[30]

Unlike the German-speaking theologians, the North Americans did not sign their names to this decree, but stated that about half of the society's fourteen hundred members voted. Of those, seventy-nine percent backed the document, seventeen percent rejected it, and twenty-two percent abstained. The voices of the American theologians were not completely united, and work on the document revealed a variety of attitudes among them regarding the best path for the future. By and large, however, the document revealed a communication gap with Rome and a decade of discontent.

Catholic Higher Education

A more ameliorative experience resolved a decade of disputes over Catholic higher education. The process began with contention and alarm but ended with statements of satisfaction by both the Vatican and Catholic educators. Not only the final papal document, issued September 35, 1990, as the *Apostolic Constitution on Catholic Universities,* but also the process and spirit of the debate contributed to the happy conclusion. Leading to this point, however, was a long road of apprehension.

In 1985 the Vatican issued its "Proposed Schema for a Pontifical Document on Catholic Universities," called the "schema" for short.[31] Vatican officials emphasized that it was only a *instrumentum laboris,* a working document, to advise the pope on his own decree. But its inclusion of rules to strengthen episcopal control of Catholic colleges and universities set off alarms. Catholic educators were invited to respond, which they did with a wholehearted critique of the schema's legalism and lack of empathy for the American context of Catholic higher education.

When the Vatican issued its second draft of the schema, Americans called it an improvement. Its section on norms, however, still seemed to undermine institutional autonomy and academic freedom. Two norms were particularly salient for how they implied church control. One said, "Those who teach theological subjects as regular teachers must have a mandate from the competent ecclesiastical authorities." Another norm was established for the hierarchy to step in to address disputes over Catholic teaching or identity: "Each episcopal conference or assembly of Catholic hierarchy, in consultation with the Catholic universities of its region, will establish procedures for such interventions, which are to be approved by the Holy See."[32]

The educators and theologians worried that the norms failed to distinguish between ecclesiastical and nonecclesiastical faculties or between types of content in "theological subjects." As a rule, the norms assuring hierarchical influence not only mirrored the Code of Canon Law's Canon 812, which allowed bishops to discipline academic clergy, but also seemed to duplicate statutes already on the books. "We've said loud and clear there is no need for another document," Sister Alice Gallin of the Association of Catholic Colleges and Universities said.[33] But the pope asked to have it. As with the first draft, the association coordinated the response of American Catholic educators to the second schema as well.

The educators were perplexed by another aspect of the second draft of the schema: It attempted to place all Catholic institutions into three categories, a hard fit for the diversity found in America. A survey of two hundred Catholic colleges and universities showed how the evolution of such institutions had created a variety of situations. The survey asked institutions to categorize themselves according to the types listed in the schema: (a) established by the Holy See (b) established by other ecclesiastical bodies, and (c) other Catholic universities. Of the one hundred fifty institutions that responded, only one said it was in category (a), twenty-one identified with category (b), and sixty-eight said they came under (c). Thirty schools could not decide in which category they fit.

Between early 1986 and early 1989, American Catholic educators had sent to the Congregation for Catholic Education two critical responses to the Vatican's two drafts of the schema. Now they took their ambivalence to Rome and hoped for the best, arriving in April 1989 to make their final recommendations. They were mindful of the Curran dispute, the legal ruling, and the public debate it had raised. Yet in their view the fate of one theologian with a canonical mission in a pontifical university set a limited precedent. The Curran case was significant, but the broader picture, the autonomy and identity of their general liberal arts institutions, was foremost in their minds.

In Rome, the American delegation of Catholic educators joined 175 other Catholic educators from 40 countries. Suspense was high; this was the first forum since the schema had appeared with its tell-tale signs of Roman intervention. During the seven-day summit, the pope spoke to the educators about a "new harmony, a closer and more trusting collaboration" between university and church.[34] To accomplish that, the educators proffered a ten-point recommendation as an alternative to the schema. At the heart was a request for a short document that was "positive, inspirational and future-oriented."

It should, they said, have few specific norms, and these should be "general in nature," making them open to interpretation by each nation.[35] The educators also wanted optimum freedom for institutional policy, research, and teaching, particularly in theology. A fifteen-member international commission, which included three North American Catholic educators, was named to forge ahead on a final document to be presented to John Paul. "We came here with somewhat of a sense we'd be met by this intransigent congregation," Gallin said in Rome. "But the opposite was true."[36]

In early September 1989 that group of fifteen met with Cardinal William Baum, head of the Congregation for Catholic Education, and agreed to a new approach on the schema. Again the pope spoke, saying that bishops should not be seen as external, like "foreign agents," to Catholic universities. He encouraged "an intimate communion with the pastors of the church."[37] The document drafted by the fifteen and left behind for Vatican consideration addressed many concerns of the Catholic universities worldwide. It incorporated the ten points made during the April summit. Part I, on the identity and mission of a Catholic university, included the fourfold test of Catholic identity, created from within an institution and first outlined in the 1972 document "The Catholic University in the Modern World." Furthermore, it reduced the seventy-two norms in the second draft of the schema to seven. "It's less juridical," Gallin said in October, the month the schema was to be sent to the pope.[38]

Key statements for both sides were written into the draft. For a Catholic college or university, the draft guaranteed the "institutional autonomy necessary to perform its functions" and said that "so long as the rights of the individual and of the community are preserved within the context of the common good, its members are guaranteed academic freedom." The hierarchy, too, was given its due as the draft exhorted colleges and universities to "recognize and accept the right of the bishops of the church, as the authentic interpreters of Catholic doctrine, to judge the conformity of their theological research and teaching with authentic catholicity and divine revelation."[39] The document had taken on a more general, exhortatory rather than legislative character.

The educators returned hopeful that what had been called a consultation had actually built a lasting consensus. Meanwhile, Gallin said, the four years of protracted debate "certainly raised the consciousness around the country about Catholic identity."[40] It apparently brought a clear message to the Vatican as well.

The pope's *Apostolic Constitution on Catholic Universities* was issued September 25, 1990, to a collective sigh of relief among the leaders of Catholic higher education.[41] The sigh was particularly strong in the United States, where about a third of the world's 925 Catholic colleges and universities function. Having already dedicated *Sapientia Christiana* for ecclesiastical faculties and universities, John Paul said he was obliged to promulgate an analogous document for Catholic universities "as a sort of 'magna carta.'" Divided between a general section on the identity and mission of the Catholic university and its general norms, the constitution reflected much that was already posited in the work of Catholic educators. Its most concrete norm, in fact, was that "non-Catholic teachers should not be allowed to constitute a majority in the institution, which is and must remain Catholic."

The university was given its autonomy, but the bishops were also given their prerogative: "If problems should arise concerning this Catholic character, the local bishop is to take initiatives necessary to resolve the matter, working with competent university authorities in accordance with established procedures and, if necessary, with the help of the Holy See."

The teaching role of the theologian was set out just as plainly: "All Catholic teachers are to be faithful to, and all other teachers respect, Catholic doctrine and morals in their research and teaching." Although these norms sounded as strict as canon law, they had a buffer in the broad strokes of the pope's vision of a mature, free, institution with academic freedom. In pursuit of a Catholic and "universal humanism," the pope said, these institutions are willing to serve the church and the world.

IN PRINCIPLE, authority and freedom found common ground in the education document. However, the desire of many academic theologians to have freedom on par with universities made consensus with the Holy See impossible. Constant battles had created a chasm between the Vatican and a large wing of theologians, a tension revealed in the Vatican's *Instruction* on the theological task.

In contrast to that, the educators had worked in consultation with the Vatican in what they called a spirit of good will. Thus, a document of their liking was produced. It was positive, visionary, and gave only general norms. If interpreted and applied that way, the document bode well for the future, suggesting an end of tension, for the time being, between American Catholic higher education and Rome.

Yet in the battle between authority and freedom in the church, such laws and papal statements can also be applied with steely precision and weight. "Every document and every law has a history of interpretation in which its ultimate meaning becomes apparent," the Jesuit president of Georgetown University, Leo O'Donovan, said about the apostolic constitution.[42] As ever, the choice of authority or freedom is not driven by perfect theories or documents. There are other forces, inspirations, and expediencies that grow out of the living relationships within the Catholic Church. There is also, according to belief, the Spirit. Hence, the documents, pro and con, may ultimately mean little. In the end, the greatest hope for both the cause of authority and of freedom lie in the church's living dynamism.

NOTES

Prologue Authority and Freedom

1. Charles Curran, *Christian Morality Today: The Renewal of Moral Theology* (Notre Dame, IN: Fides Publishers, Inc., 1966), 29.
2. Trial testimony of Charles E. Curran, December 21, 1988.
3. Wilton Wynn, *Keepers of the Keys: John Paul XXIII, Paul VI, and John Paul II: Three Who Changed the Church* (New York: Random House, 1988), 257.
4. *Lumen Gentium,* par. 9–17, and *Gaudium et spes,* par. 4, in Austin P. Flannery, ed., *Documents of Vatican II: The Conciliar and Post Conciliar Documents* (Grand Rapids, MI: William B. Eerdmans Publishing Co., 1984), 359–369, 905.
5. John 8:32; 2 Cor. 3:17.
6. Ralph Waldo Emerson, "History" in *Essays: First Series,* 1841.
7. Quoted in Martin Marty, *Modern American Religion, Volume 1: The Irony of It All, 1893–1919* (Chicago: University of Chicago Press, 1986), 64.
8. Eugene Kennedy, *Tomorrow's Catholics, Yesterday's Church: The Two Cultures of American Catholicism* (San Francisco, Harper and Row, 1988), 99–111.
9. Congregation for the Doctrine of the Faith, *Instruction on the Ecclesial Vocation of the Theologian* (Vatican City: Libreria Editrice Vaticana, June 25, 1990), par. 32.
10. Ibid., par. 31.
11. Meister Eckhart, *The Essential Sermons, Commentaries, Treatises and Defense,* translated by Edmund Colledge and Bernard McGinn (New York: Paulist, 1981), 72.
12. Quoted in Larry Witham, "Pope's choices hit for causing schism," *Washington Times,* September 30, 1988. From a Washington speech by Richard McBrien titled, "Future of the American Church."
13. Frederick H. Weisberg, Opinion and Order, *Charles E. Curran vs. The Catholic University of America,* February 28, 1989. Published in *Origins* vol. 18 (March 16, 1989): 664–72.
14. Charles Curran, *Faithful Dissent* (Kansas City, MO: Sheed and Ward, 1986), 209. Letter from Charles E. Curran to Joseph Ratzinger, June 23, 1983.
15. "John Paul holds papal speech record," *Associated Press* citing *30 Days* magazine, in the *Washington Times,* October 13, 1989.

16. See George Gallup and Jim Castelli, *The People's Religion: American Faith in the 90s* (New York: Macmillan, 1989), 252; and Wade Clark Roof and William McKinney, *American Mainline Religion: Its Changing Shape and Future* (New Brunswick, NJ: Rutgers University Press, 1987), 66–67, 170–71.
17. Roof and McKinney, *American Mainline Religion,* 148–51. Also see Dean Kelley, *Why Conservative Churches are Growing* (New York: Harper and Row, 1972), 88–90.

One Freedom in the Air

1. This brief biography of Curran is based on: Curran, *Faithful Dissent,* 3–47; Curran, "How My Mind Has Changed, 1960–1975," *Journal of the College Theology Society* vol. 2 (Fall 1975): 187–205; news reports; and Curran's testimony in D.C. Superior Court, December 21–23, 1988.
2. These figures for the William McDonald era are from the university registrar. For more on McDonald see, C. Joseph Nuesse, *The Catholic University of America: A Centennial History* (Washington D.C.: Catholic University Press, 1990), 386–401.
3. Curran, *Christian Morality Today,* 55.
4. Quoted in "Father Curran: Symbol of bishops' problem," *National Catholic Reporter,* April 26, 1967.
5. Ibid.
6. Curran, *Faithful Dissent,* 272.
7. See Erving E. Beauregard, "An Archbishop, a University, and Academic Freedom," *Records of the American Catholic Historical Society* vol. 93 (1982): 25–39.
8. Joseph Scimecca and Roland Damiano, *Crisis at St. John's: Strike and Revolution on the Catholic Campus* (New York: Random House, 1968), vii.
9. Quoted in Nuesse, *The Catholic University of America,* 400. This account of the board decision, the strike, and its aftermath is based on: Albert C. Pierce, *Beyond One Man* (Washington D.C.: Anawim Press, 1967); Curran, *Faithful Dissent,* 14–16; news accounts in the old *Washington Star* and the *Washington Post*; and testimony in the Curran trial.
10. Editorial, old *Washington Star,* April 21, 1967.
11. Curran, *Faithful Dissent,* 15.
12. "Roman Catholics: Time for a Change," *Time,* April 28, 1967, 62.
13. John Mathews, "Multiple Effort Under Way To End Catholic U. Shutdown," old *Washington Star,* April 22, 1967.
14. Ibid.
15. "Roman Catholics: Time for a Change," *Time,* April 28, 1967, 62.
16. "Priest for Students," *New York Times,* April 25, 1967.

17. This account of the dissent over *Humanae Vitae* is based on: Charles E. Curran and Robert E. Hunt, *Dissent in and For the Church: Theologians and Humanae Vitae* (New York: Sheed and Ward, 1970). 3–24; Janet E. Smith, "*Humane Vitae* at 20: New Insights Into an Old Debate," *Crisis: A Journal of Lay Catholic Opinion,* June, 1988, 16–18; testimony at the Curran trial; and interviews with personnel of Catholic University and the archdiocese of Washington D.C.
18. Paul VI, *Humanae Vitae,* par. 56.
19. Curran and Hunt, *Dissent in and For the Church,* 13.
20. Trial testimony of Charles E. Curran, December 21, 1988.
21. National Catholic News Service, August 1, 1968. Cited in Charles Curran, *Catholic Higher Education, Theology, and Academic Freedom* (Notre Dame, IN:University of Notre Dame Press, 1990), 203.
22. Curran and Hunt, *Dissent in and For the Church,* 12.
23. Trial testimony of James Brennan, December 19, 1988.
24. Trustee statement issued by chairman Carroll Hochwalt, September 5, 1968. Quoted in Curran and Hunt, *Dissent in and For the Church,* 17.
25. "Summary Report of the Faculty Board of Inquiry," April 1, 1969. The board was chaired by Donald E. Marlowe. For norms of licit theological dissent see, National Conference of Catholic Bishops, *Human Life in Our Day* (Washington D.C.: United States Catholic Conference, 1968).
26. "A Statement by the Board of Trustees of The Catholic University of America Concerning the Report of the Faculty Board of Inquiry," June 5, 1969. The board quoted from the April 30, 1969 statement of Catholic educators meeting in Rome.
27. Trial testimony of Nivard Scheel, December 15, 1988.
28. Religious News Service, "Revision Plan on Catholic Code Blasted," *Washington Post,* June 27, 1970.
29. "Charles E. Curran: A Bibliography," 1962-86. Compiled by Bonnie L. VanDelinder of Colgate Theological Seminary, Rochester, NY.
30. Letter from Cardinal Franjo Seper to Charles E. Curran, July 13, 1979. For correspondence between Curran and church authorities from 1979 to 1986 see, "Documentation," in Curran, *Faithful Dissent,* 113–276.

Two Vatican File 4866

1. See Peter Hebblethwaite, *The New Inquisition? The Case of Edward Schillebeeckx and Hans Küng* (San Francisco: Harper and Row, 1980); and Ted Schoff, ed., *The Schillebeeckx Case* (New York: Paulist Press, 1980).
2. See Paul Johnson, *Pope John Paul II and the Catholic Restoration* (New York: St. Martin's Press, 1981), 157–62; and Hebblethwaite, *The New Inquisition?*

3. Interview with a senior editor of the Catholic weekly, *The Wanderer.*
4. This account of events from the 1979 "observations" to the 1987 lawsuit is based on: Curran, *Faithful Dissent,* 26–47; Joan Barthel, "Dissent into Darkness," *Washington Post Magazine,* March 22, 1987; news reports in the *Washington Post* and the *Washington Times*; and testimony in the Curran trial.
5. Letter from Joseph Ratzinger to Charles E. Curran, September 17, 1985.
6. Trial testimony of James A. Hickey, December 14, 1988.
7. Trial testimony of Joseph Bernardin, December 16, 1988.
8. Jean-Pierre Jossua, "Jacques Pohier: A Theologian Destroyed," in Hans Küng and Leonard Swidler, *Church in Anguish: Has the Vatican Betrayed Vatican II?* (San Francisco: Harper and Row, 1987), 205–211.
9. Harvey Cox, *The Silencing of Leonardo Boff: The Vatican and the Future of World Christianity* (Oak Park, IL: Meyer Stone Books, 1989).
10. Avery Dulles, "Ratzinger's Journey," *Crisis,* December 1989. Book review.
11. Quoted in Russell Chandler, "Focus of Controversy—Ratzinger: Point Man for the Vatican," *Los Angeles Times,* November 7, 1989.
12. Dulles, "Ratzinger's Journey." For profiles on Ratzinger also see, Joseph Ratzinger with Vittorio Messori, *The Ratzinger Report: An Exclusive Interview on the State of the Church* (San Francisco: Ignatius Press, 1985), 17–20; Richard Neuhaus, *The Catholic Moment: The Paradox of the Church in the Modern World* (San Francisco: Harper and Row, 1987), 136–49; E. J. Dionne, Jr., "The Pope's Guardian of Orthodoxy," *New York Times Magazine,* November 4, 1985; and Chandler, "Focus of Controversy."
13. Quoted in Barthel, "Dissent into Darkness," *Washington Post Magazine,* March 22, 1987, 18.
14. The letters from Joseph Ratzinger to James A. Hickey and to Charles Curran were both dated July 25, 1986. Hickey sent the Ratzinger letter to Curran under his own cover letter, August 18, 1986.
15. Bernardin's action in Rome was reported by the National Catholic News Service and cited in, Joseph Berger, "Bishop Upholds Vatican in Priest Controversy," *New York Times,* March 16, 1986.
16. Editorial, *The Tower,* March 14, 1986. The next week a *Tower* poll asked 213 undergraduates "should Curran's credentials be revoked": 76 percent said no and 16 percent said yes (8 percent had no opinion). On dissent, 68 percent upheld the right and 23 percent did not. For student reactions after Curran's suspension see, Lawrence Feinberg, "CU Campus Divided on Curran," *Washington Post,* January 20, 1987.
17. Marjorie Hyer, "Tension Mounts for Theologian," *Washington Post,* March 18, 1986.
18. "Doctrine and Dissent: The Curran Case," *Commonweal,* March 28, 1986, 163.
19. Letter from Joseph Ratzinger to Charles E. Curran, July 25, 1986.

20. Roberto Suro, "Priest Censure Seen as Move To Extend Church Authority," *New York Times*, Rome, August 20, 1986.
21. Joyce Price, "Vatican Targets U.S. Dissenter," *Washington Times*, August 21, 1986.
22. Wynn, *Keepers of the Keys*, 257–58.
23. Marjorie Hyer, "Catholic Educators Back Vatican Action on Curran," *Washington Post*, September 5, 1986.
24. Russell Chandler, "Mahony Assails Censured Priest's Views," *Los Angeles Times*, October 17, 1986.
25. Letter from Charles Curran to William J. Byron, November 11, 1986. Reply letter from Byron to Curran, November 14, 1986.
26. Letter from Charles E. Curran to James A. Hickey, January 7, 1987.
27. Trial testimony of James A. Hickey, December 14, 1988.
28. Trial testimony of Charles E. Curran, December 22, 1988.
29. Robin Toner, "Censured Priest Drops Teaching Plans for Spring," *New York Times*, January 16, 1987.
30. Trial testimony of William J. Byron, December 20, 1988.
31. Nuesse, *The Catholic University of America*, 410–11. For Maguire's views see his, *The Moral Revolution: A Christian Humanist Vision* (San Francisco: Harper and Row, 1986).
32. See Marjorie Hyer, "James Provost Wins Crucial Tenure Vote at CU," *Washington Post*, August 21, 1986.

Three Magisterium and Dissent

1. Curran, *Faithful Dissent*, 271.
2. Curran, "How I Changed My Mind," 204.
3. Curran, *Faithful Dissent*, 54.
4. Ibid., 272.
5. Quoted in "Shift noted in theological leadership," *Catholic Standard*, archdiocese of Washington D.C., December 15, 1988.
6. Francis A. Sullivan, *Magisterium: Teaching Authority in the Catholic Church* (New York: Paulist Press, 1983), 24.
7. *Lumen Gentium*, par. 20, in Flannery, *Documents of Vatican II*, 372.
8. *Dei Verbum*, par. 10, in Flannery, *Documents of Vatican II*, 756.
9. This summary of the history of the magisterium is based on: Sullivan, *Magisterium*; Yves Congar, "A Brief History of the Magisterium and Its Relations to Scholars," in Charles E. Curran and Richard A. McCormick, eds., *Readings in Moral Theology No. 3: The Magisterium and Morality* (New York: Paulist Press, 1982): Richard P. McBrien, *Catholicism*, 2 vols. (Minneapolis: Winston Press, 1980), 68–72.; and *New Catholic Encyclopedia*, s.v. "Magisterium."
10. Congar, "A Brief History of the Magisterium," 315.
11. Ibid., 319.

12. Jaroslav Pelikan, *The Christian Tradition: A History of the Development of Doctrine, Volume 1–The Emergence of the Catholic Tradition (100–600)* (Chicago: Chicago University Press, 1971), 5.
13. Richard P. McBrien, "The Magisterium," part four in the twenty-four-part audio cassette series *Understanding Catholicism* (Kansas City, MO.: Creedance Cassettes, 1984). While the tape series is often based verbatim on McBrien's book *Catholicism,* I found some of his taped comments more colorful for quotation.
14. Sullivan, *Magisterium,* 29.
15. McBrien, *Catholicism,* vol. 1, 69.
16. Congregation for the Doctrine of the Faith, *Instruction,* June 1990, n. 27.
17. *Lumen Gentium,* par. 22, in Flannery, *Documents of Vatican II,* 375.
18. McBrien, *Catholicism,* vol. 2, 835.
19. Sullivan, *Magisterium,* 94–95. He cites Yves Congar's assessment of this period between the French Revolution and Vatican I.
20. These popes are cited in Curran, *New Perspectives in Moral Theology* (Notre Dame, IN: University of Notre Dame, 1976), 23.
21. Congregation for the Doctrine of the Faith, *Declaration in Defense of the Catholic Doctrine on the Church Against Certain Errors of the Present Day (Mysterium Ecclesiae),* June 24, 1973. Published in *Origins* vol. 3 (July 19, 1973): 110.
22. Hans Küng, *Infallible? An Inquiry* (Garden City, N.Y.: Doubleday, 1971), 86.
23. McBrien, "The Magisterium," part four in the tape series *Understanding Catholicism.*
24. Karl Rahner, *Theological Investigations, Volume 9: Writings of 1965–67, I,* translated by Graham Harrison (New York: Herder and Herder, 1972), 86–87. For Rahner's views see chapter 5, "Theologians and the Church's Teaching Authority After the Council."
25. Avery Dulles, *The Reshaping of Catholicism: Current Challenges in the Theology of the Church* (San Francisco: Harper and Row, 1988), 105.
26. Ibid.
27. National Conference of Catholic Bishops, "Norms of Licit Theological Dissent," in *Human Life in Our Day.*
28. This criteria for legitimate dissent is laid out in four points by McBrien in *Catholicism,* vol. 1, 72. The reference to Newman comes from Dulles, *The Reshaping of Catholicism,* 97-98
29. Thomas Aquinas, *IV Sentences,* dist. 38, a. 4. Cited in McBrien, *Catholicism,* vol. 2, 1003.
30. Thomas Aquinas, *Quodlibetal Questions,* no. 3, q. 4, art. 2. Unpublished translation by Alfred J. Freddoso, University of Notre Dame.
31. Kennedy, *Tomorrow's Catholics, Yesterday's Church,* 3–10.
32. McBrien, "Christian Moral Existence," part twenty-two in the tape series *Understanding Catholicism.*
33. *Dignitatis humanae,* par. 3, in Flannery, *Documents of Vatican II,* 801.

34. Ibid., par. 14, 811.
35. Ibid., par. 25, 379.
36. Dulles, *The Reshaping of Catholicism,* 103.
37. Vatican I, "Constitution of the Catholic Faith, 1870," chapter 4, p. 32. Cited in James J. Annarelli, *Academic Freedom and Catholic Higher Education* (New York: Greenwood Press, 1987), 7.
38. Rahner, *Theological Investigations,* vol. 9, 86.
39. *Gaudium et spes,* par. 4, in Flannery, *Documents of Vatican II,* 905.
40. Ibid., par. 5, 907.
41 Charles Curran, "Academic Freedom: The Catholic University and Catholic Theology," *The Furrow* vol. 3 (December, 1979): 750.
42. *Gaudium et Spes,* par. 17, in Flannery, *Documents of Vatican II,* 917.
43. Walter Metzger and Richard Hofstadter, *The Development of Academic Freedom in the United States* (New York: Columbia University Press, 1955), 396. Hofstadter wrote part one and Metzger wrote part two of the book.
44. This overview of academic freedom at universities is based on: Hofstadter and Metzger, *The Development of Academic Freedom,* 261–74, 383–391, 407–12; Annarelli, *Academic Freedom and Catholic Higher Education,* 2–4; and Curran, *Catholic Higher Education,* 8.
45. For a history of the AAUP see, Metzger, *Development of Academic Freedom,* 468–80.
46. American Association of University Professors, "Report: The 'Limitations' Clause in the 1940 Statement of Principles," *Academe* vol. 74 (September–October 1988): 52–59.
47. Sydney Hook, *Heresy Yes, Conspiracy No* (New York: John Day Co., 1953), 220.
48. Guthrie is quoted from Georgetown University documents in, Curran, *Catholic Higher Education,* 33–34.
49. The 1966 Notre Dame symposium produced a book: Edward Manier and John W. Houck, eds. *American Freedom and the Catholic University* (Notre Dame, IN: Fides Publishers, Inc., 1967).
50. International Federation of Catholic Universities, North American Region, "Freedom, Autonomy, and the University," *IDOC International* vol. 39 (January 1972): 79–80.
51. National Catholic Educational Association, "Relations of American Catholic Colleges and Universities with the Church," in *Occasional Papers on Catholic Higher Education* vol. 2 (April 1976): 8, 9.
52. John Paul II, "Address to U.S. Catholic university and college educators at The Catholic University of America," October 7, 1979.
53. Hofstadter, *Development of Academic Freedom,* 366.
54. Philip Gleason, "Academic Freedom and the Crisis in Catholic Universities," in Manier and Houck, eds., *American Freedom and the Catholic University,* 36.
55. John Dewey, *A Common Faith* (New Haven: Yale University Press, 1960), 51.

56. Page Smith, *Killing the Spirit: Higher Education in America* (New York: Viking, 1990), 161.
57. George A. Kelly, ed., "Introduction," *Why Should the Catholic University Survive?* (New York: St. John's University Press, 1973), xviii.
58. Theodore M. Hesburgh, *The Hesburgh Papers: Higher Values in Higher Education* (Kansas City, MO: Andrews and McNeel, 1979), 75.
59. Charles Curran, "Catholic Universities," *Texas Law Review* vol. 66 (June 1988): 1453–54.
60. Cited in Curran, *Catholic Higher Education,* 184–86.
61. Rahner, *Theological Investigations,* vol. 9, 95.
62. The critique was presented at a news conference in Washington D.C., January 28, 1990, after a two-day consultation of fifteen scholars. For their fifteen critiques see, Thomas J. Reese, ed., *The Universal Catechism Reader: Reflections and Responses* (San Francisco: Harper and Row, 1990).
63. Congregation for the Doctrine of the Faith, *Instruction,* June 1990, 12–13.
64. For an overview of the commission's history see, Smith, "*Humane Vitae* at 20," 14–21.
65. Ibid., 15.

Four Moral Theology

1. Quoted in *The Tower,* April 25, 1967.
2. Ratzinger, *The Ratzinger Report,* 87.
3. William E. May, *Moral Absolutes: Catholic Tradition, Current Trends, and the Truth* (Milwaukee: Marquette University Press, 1989), 43. The Pere Marquette Lecture in Theology, 1989.
4. McBrien, *Catholicism,* vol. 2, 997–98.
5. Charles Curran, *New Perspectives in Moral Theology* (Notre Dame: University of Notre Dame, 1976), 27. Curran cites Thomas Aquinas, *Summa Theologiae,* Ia IIae, q. 94, a. 4.
6. Thomas Aquinas, *Summa Theologiae,* translated by the Fathers of the English Dominican Province (New York: Benziger Brothers, Inc., 1947), Ia IIae, q. 100, a. 8., vol. 1, 1046.
7. Josef Fuchs, *Personal Responsibility and Christian Morality* (Washington D.C.: Georgetown University Press, 1983), 142. Cited in May, *Moral Absolutes,* 28.
8. Aquinas, *Summa Theologiae,* translated by the English Dominican Province, Ia IIae. q. 94. a. 5., vol. 1, 1012.
9. Thomas Aquinas, *De Malo,* q. 15, a. 1, ad. 15. Cited in May, *Moral Absolutes,* 63–64.
10. Curran, *Faithful Dissent,* 98.

11. Ibid., 61.
12. Ibid., 79.
13. Ratzinger, *The Ratzinger Report*, 88–89.
14. May, *Moral Absolutes*, 1.
15. This overview history of moral theology is based on: John Mahoney, *The Making of Moral Theology: A Study of the Roman Catholic Tradition* (Oxford, G.B.: Clarendon Press, 1987); Charles Curran, *Toward an American Catholic Moral Theology* (Notre Dame, IN: University of Notre Dame Press, 1987); May, *Moral Absolutes*; and *New Catholic Encyclopedia*, s.v. "Moral Theology."
16. Congregation for the Doctrine of the Faith, *Declaration on Certain Questions Concerning Sexual Ethics*, January 15, 1975, par. 10. Published in *Origins* vol. 5 (January 22, 1976): 491.
17. Saint Augustine, *De Doctrina Christiana*, I, 4; PL 34, 20–21. Cited in Mahoney, *The Making of Moral Theology*, 44.
18. Williston Walker, *A History of the Christian Church*, Third Edition (New York: Charles Scribner's Sons, 1970), 249.
19. *New Catholic Encyclopedia*, s.v. "Moral Theology, History Of, (700 to Vatican Council I)," 1119.
20. Gordon E. Leff, *Medieval Thought: St. Augustine to Ockham* (Chicago: Quadrangle Books, Inc., 1959), 113.
21. D.E. Luscombe, trans. and ed., *Peter Abelard's 'Ethics'* (Oxford: Oxford University Press, 1971,) 55.
22. While "Ockhamism" stands for rejection of both natural law and scholasticism, modern scholarship is beginning to assert that Ockham himself, while an innovator, was not that radical. Medievalist Gordon E. Leff makes this point in the introduction to his *William Ockham: The Metamorphosis of Scholastic Discourse* (Manchester, U.K.: Manchester University Press, 1975). Of past studies on Ockham, Leff said: "No distinction was made between his outlook and Ockhamism; the latter's earlier extravagances and later barrenness were transposed to this thought . . . However he may have transformed [scholastic] tradition and, whatever his place in it, the inappropriateness of the older labels of 'nominalist' and 'fideist' and the groundlessness of calling him a skeptic are now sufficiently plain."
23. Quoted in Joyce Price, "Catholic Educators call Curran ouster necessary action," *Washington Times*, September 5, 1986. From a statement by George A. Kelly, president of the Fellowship of Catholic Scholars.
24. Quoted in Mahoney, *The Making of Moral Theology*, 136.
25. Ibid., 140–41.
26. Blaise Pascal, *Les Provinciales*, L. Dogent, ed. (Paris, 1965), 101. Cited in Mahoney, *The Making of Moral Theology*, 139.
27. Albert Jonsen and Stephen Toulmin, *The Abuse of Casuistry: A History of Moral Reasoning* (Berkeley, CA: University of California Press, 1988), 238–239.

28. Paul Tillich, *A History of Christian Thought: From Its Judaic Origins to Existentialism* (New York: Simon and Schuster, 1967), 213.
29. The 1985 poll is cited in, George Gallup and Jim Castelli, *The American Catholic People: Their Beliefs, Practices, and Values* (Garden City, NY: Doubleday and Company, 1987), 51. The 1989 poll is cited in, Larry Witham, "Poll: Faith can't predict moral values," *Washington Times,* May 26, 1989.
30. Gallup and Castelli, *The American Catholic People,* 59–65, 189.
31. See Andrew Greeley, William C. McCready, and Kathleen McCourt, *Catholic Schools in a Declining Church* (Kansas City, MO: Sheed and Ward, 1976). In a later work, *Crisis in the Church: A Study of Religion in America* Chicago: Thomas More Press, 1979), 43–44, Greeley clarified that the school study only claimed "sexuality and doctrinal positions on the nature of church authority will be *partial* explanations for Catholic religious behavior."
32. Ratzinger, *The Ratzinger Report,* 83.
33. Quoted in Jaroslav Pelikan, *A History of the Development of Doctrine, Volume 5—Christian Tradition and Modern Doctrine (Since 1700)* (Chicago: University of Chicago Press, 1989), 174.
34. Allan Bloom, *The Closing of the American Mind: How Higher Education has Failed Democracy and Impoverished the Souls of Today's Students* (New York: Simon and Schuster, 1987), 194–216.
35. Bernard Lonergan, "The Transition from a Classicist World-View to Historical-Mindedness," in *A Second Collection,* William F.J. Ryan and Bernard J. Tyrrell, eds. (Philadelphia: Westminster Press, 1975), 5–6.
36. Ratzinger, *The Ratzinger Report,* 96.
37. Josef Fuchs, *Christian Ethics in a Secular Arena* (Washington D.C.: Georgetown University Press, 1984), 72.
38. Quoted in May, *Moral Absolutes,* 24. He cites Timothy O'Connell, *Principles for Catholic Morality* (New York: Seabury, 1978), 157–58.
39. See this analysis of the "majority report" in May, *Moral Absolutes,* 21–22; and Smith, "*Humane Vitae* at 20," 16.
40. Jonsen and Toulmin, *The Abuse of Casuistry,* 304.
41. Bernard Häring, "The Master Idea of Christian Morality," in Walter I. Burghardt and William F. Lynch, eds., *The Idea of Catholicism: An Introduction to the Thought and Worship of the Church* (Cleveland: The World Publishing Company, 1964), 42, 46–52.
42. May, *Moral Absolutes,* 69–70, 71, 75.
43. Curran, *New Perspectives in Moral Theology,* 66.
44. Curran, *A New Look at Christian Morality* (Notre Dame, IN: Fides Publishers, 1968), 169–73, 232–33; and *Catholic Moral Theology in Dialogue* (Notre Dame, IN:Fides Publishers, 1972), 209–19. Also see Curran's analysis of sin in, *New Perspectives in Moral Theology,* 65–75.
45. Curran, *New Perspectives in Moral Theology,* 75.
46. Ibid., 14–15.

47. Curran, *Faithful Dissent,* 87.
48. Ratzinger, *The Ratzinger Report,* 98.
49. Ibid., 86.
50. Ibid.

Five Catholic Higher Education

1. Edward J. Power, *Catholic Higher Education in America: A History* (New York: Appleton-Century-Crofts, 1972), 370.
2. Quoted in George W. Hunt, "American Catholic Intellectual Life," *America,* May 6, 1989.
3. National Catholic Educational Association. "Relations of American Catholic Colleges and Universities with the Church," 6.
4. These types of Catholic institutions are suggested in Annarelli, *Academic Freedom and Catholic Higher Education,* 45–48.
5. John Paul II, *Redemptor Hominis,* March 1979 (Washington D.C.: United States Catholic Conference, 1979).
6. John Paul II, *Apostolic Constitution Sapientia Christiana: On Ecclesiastical Faculties and Universities,* 1979. Published in *Origins* vol. 9 (June 7, 1979).
7. John Paul II, "Address to U.S. Catholic university and college educators at the Catholic University of America," 1979.
8. This overview of Christianity and education is based on: Hofstadter, *Development of Academic Freedom*; Kelly, *Why Should the Catholic University Survive?*; Johnson, *A History of Christianity*; Nicolas Cheetham, *Keepers of the Keys: A History of the Popes from St. Peter to John Paul II* (New York, Charles Scribner's Sons, 1983); Christopher Dawson, *Religion and the Rise of Western Culture* (New York: Doubleday, Image Books, 1958); and *Encyclopaedia Britannica* s.v. "Education, History of," 333–39.
9. Kelly, *Why Should the Catholic University Survive?,* xi.
10. Dawson, *Religion and the Rise of Western Culture,* 185.
11. Brian Tierny, "Popes and Bishops Before Trent: An Historical Survey," in Bernard Cooke, ed., *The Papacy and the Church in the United States* (New York: Paulist Press, 1989), 17.
12. Hofstadter, *The Development of Academic Freedom,* 62.
13. Charles Frederick Harrold, "Forward," in John Henry Newman, *The Idea of a University* (London: Longmans, Green and Co., 1947), xxi.
14. Ibid., xxii.
15. John Henry Newman, *The Idea of a University,* (London: Longmans, Green and Co., 1947), 190, 192.
16. Professor Friedrich Paulsen, *The German University and University Study,* cited by Ralph F. Fuchs, "Academic Freedom: Its Basic Phi-

losophy, Function and History," in Louis Jonghin, ed., *Academic Freedom and Tenure* (Madison, WI: University of Wisconsin, 1967), 249.

17. This summary of Catholic higher education in the United States is based on: Power, *Catholic Higher Education*; Philip Gleason, "American Catholic Higher Education: A Historical Perspective," and Robert Hassenger, "College and Catholic: An Introduction" and "The Future of Catholic Higher Education," in Robert Hassenger, ed., *The Shape of Catholic Higher Education* (Chicago: University of Chicago Press, 1967); Gleason, "Academic Freedom and the Crisis in Catholic Universities"; Andrew M. Greeley, *From Backwater to Mainstream: A Profile of Catholic Higher Education* (New York: McGraw-Hill, 1969); James Hennesey, *American Catholics: A History of the Roman Catholic Community in the United States* (New York: Oxford University Press, 1981); National Catholic Educational Association, "Relations of American Catholic Colleges and Universities with the Church"; Edmund D. Pellegrino, "Catholic Universities and the Church's Intellectual Ministry: The Crisis of Identity and Justification," *Thought* vol. 57 (June 1982): 165–81.
18. Quoted in Paul Johnson, *Modern Times: The World From the Twenties to the Eighties* (New York: Harper and Row, 1983), 641.
19. Johnson, *Modern Times,* 225.
20. Quoted in Hennesey, *American Catholics,* 249.
21. Gleason, "American Catholic Higher Education," 46.
22. Fulton J. Sheen, "Educating for a Catholic Renaissance," *National Catholic Educational Association Bulletin* 26 (1929), 45–54. Cited in Hennesey, *American Catholics,* 255.
23. *National Catholic Educational Association Bulletin* 32 (1935), 70–71. Cited in Hennesey, *American Catholics.*
24. Johnson, *Modern Times,* 641.
25. Edward F. Denison, *Sources of Economic Growth in the United States and the Alternatives Before Us* (New York: Committee for Economic Development, 1962).
26. Clark Kerr, "The Uses of the University" (Cambridge, MA: Harvard University Press, 1964), 88. The 1963 Godkin Lectures at Harvard University.
27. John Tracy Ellis, "American Catholics and the Intellectual Life," *Thought* vol. 30 (September 1955): 377–78.
28. Bernard Berelson, *Graduate Education in the United States* (New York: McGraw-Hill, 1960); and John L. Chase, *Doctors Degrees Conferred by U.S. Institutions* (Washington D.C.: n.d). Cited in Gleason, "American Catholic Higher Education," 42–43.
29. Theodore Hesburgh, "The Work of Mediation," *Commonweal* vol. 75 (October 6, 1961): 33–35. Originally presented as an address in 1961 to the National Catholic Educational Association.
30. *Gaudium et spes,* par. 4, 36, 62, in Flannery, *Documents of Vatican II,* 905, 935, 968.

31. Smith, *Killing the Spirit,* 115.
32. Frank D. Schubert, "Theology Without God: A New Study Documents the Secularization of the Catholic Curriculum," *Crisis,* June, 1989, 22–26.
33. Research by Andrew Greeley cited in Hassenger, *The Shape of Catholic Higher Education,* 7.
34. Harold A. Beutow, *The Catholic School: Its Roots, Identity and Future* (New York: Crossroad, 1988), 311.
35. John Paul II, *Apostolic Constitution on Catholic Universities* (Vatican City, September 25, 1990), 23.
36. Scimecca and Damiano, *Crisis at St. John's,* vii.
37. Walter Lippmann, "The University," *New Republic,* May 28, 1966, 17–20.
38. Beutow, *The Catholic Schools,* 106.
39. Pellegrino, "Catholic Universities and the Church's Intellectual Ministry," 70.
40. Johnson, *Modern Times,* 643.
41. Quoted in Lionel Trilling, *Last Decade: Essays and Reviews, 1965–75,* Diana Trilling ed. (New York: Harcourt Brace Jovanovich, 1978), 111. Louis Kampf gave his presidential address to the Modern Languages Association in 1971.
42. See Bloom's "Tocqueville on Democratic Intellectual Life" and "Liberal Education," in *The Closing of the American Mind,* 246–56, 336–47.
43. National Catholic Educational Association, "Relations of American Catholic Colleges and Universities with the Church," 6.
44. Charles H. Wilson Jr., *Tilton vs. Richardson: The Search for Sectarianism in Education* (Washington D.C.: Association of American Colleges, 1971).
45. Land O'Lakes Statement, in Neil McCluskey, ed., *The Catholic University: A Modern Appraisal* (Notre Dame: University of Notre Dame Press, 1970).
46. 1969 Congress of Delegates of the Catholic Universities of the World, "The Rome Statement: The Catholic University and the Aggiornamento," May 1, 1969, in McCluskey, *The Catholic University,* 346–365.
47. Second Congress of Delegates of the Catholic Universities of the World, "The Catholic University in the Modern World," in Kelly, *Why Should the Catholic University Survive?,* 108–129.
48. Ibid.
49. Letter from Cardinal Gabriel Marie Garrone to presidents of Catholic universities, April 25, 1973. Published in National Catholic Educational Association, *College Newsletter,* March 1973.
50. Alice Gallin, "On the Road: Toward a Definition of a Catholic University," *The Jurist* vol. 48 (1988): 547.
51. National Catholic Educational Association, "Relations of American Catholic Colleges and Universities with the Church," 8.
52. Gallin, "On the Road," 552–53.
53. Canon 59, in Pontifical Commission on the Revised Code of Canon Law,

Schema Canonum Libri III De Ecclesiae Munere Docendi. Cited in Gallin, "On the Road," 553. The other troublesome canon, 64, read: "Those who, in any kind of institution of higher education, give courses in theology or courses related to theology require a canonical mission." That language was changed to "mandate" in the final code.

54. Congregation for Catholic Education, "Proposed Schema for a Pontifical Document on Catholic Universities," April 15, 1985. Published in *Origins* vol. 15 (April 10, 1986): 706–11
55. Gallin, "On the Road," 542.

Six Catholic University

1. For an overview see Nuesse, *The Catholic University of America*.
2. Larry Witham, "CUA-church tension not new, historian says," *Washington Times*, July 18, 1986.
3. Nuesse, *The Catholic University of America*, 479–80.
4. John Paul II, "Address to Leaders of Catholic Higher Education," September 12, 1987, Xavier University, New Orleans.
5. William J. Byron, "An American Catholic Perspective on Academic Freedom." Address to the Association of Catholic Colleges and Universities, February 1, 1989, Washington D.C. Published in *Origins* vol. 18 (February 16, 1989): 596–604.
6. This brief history of The Catholic University of America is based on: Nuesse, "CUA's First One Hundred Years," *CUA Magazine* vol. 1 (Fall 1989); The Catholic University of America, "History," in *Announcements: School of Religious Studies, 1987–88*; Hennesey, *American Catholics*; trial testimony; and *New Catholic Encyclopedia*, s.v. "The Catholic University of America."
7. Hennesey, *American Catholics*, 198.
8. *Announcements*, 18–19.
9. Gleason, "American Catholic Higher Education," 40.
10. *Announcements*, 18.
11. James Hitchcock, "The Curran Case and the 'American Church'," in William May, ed., *Vatican Authority and American Catholic Dissent: The Curran Case and its Consequences* (New York: Crossroad, 1988), 56.
12. For the Poels case at Catholic University see, Gerald P. Fogarty, *American Catholic Biblical Scholarship: A History from the Early Republic to Vatican II* (San Francisco: Harper and Row, 1989), 108–116.
13. See Nuesse, *The Catholic University of America*, 279–81.
14. *New Catholic Encyclopedia*, s.v. "The Catholic University of America," 333.
15. Gleason, "American Catholic Higher Education," 41.

16. For this account see, "Universities: Crisis at Catholic U.," *Time,* March 29, 1963, 58.
17. Quoted in "Crisis at Catholic U.," 58. See also, Nuesse, *The Catholic University of America,* 394–96.
18. Catholic University of America Board of Trustees, "The Objectives of the Catholic University of America," *Manual of Information for the Faculty* Washington D.C., 1968, ii. The objectives were adopted by the board July 26, 1968.
19. The clause "faithful to the Christian message" was included in, "Statement of University Objectives," *Documents of the Catholic University of America, 1970.* These document were promulgated February 6, 1970, after approval by the board of trustees and the Holy See.
20. Quoted in "Purposes and Objectives," *The Catholic University of America Self Evaluation for the Middle States Association,* January 1970, 3.
21. "The Juridical Status of the University," article 8, *Statutes of The Catholic University of America, 1937.* Reprinted in 1964.
22. Letter of Frank Gallagher to Lawrence Shehan, April 23, 1968.
23. Ibid.
24. Quoted in "Revision of the Statutes," an analysis paper by the Congregation for Catholic Education, November 25, 1969. It is responding to the proposed revision.
25. Letter of F. Taylor Jones to Clarence Walton, January 28, 1970.
26. Ibid. Walton's comment is written on the Jones letter, directing his secretary to reply.
27. Pope Pius XI, *Deus scientiarum Dominus,* 1931.
28. Congregation for Catholic Education, *Normae Quaedam,* 1968.
29. Ibid., see "Principles," par. 2.
30. Trial testimony of Frederick McManus, December 16, 1988. In the norms of *Normae Quaedam,* a more specific phrase is used in paragraph 20: "in full communion with the magisterium of the church."
31. Letter from Gabriel Marie Garrone to Patrick O'Boyle, November 27, 1969.
32. "Special Statutes for Pontifical Schools," par. 10, *Documents of The Catholic University of America, 1970.*
33. Letter from Gabriel Marie Garrone to Lawrence J. Shehan, November 28, 1969. Cited in the minutes of the board of trustees meeting, December 6, 1969.
34. Trial testimony of Charles E. Curran, December 22, 1988.
35. Trial testimony of Frederick McManus, December 16, 1988.
36. "Members and Associates of Faculties," par. 4, *Canonical Statutes for the Ecclesiastical Faculties of The Catholic University of America.* The statutes were adopted by the academic senate and board of trustees in January 1981.
37. Ibid., see "Preamble and General Statutes," par. 1.

38. Ibid., see "Members and Associates of Faculties," par. 8.
39. Letter from Charles E. Curran to Frederick McManus, provost, August 12, 1982.

Seven From Campus to Court

1. Much of the account in this chapter is based on interviews with Kevin Baine, lawyer for Catholic University, and Paul Saunders, lawyer for Charles Curran. The interviews took place in the fall of 1989.
2. "Report to the Chancellor from the Ad Hoc Committee of the Academic Senate of The Catholic University of America In the Matter of Professor Charles E. Curran," October 9, 1987, 59.
3. Letter from James A. Hickey to Urban A. Lester, chairman of the faculty ad hoc committee, December 14, 1987.
4. Deposition of William J. Byron, *Curran vs. Catholic University,* June 23, 1988, 141–52.
5 Bruce D. Beaudin, Judge's Order, *Curran vs. Catholic University,* April 5, 1988.
6. Trial testimony of James A. Hickey, December 14, 1988.
7. Press release by the trustees, April 12, 1988.
8. Trial testimony of James A. Hickey, December 14, 1988.
9. Trial testimony of Joseph Bernardin, December 16, 1988.
10. Letter from Joseph Bernardin to James A. Hickey, December 11, 1987.
11. The so-called oath was one of three documents drafted by the trustees, April 12, 1988. First was the, "Statement of the Board of Trustees of The Catholic University of America to the Ad Hoc Committee of the Academic Senate." This was accompanied by an "Agreement" on how Curran could teach in the department of sociology, which included the attached one page "oath."
12. Baine and Saunders dispute whether there was poor communication and why on this point. This is largely Baine's account.
13. Statement of Charles Curran released by his lawyers, April 12, 1988. Quoted in Marjorie Hyer, "Curran Retains Teaching Job, Must Leave Theology School," *Washington Post,* April 13, 1988.
14. Letter from John Hunt and Paul Saunders to Kevin Baine, April 19, 1988.
15. Letter from John Hunt and Paul Saunders to Kevin Baine, May 10, 1988.
16. Larry Witham, "Curran terms CUA's teaching offer 'cynical,'" *Washington Times,* May 18, 1988.
17. Letter from William J. Byron to Charles E. Curran, May 25, 1988.
18. Letter from Charles E. Curran to William J. Byron, May 25, 1988.
19. Letter from William J. Byron to Charles E. Curran, May 26, 1988.
20. Trial testimony of Joseph Bernardin, December 16, 1988.
21. Trial testimony of William J. Byron, December 20, 1988.

22. Catholic University Board of Trustees, "Resolution," June 2, 1988.
23. Letter from William J. Byron to Charles E. Curran, June 3, 1988.
24. Charles Curran, "Does Academic Freedom Exist at Catholic U?" *Washington Post,* May 29, 1988; William Byron, "At Catholic U. the Issue is Religious, not Academic Freedom," *Washington Post,* June 5, 1988.
25. Trial testimony of William J. Byron, December 21, 1988.
26. Letter from Charles E. Curran to William J. Byron, June 9, 1988.
27. Quoted in Marjorie Hyer, "Curran to Sue Catholic University," *Washington Post,* May 18, 1988.
28. Interview with Saunders.
29. Susan Schmidt, "Evangel Temple Suit Reluctantly Dismissed," *Washington Post,* December 9, 1988.
30. Brief interview with Bernardin, June 17, 1989, at the National Conference of Catholic Bishops meeting, Seton Hall University.

Chapters Eight to Thirteen— A Cardinal's View • Two Sides of the Story • Four Witnesses • The Ecclesial Limit • "I Can't Deny Who I Am" • Past Presidents

See bibliography for all the legal documents on which the trial testimony is based.

Fourteen Verdict

1. Interviews with Kevin Baine and Paul Saunders.
2. Weisberg, Opinion and Order, *Curran vs. Catholic University.*
3. Interview with Baine.
4. Interview with Saunders.
5. Quoted in "Academic Freedom and The Catholic University of America," *America,* May 27, 1989, 506. The resolution was issued March 6, 1989.
6. Religious News Service, "14 CU Professors Stage Protest," *Washington Post,* April 22, 1987.
7. Joseph A. O'Hare, "Faith and Freedom in Catholic Universities," in May, ed., *Vatican Authority and American Catholic Dissent,* 161–62.
8. Tim Unsworth, "Not Much Cooking at post-Curran Catholic U," *National Catholic Reporter,* June 2, 1989.
9. Byron's remarks to the National Conference of Catholic Bishops, November 15, 1988, Washington D.C.
10. See Larry Witham, "Catholic educators assess boundaries of their freedom," *Washington Times,* February 3, 1989. A version of Willaim J.

Byron's talk is published as "Academic Freedom," in his, *Quadrangle Considerations* (Chicago: Loyola University Press, 1989), 29–44.

11. Poll cited in Byron's remarks to the National Conference of Catholic Bishops, November 6, 1989, Baltimore.
12. National Conference of Catholic Bishops, "Doctrinal Responsibilities: Approaches to Promoting Cooperation and Resolving Misunderstandings between Bishops and Theologians," (Washington D.C.: United States Catholic Conference, 1989). The process of forming the guidelines began with a report by canon law experts see, Leo J. O'Donovan, ed. *Cooperation Between Theologians and the Ecclesiastical Magisterium* (Washington D.C.: Canon Law Society of America, 1982).
13. News conference, June 19, 1989, Seton Hall University.
14. Curran, *Catholic Higher Education,* 140.
15. Interviews with Catholic University officials.
16. Trial testimony of Charles E. Curran, December 21, 1988.
17. See "Entire University on trial in Curran case," *The Tower,* December 2, 1988; and "Total Annual Giving Sets Record," *CUA Magazine* vol. 1 (Fall 1989): 6.
18. American Association of University Professors, "Academic Freedom and Tenure: The Catholic University of America," *Academe* vol. 75 (September–October, 1989): 27–40.
19. Byron's remarks to the National Conference of Catholic Bishops, November 6, 1989.
20. Curran, *Catholic Higher Education,* 238.
21. Ibid.
22. Quoted in Richard Ostling, "The Pope Wins In Court," *Time,* March 13, 1989, 70.
23. Curran, *Catholic Higher Education,* 239.
24. Editorial, *National Catholic Reporter,* September 7, 1990. The first report on the Auburn dispute appeared in, Adam Nossiter, "Auburn Rejects Tenure for Maverick Theologian," *Atlanta Constitution,* September 11, 1990.
25. Richard P. McBrien and Richard A. McCormick, "L'Affaire Curran II," *America,* September 15, 1990.
26. Quoted in Pat Windsor, "Curran is denied tenure at Auburn," *National Catholic Reporter,* September 21, 1990.
27. Interview with Gary Mullen, Auburn's university senate chairman, November 20, 1990.
28. Jay Reeves, *Associated Press,* December 11, 1990.
29. Jay Reeves, "Theologian in Tenure Dispute to Take Post at Southern Methodist University," *Associated Press,* December 13, 1990.
30. Press statements by Southern Methodist University and by Charles Curran, both on December 13, 1990.

Epilogue Sparks but not Fire

1. Weisberg, Opinion and Order, *Curran vs. Catholic University.*
2. "Theologian cites 'creeping restoration,'" *National Catholic Reporter,* April 28, 1989.
3. "The Cologne Statement," January 6, 1989. Printed in *Commonweal,* February 24, 1989, 102–4.
4. Alan Riding, "Theologians in Europe Challenge Pope's Conservative Leadership," *New York Times,* July 14, 1989.
5. Ibid.
6. Congregation for the Doctrine of the Faith, "Profession of Faith and 'Oath of Fidelity.'" Published in *Origins* vol. 18 (March 16, 1989) 661–63. The oath appeared originally in *L'Osservatore Romano,* February 25, 1989.
7. Canon 833, nos. 5–8, *The Code of Canon Law: A Text and Commentary,* James A. Coriden, Thomas J. Green, and Donald J. Heintschel, eds. (New York: Paulist Press, 1985).
8. Quoted in Todd Ackerman, "New Oath leaves many puzzled, indifferent," *National Catholic Register,* April 9, 1989.
9. Ladislas Orsy, "Profession of Faith and the 'Oath of Fidelity,'" *America,* April 15, 1989, 347.
10. Quoted in "We cannot but express our dismay...," *National Catholic Reporter,* June 30, 1989.
11. See "Summary," *Report of the Catholic Theological Society of America's Commission on the Profession of Faith and Oath of Fidelity,* (Washington D.C.: Office of CTSA Treasurer, Washington Theological Union, April 15, 1990), 115–17.
12. Quoted in Marjorie Hyer, "Pope, U.S. Archbishops Open Critical Talks," *Washington Post,* Rome, March 9, 1989.
13. Quoted in Victor L. Simpson, "Differences Emerge But Business As Usual Promised," *Associated Press,* Rome, March 13, 1989.
14. Quoted in Tom Fox, "Archbishop May defends U.S. theologians," *National Catholic Reporter,* June 30, 1989.
15. Quoted in John Wilkins, "Italian theologians echo Cologne," *National Catholic Reporter,* June 2, 1989.
16. Quoted in Peter Hebblethwaite, "Italian and Cologne statements differ," *National Catholic Reporter,* July 28, 1989.
17. For Häring's actions between January and April see, Riding, "Theologians in Europe Challenge Pope's Conservative Leadership," and Pat Windsor, "Häring fears 'psychological exodus' from church," *National Catholic Reporter,* April 28, 1989. Häring's remarks on reforming the Congregation for the Doctrine of the Faith appeared in an interview with the Milan-based Italian daily, *Corriere della Sera,* April 18, 1989.

18. "No Dissent From Church Authority, Vatican Tells Theologians," *Reuters News Service,* Rome, June 5, 1989.
19. Editorial, *National Catholic Reporter,* June 2, 1989.
20. See Dulles, "Extraordinary Synod of 1985," in his *The Reshaping of Catholicism,* 184–206
21. Synod of Bishops, "The Final Report." Published in *Origins* vol. 15 (December 19, 1985): 488.
22. For a brief history of the catechism and the debate it raised see, Reese, "Introduction," *The Universal Catechism Reader.*
23. Larry Witham, "Catholic scholars debate catechism," *Washington Times,* January 29, 1990.
24. William C. Spohn, "The Moral Vision of the Catechism: Thirty Years That Did Not Happen," *America,* March 3, 1990, 189–92.
25. Avery Dulles, "The Church and the Universal Catechism," *America,* March 3, 1990, 219.
26. Quoted in "Vatican bars public dissent by theologians," *Associated Press,* in the *Washington Times,* June 29, 1990.
27. Congregation for the Doctrine of the Faith, *Instruction,* June 1990, par. 12, 11.
28. Ibid., par. 32.
29. Ibid., par. 16.
30. Catholic Theological Society of America, "Do Not Extinguish the Spirit," December 8, 1990, par. 20, 24.
31. Congregation for Catholic Education, "Proposed Schema for a Pontifical Document on Catholic Universities," April 15 1985. Published in *Origins* vol. 15 (April 10, 1986): 706.
32. Congregation for Catholic Education, "A Draft Document on Catholic Higher Education," November 8, 1988. Published in *Origins* vol. 18 (December 22, 1988), 445–64.
33. Witham, "Catholic educators assess boundaries."
34. Quoted in Jennifer Parmelee, "Catholic Educators Ask Pope to Protect Academic Freedom," *Washington Post,* Rome, April 29, 1989.
35. Catholic Higher Education Congress, "Ten Recommendations." Published in *Origins* vol. 19 (May 18,1989): 16.
36. Quoted in Parmelee, "Catholic Educators Ask Pope to Protect Academic Freedom."
37. Quoted in Cindy Wooden, "Bishops must not be seen as 'foreign agents,' pope tells universities," Catholic News Service, Rome, the *Catholic Standard,* archdiocese of Washington D.C. September 14, 1989.
38. Larry Witham, "Vatican revises education draft to satisfy Americans," *Washington Times,* October 20, 1989.
39. Congregation for Catholic Education, "A Draft Document on Catholic Higher Education," July 13, 1989, 2, 14. This third draft was modestly revised during the September 6–9, 1989, Rome meeting of Cardinal

Baum and the fifteen-member commission and was then sent to John Paul II as an advisory document.

40. Witham, "Vatican revises education draft."
41. John Paul II, *Apostolic Constitution on Catholic Universities,* September 25, 1990.
42. Interview with Leo O'Donovan, December 18, 1990.

BIBLIOGRAPHY

Books

Annarelli, James J. *Academic Freedom and Catholic Higher Education*. New York: Greenwood Press, 1987.

Aquinas, Thomas. *Summa Theologiae*. 3 vols. Translated by the Fathers of the Dominican Province. New York: Benziger Brothers, Inc., 1947.

Beutow, Harold A. *The Catholic School: Its Roots, Identity and Future*. New York: Crossroad, 1988.

Bloom, Allan. *The Closing of the American Mind: How Higher Education has Failed Democracy and Impoverished the Souls of Today's Students*. New York: Simon and Schuster, 1987.

Byron, William J. *Quadrangle Considerations*. Chicago: Loyola University Press, 1989.

Cheetham, Nicolas. *Keepers of the Keys: A History of the Popes from St. Peter to John Paul II*. New York, Charles Scribner's Sons, 1983.

Coriden, James A., Green, Thomas J., and Heintschel, Donald J., eds. *The Code of Canon Law: A Text and Commentary*. New York: Paulist Press, 1985.

Cox, Harvey. *The Silencing of Leonardo Boff: The Vatican and the Future of World Christianity*. Oak Park, IL: Meyer Stone Books, 1989.

Curran, Charles E. *Christian Morality Today: The Renewal of Moral Theology*. Notre Dame, IN: Fides Publishers, Inc., 1966.

———. *A New Look at Christian Morality: Christian Morality Today II*. Notre Dame, IN: Fides Publishers, Inc., 1968.

———, and Hunt, Robert E. *Dissent in and For the Church: Theologians and Humanae Vitae*. New York: Sheed and Ward, 1970.

———. *New Perspectives in Moral Theology*. Notre Dame: University of Notre Dame Press, 1976.

———, and McCormick, Richard A., eds. *Moral Norms and Catholic Tradition: Readings in Moral Theology No. 1*. New York: Paulist Press, 1979.

———, and McCormick, Richard A., eds. *The Magisterium and Morality: Readings in Moral Theology, No. 3*. New York: Paulist Press, 1980.

———, and McCormick, Richard A., eds. *Dissent in the Church: Readings in Moral Theology No. 6*. New York: Paulist Press, 1982.

———. *Faithful Dissent*. Kansas City, MO: Sheed and Ward, 1986.

———. *Toward an American Catholic Moral Theology*. Notre Dame: University of Notre Dame Press, 1987.

———. *Catholic Higher Education, Theology, and Academic Freedom*. Notre Dame, IN: University of Notre Dame Press, 1990.

Dawson, Christopher. *Religion and the Rise of Western Culture*. New York: Doubleday, Image Books, 1958.

Denison, Edward F. *Sources of Economic Growth in the United States and the Alternatives Before Us*. New York: Committee for Economic Development, 1962.

Dulles, Avery. *The Reshaping of Catholicism: Current Challenges in the Theology of the Church*. San Francisco: Harper and Row, 1988.

Eckhart, Meister. *The Essential Sermons, Commentaries, Treatises and Defense*. Translated by Edmund Colledge and Bernard McGinn. New York: Paulist, 1981.

Flannery, Austin P., ed. *Documents of Vatican II: The Conciliar and Post Conciliar Documents*. Grand Rapids, MI: William B. Eerdmans Publishing Co., 1984.

Fogarty, Gerald P. *American Catholic Biblical Scholarship: A History from the Early Republic to Vatican II*. San Francisco: Harper and Row, 1989.

Fuchs, Josef. *Christian Ethics in a Secular Arena*. Washington D.C.: Georgetown University Press, 1984.

———. *Personal Responsibility and Christian Morality*. Washington D.C.: Georgetown University Press, 1983.

Gallup, George, and Castelli, Jim. *The American Catholic People: Their Beliefs, Practices, and Values*. Garden City, NY: Doubleday and Company, 1987.

———. *The People's Religion: American Faith in the 90s*. New York: Macmillan, 1989.

Greeley, Andrew M. *From Backwater to Mainstream: A Profile of Catholic Higher Education*. New York: McGraw-Hill, 1969.

———, McCready, William C., and McCourt, Kathleen. *Catholic Schools in a Declining Church*. Kansas City, MO: Sheed and Ward, 1976.

———. *Crisis in the Church: A Study of Religion in America*. Chicago: Thomas More Press, 1979.

Häring, Bernard. *Fede, Storia, Morale*. Interview with Gianni Licheri. Rome: Edizioni Borla, 1989.

Hassenger, Robert, ed. *The Shape of Catholic Higher Education*. Chicago: The University of Chicago Press, 1967.

Hebblethwaite, Peter. *The New Inquisition? The Case of Edward Schillebeeckx and Hans Küng*. San Francisco: Harper and Row, 1980.

Hennesey, James. *American Catholics: A History of the Roman Catholic Community in the United States*. New York: Oxford University Press, 1981.

Hesburgh, Theodore M. *The Hesburgh Papers: Higher Values in Higher Education*. Kansas City, MO: Andrews and McNeel, 1979.

Hofstadter, Richard, and Metzger, Walter. *The Development of Academic Freedom in the United States*. New York: Columbia University Press, 1955

Hook, Sidney. *Heresy Yes, Conspiracy No*. New York: John Day Co., 1953.

Hunt, John F., and Connelly, Terrence R., et al. *The Responsibility of Dissent: The Church and Academic Freedom*. New York: Sheed and Ward, 1970.

Jonghin, Louis, ed. *Academic Freedom and Tenure*. Madison, WI: University of Wisconsin, 1967.

Johnson, Paul. *A History of Christianity*. New York: Atheneum, 1977.

———. *Pope John Paul II and the Catholic Restoration*. New York: St. Martin's Press, 1981.

———. *Modern Times: The World From the Twenties to the Eighties*. New York: Harper and Row, 1983.

Jonsen, Albert R., and Toulmin, Stephen. *The Abuse of Casuistry: A History of Moral Reasoning*. Berkeley, CA: University of California Press, 1988.

Kelley, Dean. *Why Conservative Churches are Growing*. New York: Harper and Row, 1972.

Kelly, George A., ed. *Why Should the Catholic University Survive?* New York: St. John's University Press, 1973.

Kennedy, Eugene. *Tomorrow's Catholics, Yesterday's Church: The Two Cultures of American Catholicism*. San Francisco, Harper and Row, 1988.

Kerr, Clark. *The Uses of the University*. Cambridge, MA: Harvard University Press, 1964.

Küng, Hans. *Infallible? An Inquiry*. Garden City, NY: Doubleday, 1971.

Leff, Gordon E. *Medieval Thought: St. Augustine to Ockham*. Chicago: Quadrangle Books, Inc., 1959.

———. *William Ockham: The Metamorphosis of Scholastic Discourse*. Manchester, U.K.: Manchester University Press, 1975.

Luscombe, D.E., trans. and ed. *Peter Abelard's 'Ethics.'* Oxford: Oxford University Press, 1971.

Maguire, Daniel C. *The Moral Revolution: A Christian Humanist Vision*. San Francisco: Harper and Row, 1986.

Mahoney, John. *The Making of Moral Theology: A Study of the Roman Catholic Tradition*. Oxford: Clarendon Press, 1987.

Manier, Edward, and Houck, John W., eds. *American Freedom and the Catholic University*. Notre Dame, IN: Fides Publishers, Inc., 1967.

Marty, Martin E. *Modern American Religion, Volume 1: The Irony of It All, 1893–1919*. Chicago: University of Chicago Press, 1986.

May, William E., ed. *Vatican Authority and American Catholic Dissent: The Curran Case and its Consequences*. New York: Crossroad, 1988.

———. *Moral Absolutes: Catholic Tradition, Current Trends, and the Truth*. Milwaukee: Marquette University Press, 1989.

McBrien, Richard P. *Catholicism*. 2 vols. Minneapolis: Winston Press, 1980.

———. *Understanding Catholicism*. Twenty-four-part audio tape series. Kansas City, MO.: Creedance Cassettes, 1984.

McCluskey, Neil, ed. *The Catholic University: A Modern Appraisal*. Notre Dame: University of Notre Dame Press, 1970.

Neuhaus, Richard John. *The Catholic Moment: The Paradox of the Church in the Postmodern World*. San Francisco: Harper and Row, 1987.

Newman, John Henry. *The Idea of a University*. Forward by Charles Frederick Harrold. London: Longmans, Green and Co., 1947.

Nuesse, Joseph C. *The Catholic University of America: A Centennial History*. Washington D.C.: Catholic University Press, 1990.

O'Connell, Timothy. *Principles for Catholic Morality*. New York: Seabury, 1978.

O'Donovan, Leo J. *Cooperation Between Theologians and the Ecclesiastical Magisterium*. Washington D.C.: Canon Law Society of America, 1982.

Pierce, Albert C. *Beyond One Man*. Washington D.C.: Anawim Press, 1967.

Pelikan, Jaroslav. *The Christian Tradition: A History of the Development of Doctrine. Volume 1, The Emergence of the Catholic Tradition (100–600)*. Chicago: University of Chicago Press, 1971.

———. *The Christian Tradition: A History of the Development of Doctrine. Volume 5, Christian Doctrine and Modern Culture (Since 1700)*. Chicago: University of Chicago Press, 1989.

Power, Edward J. *Catholic Higher Education in America: A History*. New York: Appleton-Century-Crofts, 1972.

Rahner, Karl. *Theological Investigations, Volume 9: Writings of 1965–67, I*. Graham Harrison trans. New York: Herder and Herder, 1972.

Ratzinger, Joseph, with Messori, Vittorio. *The Ratzinger Report: An Exclusive Interview on the State of the Church*. San Francisco: Ignatius Press, 1985.

Reese, Thomas J., ed. *The Universal Catechism Reader: Reflections and Responses*. San Francisco: Harper and Row, 1990.

Roof, Wade Clark, and McKinney, William. *American Mainline Religion: Its Changing Shape and Future*. New Brunswick, NJ: Rutgers University Press, 1987.

Scimecca, Joseph, and Damiano, Roland. *Crisis at St. John's: Strike and Revolution on the Catholic Campus*. New York: Random House, 1968.

Smith, Page. *Killing the Spirit: Higher Education in America*. New York: Viking, 1990.

Sullivan, Francis A. *Magisterium: Teaching Authority in the Catholic Church*. New York: Paulist Press, 1983.

Tillich, Paul. *A History of Christian Thought: From Its Judaic Origins to Existentialism*. New York: Simon and Schuster, 1967.

Trilling, Lionel. *Last Decade: Essays and Reviews, 1965–75*. Diana Trilling ed. New York: Harcourt Brace Jovanovich, 1978.

Walker, Williston. *A History of the Christian Church*. Third Edition. New York: Charles Scribner's Sons, 1970.

Wilson, Charles H. *Tilton vs. Richardson: The Search for Sectarianism in Education*. Washington D.C.: Association of American Colleges, 1971.

Wynn, Wilton. *Keepers of the Keys: John Paul XXIII, Paul VI, and John Paul II—Three Who Changed the Church*. New York: Random House, 1988.

Main Articles and Documents

American Association of University Professors. "Report of the Special Committee on Academic Freedom in Church-Related Colleges and Universities." *AAUP Bulletin* vol. 53, 1967.

———, "Report: The 'Limitations' Clause in the 1940 Statement of Principles." *Academe* vol. 74, September–October, 1988.

———. "Academic Freedom and Tenure: The Catholic University of America." *Academe* vol. 75, September–October, 1989.

Barthel, Joan. "Dissent Into Darkness." *Washington Post Magazine,* March 22, 1987.

Beauregard, Erving E. "An Archbishop, a University, and Academic Freedom." *Records of the American Catholic Historical Society* vol. 93, 1982.

Byron, William J. "An American Catholic Perspective on Academic Freedom." February 1, 1989. In *Origins* vol. 18, February 16, 1989.

Catholic Theological Society of America. "Don't Extinguish the Spirit." December 8, 1990. Washington D.C.: Office of CTSA Treasurer, Washington Theological Union, 1990.

———. Report of the Catholic Theological Society of America Commission on the Profession of Faith and Oath of Fidelity. April 15, 1990. Washington D.C.: Office of CTSA Treasurer, Washington Theological Union. 1990.

Catholic University of America. *Canonical Statutes for the Ecclesiastical Faculties of the Catholic University of America.* January, 1981.

———. *Announcements—School of Religious Studies, 1987–88* vol. 73, March 15, 1987.

"Cologne Statement." January 6, 1989. *Commonweal,* February 24, 1989.

Congar, Yves. "A Brief History of the Magisterium and Its Relations to Scholars," in Curran, Charles E., and McCormick, Richard A., eds. *Readings in Moral Theology, No. 3: The Magisterium and Morality.* New York: Paulist Press, 1980.

Congregation for the Doctrine of the Faith. *Declaration in Defense of the Catholic Doctrine on the Church Against Certain Errors of the Present Day (Mysterium Ecclesiae).* June 24, 1973. In *Origins* vol. 3, July 19, 1973.

———. *Declaration on Certain Questions Concerning Sexual Ethics.* January 15, 1975. In *Origins* vol. 5, January 22, 1976.

———. "Profession of Faith and 'Oath of Fidelity.'" *L'Osservatore Romano,* February 25, 1989. In *Origins* vol. 18, March 16, 1989.

———. *Instruction on the Ecclesial Vocation of the Theologian.* June 25, 1990. Vatican City: Libreria Editrice Vaticana, 1990.

Congregation for Catholic Education. *Normae Quaedam.* 1968.

———. "Proposed Schema for a Pontifical Document on Catholic Universities." April 15, 1985. First draft. In *Origins* vol. 15, April 10, 1986.

———. "A Draft Document on Catholic Higher Education." November 8, 1988. Second draft. In *Origins* vol. 18, December 22, 1988.

———. "A Draft Document on Catholic Higher Education." July 13, 1989. Third draft.

Congress of Delegates of the Catholic Universities of the World, 1969. "The Rome Statement: The Catholic University and the Aggiornamento." In McCluskey, Neil, ed. *The Catholic University: A Modern Appraisal.* Notre Dame: University of Notre Dame Press, 1970.

———. Second Congress, 1972. "The Catholic University in the Modern World." In Kelly, George A., ed. *Why Should the Catholic University Survive?* New York: St. John's University Press, 1973.

Curran, Charles. "How My Mind Has Changed." *Journal of the College Theology Society* vol. 23, Fall 1975.

———. "Academic Freedom: The Catholic University and Catholic Theology." *The Furrow* vol. 3, December 1979.

———. "Catholic Universities." *Texas Law Review* vol. 66, June 1988.

Dionne, Jr., E. J. "The Pope's Guardian of Orthodoxy." *New York Times Magazine,* November 4, 1985.

Dulles, Avery. "Ratzinger's Journey." *Crisis: A Journal of Lay Catholic Opinion,* December 1989.

———. "The Church and the Universal Catechism." *America,* March 3, 1990.

———. "The Teaching Mission of the Church and Academic Freedom." *America,* April 21, 1990.

Ellis, John Tracy. "American Catholics and the Intellectual Life." *Thought* vol. 30, September 1955.

———. "A Tradition of Autonomy," in McCluskey, Neil, ed. *The Catholic University: A Modern Appraisal.* Notre Dame: University of Notre Dame Press, 1970.

Gallin, Alice. "On the Road: Toward a Definition of a Catholic University." *The Jurist* vol. 48, 1988.

Gleason, Philip. "Academic Freedom and the Crisis in Catholic Universities," in Manier, Edward, and Houck, John W., eds. *American Freedom and the Catholic University.* Notre Dame, IN: Fides Publishers, Inc., 1967.

———. "American Catholic Higher Education: A Historical Perspective," in Hassenger, Robert, ed. *The Shape of Catholic Higher Education.* Chicago: University of Chicago Press, 1967.

Häring, Bernard. "The Master Idea of Christian Morality," in Burghardt, Walter I., and Lynch, William F. eds., *The Idea of Catholicism: An Introduction to the Thought and Worship of the Church.* Cleveland: The World Publishing Company, 1964.

Hesburgh, Theodore. "The Work of Mediation." *Commonweal,* October 6, 1961.

Hitchcock, James. "The Curran Case and the 'American Church'," in May, William, ed., *Vatican Authority and American Catholic Dissent: The Curran Case and its Consequences.* New York: Crossroad, 1988.

Hunt, George W. "American Catholic Intellectual Life." *America,* May 6, 1989.

International Federation of Catholic Universities, North American Branch. Land O Lakes Statement, in McCluskey, Neil, ed. *The Catholic University: A Modern Appraisal.* Notre Dame: University of Notre Dame Press, 1970.

John Paul II. *Redemptor Hominis.* March 4, 1979. Washington D.C.: United States Catholic Conference, 1979.

———. *Apostolic Constitution Sapientia Christiana: On Ecclesiastical Faculties and Universities.* Washington D.C.: United States Catholic Conference, 1979.

———. "Address to U.S. Catholic university and college educators at The Catholic University of America." October 7, 1979. Washington D.C.: United States Catholic Conference, 1979.

———. "Address to Leaders of Catholic Higher Education." September 12, 1987. Xavier University, New Orleans. *John Paul II in America: Talks Given on the Papal Tour.* Boston: St. Paul Books and Media, 1987.

———. *Apostolic Constitution on Catholic Universities.* Vatican City: Libreria Editrice Vaticana, 1990.

Jossua, Jean-Pierre. "Jacques Pohier: A Theologian Destroyed," in Küng, Hans, and Swidler, Leonard. *Church in Anguish: Has the Vatican Betrayed Vatican II?* San Francisco: Harper and Row, 1987.

Lippmann, Walter. "The University." *New Republic,* May 28, 1966.

Lonergan, Bernard. "The Transition from a Classicist World-View to Historical-Mindedness," in *A Second Collection,* Ryan, William F.J., and Tyrrell, Bernard J., eds. Philadelphia: Westminster Press, 1975.

National Catholic Educational Association, "Relations of American Catholic Colleges and Universities with the Church." *Occasional Papers on Catholic Higher Education* vol. 2, April 1976.

National Conference of Catholic Bishops. "Norms of Licit Theological Dissent," in *Human Life in Our Day.* Washington D.C.: United States Catholic Conference, 1968. Par. 49–54.

———. "Doctrinal Responsibilities: Approaches to Promoting Cooperation and Resolving Misunderstandings between Bishops and Theologians." Washington D.C.: United States Catholic Conference, 1989.

Nuesse, C. Joseph. "CUA's First One Hundred Years." *CUA Magazine* vol. 1, Fall 1989.

O'Hare, Joseph A. "Faith and Freedom in Catholic Universities," in May, William, ed. *Vatican Authority and American Catholic Dissent: The Curran Case and its Consequences.* New York: Crossroad, 1988.

Orsy, Ladislas. "Profession of Faith and the 'Oath of Fidelity.'" *America,* April 15, 1989.

———. "Magisterium and Theologians: A Vatican Document." *America,* July 14–21, 1990.

Pellegrino, Edmund D. "Catholic Universities and the Church's Intellectual Ministry: The Crisis of Identity and Justification." *Thought* vol. 57, June 1982.

Pope Pius XI. *Deus scientiarum Dominus*. 1931.

Provost, James A. "Canonical Mission in Catholic Universities." *America*, June 7, 1980.

Riding, Alan. "Theologians in Europe Challenge Pope's Conservative Leadership." *New York Times*, July 14, 1989.

"Roman Catholics: Time for a Change." *Time*, April 28, 1967.

Schubert, Frank D. "Theology Without God: A New Study Documents the Secularization of the Catholic Curriculum." *Crisis*, June, 1989.

Smith, Janet E. "*Humane Vitae* at 20: New Insights Into an Old Debate." *Crisis*, June, 1988.

Spohn, William C. "The Moral Vision of the Catechism: Thirty Years That Did Not Happen." *America*, March 3, 1990.

Suro, Roberto. "Priest Censure Seen as Move To Extend Church Authority." *New York Times*, August 20, 1986.

Tierny, Brian. "Pope and Bishops Before Trent: An Historical Survey," in Cooke, Bernard, ed. *The Papacy and the Church in the United States*. New York: Paulist Press, 1989.

VanDelinder, Bonnie L. "Charles E. Curran: A Bibliography," 1962–86. Rochester, NY: Colgate Theological Seminary, 1986.

Legal Documents

First Complaint. *Charles E. Curran vs. The Catholic University of America*. February 27, 1987. Civil case no. 1562-87. Superior Court of the District of Columbia, Washington D.C.

Defendant's Motion for Summary Judgement. *Curran vs. Catholic University*. March 1, 1989.

Plaintiff's Memorandum in Opposition to Defendant's Motion. *Curran vs. Catholic University*. March 18, 1988.

Beaudin, Bruce D. Judge's Order. *Curran vs. Catholic University*. April 5, 1988.

First Amended Complaint. *Charles E. Curran and Julia Fleming et. al. vs. The Catholic University of America*. June 10, 1988.

Defendant's Motion to Dismiss or for Summary Judgement. *Curran vs. Catholic University*. November 2, 1988.

Plaintiff's Trial Brief and Memorandum in Opposition to Defendant's Motion for Summary Judgement. *Curran vs. Catholic University*. November 17, 1988.

Trial Testimony. *Charles E. Curran and Julia Fleming et. al. vs. The Catholic University of America*. December 14–23, 1988. Pages 1–1933. Washington D.C.: Superior Court for the District of Columbia.

Index to Plaintiff's Trial Exhibits. *Curran vs. Catholic University*. 33 pp. Index for 303 exhibits.

Index to Defendant's Exhibits. *Curran vs. Catholic University*. 10 pp. Index for 156 exhibits.

Defendant's Post Trial Memorandum. *Curran vs. Catholic University*. January 25, 1989.

Defendant's Proposed Findings of Fact and Conclusions of Law. *Curran vs. Catholic University*. January 25, 1989.

Plaintiff's Post Trial Brief. *Curran vs. Catholic University*. January 25, 1989.

Plaintiff's Proposed Finding of Fact. *Curran vs. Catholic University*. January 25, 1989.

Weisberg, Frederick H. Opinion and Order. *Curran vs. Catholic University*. February 28, 1989.

INDEX